Instructor's Resource Manual
THE RIVERSIDE READER

Eighth Edition

Rai Peterson
Ball State University

Joseph F. Trimmer
Ball State University

Maxine Hairston
University of Texas at Austin

HOUGHTON MIFFLIN COMPANY   **Boston**   **New York**

Senior Sponsoring Editor: Suzanne Phelps Weir
Development Editor: Sarah Helyar Smith
Editorial Assistant: Anne Leung
Associate Project Editor: Jane Lee
Manufacturing Manager: Florence Cadran
Marketing Manager: Cindy Graff Cohen

Printed in the U.S.A.

ISBN: 0-618-43386-4

456789-VHO-09 08 07 06

Contents

Preface

Using the Instructor's Guide

The instructor's guide provides several aids that help in teaching *The Riverside Reader:*

- **Three approaches** to using *The Riverside Reader* in a process-centered writing class.
- **Suggestions for** *new* **teachers** about how to organize and teach a writing class.
- A **brief analysis of each rhetorical strategy** in the text, summarizing the purposes a teacher might consider in planning the sequence of reading and writing assignments in a writing course, including a discussion of the visual text.
- A **descriptive analysis of every essay and story** in the anthology, pointing out the salient features (purpose, audience, strategy) that a teacher might want to emphasize in a rhetorical analysis of the text.
- A **reading quiz** for each essay. These questions can be answered and graded quickly, perhaps even graded by students in class. Each quiz contains at least one question based on the essay's headnote to encourage students to discover something about the background and credentials of the author. These quizzes are *not* intended as tests of a students ability to read rhetorically. That task comes in the give-and-take of class discussion. But these quizzes do offer a convenient way to see whether there is any point in beginning such a discussion—that is, to see whether the students have read the assignment. An answer key is included at the back of this guide.
- A **vocabulary list** for each essay. In addition to encouraging students to read with a dictionary at hand, such vocabulary lists emphasize the importance of diction in the crafting of each essay. As Mark Twain once said, "the difference between the right word and the nearly right word is the difference between lightning and the lightning bug."

Introduction

Most instructors who teach college writing courses use an essay anthology for at least three reasons. First, they want to introduce their students to the rhythms, patterns, and images of good nonfiction, a genre that William Zinsser has called the "new American literature." Second, they want to engage their students in reading and responding to rigorous assessments of the issues that affect their lives. Third, they want to help their students study and discuss how good nonfiction writers employ a variety of rhetorical strategies. They hope that by reading and talking about these models, their students will learn to incorporate some of these strategies into their own writing.

But instructors who use essay anthologies often encounter problems, particularly if they want to teach a process-centered writing course. One problem may be that when students are introduced to professional essays, they become passive spectators. Because they have no sense of the slow process by which an essay comes into existence, they are intimidated rather than inspired by the finished product. Another problem may be that students want to react to one or two isolated opinions in an essay. Because they are unfamiliar with the principles of rhetorical context, they see an essay as an occasion for declaring rather than developing their ideas. A third problem may be that students have had so little practice in rhetorical analysis that they don't know how to decipher the strategies an author uses to accomplish his or her purpose. Because they do not see how these strategies work in their reading, they find it difficult to employ them in their writing.

The Riverside Reader is a rhetorical reader designed to help students overcome these problems by emphasizing the relationships between reading and writing, analyzing the reading in a context that helps them understand the craft of writing, and assigning the writing in a way that helps them understand the process by which reading comes into existence. The special benefit of a *rhetorical reader* is that it focuses on all the elements involved when readers and writers try to communicate with each other. Students are invited to pay attention to the *author* of the message, the *purpose* of the message, the *audience* for the message, and the *strategies* by which the meaning of the message is constructed. *The Riverside Reader* stresses the constant interaction between these elements in each essay and suggests ways in which that interaction may also be at work in several short stories. When your students approach this reading from a rhetorical point of view, they can discover the strategies of the writing process and still enjoy the intellectual and aesthetic rewards of well-written, stimulating prose. Here are some suggestions about ways you can use a rhetorical approach in your classroom.

THREE APPROACHES TO USING A READER

Analyzing the Rhetorical Situation for an Essay

Encourage your students to see that every essay is written in response to what Lloyd Bitzer calls a "rhetorical situation." Bitzer says that each rhetorical situation must have three components:

1

1. The *occasion* that creates the need for a response. Rhetoric can exist only when a writer has identified some problem or issue that needs to be addressed or some change that needs to be made.
2. The *audience* to which the writing is directed. Rhetoric requires an audience that can act or be influenced.
3. The *constraints* under which the writer works. These include the amount of information the writer has, the strategies available for persuading the audience, and the limitations of time and space under which the writer is working.

Consider, for example, Paco Underhill's " Shop Like a Man." Start by asking your students to speculate about the occasion, or need, that prompted Underhill to write such an essay. What problem did he want to address, or what situation did he hope to change by writing it? There are several. Certainly, Underhill wants to change the way stores market certain products directly to men in order to increase their sales, but he also wants readers of both sexes to learn from and learn to tolerate the way their counterparts view shopping.

For whom is Underhill writing? Are they people who market products or consumers who buy them? Can they be influenced? Will they sell or shop differently after reading his essay? As a researcher, he routinely advises retailers about how to best present their merchandise and organize their stores, but what can shoppers learn from an analysis of typical shopping behavior? Also, how does knowing what a research firm like Underhill's tells retailers help buyers outsmart clever marketing?

What are the constraints on Underhill? What *can't* he do? For one thing, he can't name specific retailers or talk too specifically about the products they sell. He can't give information that will help shoppers spot researchers in the stores they enter. However, he does have years of experience at analyzing shopping behavior, and his observations are generally useful to anyone with a product to sell or a shopping list to check off. How does he gear his essay toward both buyers and sellers?

This kind of analysis gives students insights into what goes on when all writers—not just professionals—write. They must draw on their own knowledge and experience and use it to address a problem that will interest and influence readers.

Constructing a Process Scenario

A second way to teach the essays in this anthology is to construct an imaginary scenario in which you and your students try to put yourselves in the writer's place as he or she creates an essay. This kind of analysis sorts out the various methods the author uses for making meaning.

Try to re-create some of a writer's actions as he or she worked through the various stages of the writing process. Stress that any scenario you develop is necessarily contrived because no one knows exactly what goes on in an author's mind and that any scenario leaves out many steps. Indeed, most authors find it difficult to remember all the procedures they explored in composing a given essay. But even if your imaginary scenario is sketchy and tentative, it can be useful in giving students some insights into how writers work. The method is similar to the composing-aloud protocols developed by Linda Flower and John Hayes in their research on the writing process.

For example, you might select George Orwell's "Shooting an Elephant." Start by asking your students to read the essay carefully, first to get the gist of the narrative, and second, with the help of the study questions, to identify some of the issues Orwell is trying to illustrate. Most likely you should use the headnote to give the class some background information about Orwell's lifelong interest in Third World culture. Then members of the class should try to analyze the context for this particular essay. Why did this incident, among the many Orwell probably experienced in his years in Burma, make him so befuddled or furious that he wanted to write about it to explain its meaning?

Then imagine Orwell asking himself, "Who am I writing this for? Who needs to read what I have to say about 'the real motives for which despotic governments act'?" The people he would want to reach would be Englishmen and other white Europeans who have implicated themselves in the economics and politics of imperialism. Some might suggest that Orwell would be far too cynical to believe that he could influence such people, but that reinforces the point that an author sometimes writes to express anger and frustration. Anticipating his readers' indifference, he may adjust his arguments to engage them more directly.

Now that Orwell has decided to reconstruct an incident for an audience, he must answer two questions: How is he going to interpret the incident, to underline its meaning? What resources does he have to draw on? First, he has to catch his readers' attention and gain their sympathy. Can he hook their attention from the beginning? He digs back in his memories of his life in Burma and composes a powerful opening sentence that captures the essence of his experience: "In Moulmein, in lower Burma, I was hated by large numbers of people—the only time in my life that I have been important enough for this to happen to me."

Next Orwell would ask himself, "What shall I follow that with to make my point about the problems of authority and hatred?" His answer, of course, is to use an extended example from his own experience—shooting the elephant. But he might ask himself, "How can I demonstrate how this experience affected me and other people I knew?" One answer is to record his reaction to the agonizing death of the elephant; another is to report the varied reactions of the crowd, the owner, and the older and younger Europeans. In dramatizing these reactions, he might think to himself, "I've got it. The whole event was an extraordinary drama. I can portray the crowd as the audience and myself and the elephant as the chief actors." His last sentence suggests how he interpreted his role in this drama: "I often wondered whether any of the others grasped that I had done it solely to avoid looking a fool."

This speculative scenario reflects the way Orwell could have started to write his essay, gradually accumulating his material and shaping it through a number of drafts. You might go on to analyze some of the paragraphs in the essay, talking about why he selected certain details, why he uses dialogue in some places, and how he uses observations to support and qualify his judgments.

Of course, students might come up with several different scenarios for a single essay or might disagree about the author's reasons for writing. If they do, that's healthy and productive because they are showing that they realize that writers have options and might use different approaches to reach the same goal. The essence of the writing process is making and remaking choices. Constructing a scenario raises your students' consciousness about such choices and how they advance the writing process.

A Variant on the Process Scenario. You can introduce an important variant on the process scenario by bringing your own writing into class and talking about it. Doing so gives you the opportunity to create a scenario that has real authority and perhaps considerable drama. Tell your students what you are writing and why. What biases or expectations does your audience have? What is your deadline? What kind of argument are you making, and how are you supporting your case?

For example, you may be writing a request for a sabbatical leave that requires you to describe a research project in such a way that your university will want to invest its money in your work. Or you may be making a grant application to the National Endowment for the Humanities that requires you to present your ideas in a specific format and within a certain number of pages. Or you might be working on an article for *College English* or *College Composition and Communication* that addresses other writing teachers about some aspect of the writing process.

If you are engaged in any writing task, you can make good use of it to illustrate a specific rhetorical situation and to trace the process you are going through as you compose. For example, we brought drafts of the introductions, study questions, and writing assignments for *The Riverside Reader* into our classroom and shared them with our students. We wanted their reactions to some problems we were having with tone. Often such writing problems stem from not knowing (or forgetting) the assumptions and expectations of your audience. By sharing our writing with writing students, the intended audience for our book, we were able to revise our own writing and help our students understand the process authors go through as they work on a project. You can accomplish the same objectives with your writing.

Using Essays to Illustrate Strategies

A third way you can use an essay anthology to support a process approach to teaching writing is to follow Paul Escholz's advice in "The Prose Models Approach: Using Product in the Process," printed in the NCTE book *Eight Approaches to Teaching Writing* (1980), edited by Timothy R. Donovan and Ben W. McClelland. Escholz suggests that an instructor use professional prose models once a student has completed one or two drafts of a paper. At that time a student is likely to have problems that an instructor can respond to by illustrating how professional writers have used specific strategies to solve similar problems. The advantage of this approach is that it enables you to demonstrate several strategies—the one a writer uses to shape the dominant pattern for an essay and the other strategies he or she uses to extend and enrich the essay.

Suppose, for instance, a student is writing an essay on the relationship between humankind and nature. In her first draft, she has had trouble getting into her topic and has written a rather dull opening paragraph that generalizes about comparisons. You could certainly suggest that she reread how a writer in the comparison and contrast section, Mark Twain, handles the problem. But you might also suggest that she look at the way authors in other sections use personal narrative in an analysis. George Orwell's observations about the elephant when he first comes upon her munching grass in "Shooting an Elephant" or Stephen Harrigan's description of confronting Miguel, the tiger who killed a man at the Houston Zoo in "The Tiger Is God" are good examples of this strategy.

Or you might have a student who is writing a paper on how to solve an interpersonal problem. In the first draft the student relies primarily on abstract nouns and adjectives to describe the problem and thus fails to give his readers images and details that would help them understand the solution. You would certainly refer that student to Jill McCorkle's "The Mullet Girls" or Judith Ortiz Cofer's "The Myth of the Latin Woman," but you might also recommend Flannery O'Connor's "Revelation" or Alice Walker's "Everyday Use" to show how a writer selects details that sketch a picture of a person, or Witi Ihimaera's "His First Ball" to show how a writer can record the internal processing that a person undergoes after an unpleasant interaction.

Professional essays can be particularly useful when you want to show students how to support generalizations with concrete examples and specific information. Readers what to learn something when they read, and they learn more effectively when they are given illustrations that explain the author's points. You can use almost any essay in *The Riverside Reader* to demonstrate this principle, but several that would be especially effective are Paco Underhill's "Shop like a Man" or Sarah Vowell's "Cowboys v. Mounties" (in Comparison and Contrast), James H. Austin's "Four Kinds of Chance" and James Q. Wilson's "Democracy for All?" (in Division and Classification), and Joan Acocella's "Under the Spell" (in Persuasion and Argument).

If you take time to become thoroughly familiar with the essays in *The Riverside Reader* early in the term, you will have at your fingertips a supply of examples to which you can refer students when you comment on their drafts. In time, as you and they work back and forth between reading and writing, both of you will learn to use the essays in this anthology as a source book for writing strategies.

HELPING STUDENTS TO READ RHETORICALLY

When your students read the essays according to one of these methods, you are teaching them to read rhetorically. They will thus avoid the pitfall of identifying with only one or two notions in an essay. Such identification is often necessary. Indeed, the response questions encourage students to connect their experience with the experience analyzed in the essay. But a more sophisticated reading requires students to see how a writer has shaped an experience for a rhetorical purpose.

For example, Alice Walker' story "Everyday Use" is a narrative about cultural values and perceptions. But it wasn't written in a vacuum. If you ask students to think about what they know about Alice Walker as a contemporary African American woman, or which of her other texts they have read (or seen the movie version of, e.g., *The Color Purple*), they will see the content of the essay in a larger context. And, if you ask them to think about their response to the essay, particularly since many of them, like the character Dee, have gone to college hoping to "better" themselves, they will see again the complexity of rhetorical context. Different readers see the story differently. This approach recognizes that reading an essay or a story is not a neutral experience: A reader is not uninformed, and a story is not inert. Readers must negotiate a connection between their own experience and the experience the author has shaped by the rhetorical strategies.

You might discuss, for example, how Walker seems to want her readers to respond to Dee's apparent selfishness or Maggie's reticence. Why does she tell about Mrs. Johnson's dream in which she and Dee are reunited on Johnny Carson's show and she looks exactly as Dee would want her to look? How does she use dialogue to demonstrate the differences between Dee and Maggie? How does she compare the sisters' attitudes toward handmade heirlooms? Discussing an essay in this way helps students read on two levels: At one level, they are absorbing the ideas in the essay and connecting them to their own experience, but at another level, they are standing back and observing how the writer uses specific strategies to influence their understanding.

Probably the best way to start this process is to ask your students to read the general introduction to *The Riverside Reader*. Go over the "Guidelines for Reading an Essay." These questions are the key to helping students read from a *rhetorical* point of view. If you encourage your students to ask these questions as they read, they will anticipate the kind of study questions posed at the end of each essay. A good way to demonstrate this process is to apply these questions to Gloria Naylor's "Beginning." This exercise will help students see how to analyze and annotate an essay, how to become an active reader rather than a passive reader.

The bonus that should come when students become active readers is that they will gradually learn to ask these same questions about their own writing. They will begin to see writing as a process made up of a number of interrelated activities, a process in which they have been engaging themselves, and one at which they can gradually become more confident and competent.

TEACHING THE INDIVIDUAL SECTIONS

We have organized *The Riverside Reader* according to the traditional pattern that begins with Narration and Description and ends with Persuasion and Argument. We have also added a special section, Resources for Writing, that recapitulates the pattern of the text but focuses on one theme. Our rationale is that students should write expressive essays at the beginning of the course, progress through more complex forms of informative and argumentative discourse, and then combine strategies at the end of the term. But we have no proof for this hypothesis, and certainly there is no magic about the arrangement. You might well want to start with the essays in the last section, Resources for Writing, to show your students how each strategy serves as a means for discovering as well as developing their ideas.

We have tried to arrange each section in an ascending order of complexity, beginning with the simpler essays and concluding with the most difficult piece. You shouldn't assume, however, that you will always agree with us or that our arrangement will work well in your class. By all means, read and evaluate the essays (and the story) in each section before you decide which ones you want to assign. The addition of the short story at the end of each section may prove unsettling at first because it does not fit precisely into the rhetorical scheme established for the essays. But we have included a story for each section to enrich your students' sensitivity to the thinking processes expressed by each strategy. These processes are so fundamental to the way we perceive, explain, and interact with the world that they can be dramatized in the story.

At the beginning of each section we have tried to identify the major characteristics of each form, explaining the purposes for which it is used, the audiences for which it is intended, and the strategies it employs. We have demonstrated how these characteristics are developed in a restricted space by providing an annotated paragraph at the end of the introduction. The explanation and the example should help students understand how they should approach the essays in the section.

After each essay we have provided five types of questions: (1) Questions for Response to encourage students to negotiate some sort of personal connection between their own experience and the experience analyzed in the essay, (2) Questions About Purpose to help students identify the author's guiding purposes, (3) Questions About Audience to show students that the essay was written for a variety of readers, (4) Questions about Strategies to demonstrate to students how writers use specific techniques to develop their ideas, and (5) Questions for Discussion to invite students to place the ideas raised by the essay in a larger context. We have not provided answers to these questions because many of them are intended to stimulate varied answers and further questions.

At the end of each section we have provided six writing assignments. Each assignment has been placed in a rhetorical context by suggesting possible purposes, audiences, and strategies other than the classroom. Each of the assignments also evokes one or more of the essays in the section, thus providing one more connection between reading and writing. The first two assignments ask students to write from their own personal experience in the strategy of the section. The second two ask the students to perform some sort of rhetorical analysis of one or more of the essays. And the last two assignments ask the students to use the information and ideas in the essays as the starting point for an essay in a slightly different context. These assignments are merely suggestive of the kind of writing that might occur to students after they have read an essay: (1) *imitate* it with an experience of their own, (2) *analyze* it with the tools of rhetorical analysis, or (3) *argue* with it or from it to create another perspective. But surely you and your students will be able to mix and match assignments from other sections or draft original assignments that will enable a student to identify his or her own way of writing in response to reading.

Suggestions
for New Writing Teachers

If you are starting out as a writing teacher, you are indeed fortunate because in the past few decades, teaching writing has come into its own as a field of study. Researchers have published reports on every aspect of the writing process, from strategies for invention to error analysis. And teachers have written about a wide range of pedagogical issues, including conducting student conferences and teaching writing across the curriculum. Unfortunately, many graduate students do not encounter this literature in their course of study and so feel unprepared to teach their first writing course. For that reason, you may want to read the nine books in the following list to give you some sense of the range of information available to new teachers. If you want to become a professional writing teacher, you will want to move beyond this basic list with the assistance of the bibliographies cited at the end of this chapter. But these nine books should give you a good grounding in the theory and practice of teaching writing.

BASIC BOOKS

Bishop, Wendy and Deborah Coxwell Teague. *Finding Our Way: A Writing Teacher's Sourcebook.* Boston: Houghton Mifflin, 2005.
 A provocative new collection of essays on seldom-discussed issues such as student-teacher relationships and power struggles, politics in the classroom, and teaching and attending graduate school simultaneously.

Elbow, Peter. *Embracing Contraries: Explorations in Learning and Teaching.* New York: Oxford UP, 1986.
 A collection of essays that set forth Elbow's theories, at once imaginative and down-to-earth, about the processes of learning, teaching, and evaluating writing. The book gains its power by Elbow's references to his own perplexities as a student and teacher.

Lindemann, Erika. *A Rhetoric for Writing Teachers.* 3rd ed. New York: Oxford UP, 1995.
 A brief but lucid history of rhetoric that covers both theory and practice. Sensible treatment of issues such as writing assignments and evaluating papers.

Moffett, James. *Active Voice: A Writing Program Across the Curriculum.* 2nd Ed. Portsmouth, N.H.: Boynton/Cook, 1992.
 A useful book about the designing and sequencing of assignments. A fuller treatment of Moffett's theories about the "discursive spectrum" can be found in *Teaching the Universe of Discourse* (Portsmouth, N.H.: Boynton/Cook, 1983).

Murray, Donald. *A Writer Teaches Writing.* Revised 2nd ed. Boston: Heinle, 2003.
 An important book on the writing process by a former journalist who won the Pulitzer Prize for editorial writing. Insightful on the place of individual conferences and workshops as alternatives to more traditional classroom practice.

North, Stephen M. *The Making of Knowledge in Composition: Portrait of an Emerging Field.* Portsmouth, N.H.: Boynton/Cook, 1987.
 A controversial overview of the assumptions that guide the research of different composition scholars. Helpful as a method for thinking about how to catalogue and evaluate research in the field.

Peterson, Rai. *The Writing Teacher's Companion: Planning, Teaching, and Evaluating in the Composition Classroom.* Boston: Houghton Mifflin, 1995.

A comprehensive guide to organizing and teaching writing, including advice about everything from writing syllabi to evaluating student work. The conversational style of this book makes it one of the easiest to read on the topics of composition theory and teaching practice.

Rose, Mike. *Lives on the Boundary: The Struggles and Achievements of America's Underprepared.* New York: Free Press, 1989.

A thoughtful and inspirational book that blends autobiography, case studies, and cultural criticism. Excellent for its revelation of the intellectual, emotional, and social forces that prevent and propel student learning.

Shaughnessy, Mina. *Errors and Expectations: A Guide for the Teacher of Basic Writing.* New York: Oxford UP, 1977.

This extended analysis of the errors made by open-admission students is still the best of its kind for writing teachers. Teachers working with unprepared students find it especially useful as a guide to illuminating their students' thinking processes.

These nine books, which can be read in a few weeks, provide a cram course that should help you get started as a writing teacher. Of course, you can't learn to teach writing from books, but reading through these books should give you a feel for the current thinking about teaching writing and introduce you to some basic procedures and terminology. Probably the best way to expand your knowledge about teaching writing is to join the National Council of Teachers of English (**www.ncte.org**). You can join the subsidiary organization, the Conference of College Composition and Communication. The two major journals in the field, *College English* and *College Composition and Communication,* are included as part of your membership. Furthermore, NCTE and CCCC sponsor and publish much of the research conducted in the field, and you can purchase many of the major books and monographs only through NCTE. You will receive a catalogue when you join and may buy books at a discount. The organization is invaluable, and a great bargain to boot.

THREE GUIDING PRINCIPLES

Even if you read the publications just cited before you begin to teach writing, you will need several months to understand the significance of their suggestions and to adapt them to your own teaching style. In the meantime, keep three principles in mind.

1. *A writing teacher should write.* Over the years, you have probably absorbed a good deal of folklore and conventional wisdom about how people write. The only way to test these precepts is to analyze your own writing process; only then can you give your students honest advice. If you are not currently working on academic or professional writing projects, you should work on the assignments you give your students. The experience will help you understand the difficulties they encounter as they try to develop their papers. (See Jim Corder's "What I Learned in School," *College Composition and Communication,* December 1975.) As you write, share your experiences with your students. Talk with them about the strategies you use for getting started and revising drafts. Bring in two or three opening paragraphs and invite them to help you decide which one works best. Talk candidly about the excuses you use to avoid work and the time it takes you to write an acceptable draft. Such information will usually shock them because they see you as an expert who has no trouble writing. The important point here is to present yourself as a working writer who is "doing it *with* them, not *to* them." Both of you are learning something from struggling with common writing problems. As Donald Murray says, "Act like a coach, not a judge."

2. *Focus your teaching on the writing process, not the written product.* A professional football coach would not try to train his rookie players by showing them a film of a championship

game and then leaving them to figure out what to do. Neither can you expect apprentice writers to improve their writing simply by giving them good writing to read and expecting them to imitate it. You can't just specify the product—you have to show them how the process works and then help them *as* they write. This is not to suggest that the final product is unimportant; ultimately, writers are judged on what they produce, and you need to evaluate their finished work. But you should do so only after you have worked with them during the process and given them useful suggestions that they can incorporate into their papers.

You can intervene in your students' writing processes at several points. First, you can help them find and focus their topics by teaching them various strategies for generating information. At this stage you can also help them by showing them options for organizing their writing. *The Riverside Reader* provides extensive assistance at this point by showing students various procedures for conceptualizing and arranging a topic. Second, you can intervene during the process itself by encouraging them to compose several drafts and by commenting on those drafts or talking about them in a conference. Third, you can help your students develop a sense of the audience for their writing by organizing your students into small groups and using class time for them to discuss their papers with one another.

3. *Don't be a composition slave.* Composition teachers often set themselves up as faculty martyrs, believing that they must mark every error on a paper and add copious marginal comments. As a result, they become bogged down in their grading, become frustrated when students don't appreciate their diligence, and wind up feeling angry and guilty. Worse, this method of meticulous proofreading doesn't help students improve their writing. First, teachers who become composition slaves usually hate teaching composition. They inevitably communicate their negative attitudes to their students, and the students will lose any enthusiasm they might have had for writing. Second, students can absorb only so much instruction at one time. If by marking every error you set so many goals for a student that he or she cannot possibly achieve them all, the student is more likely to give up than to try to improve. Third, as psychologist Carl Rogers points out, "When people are bombarded with negative messages, they will stop listening in order to protect their self-images." Students' reluctance to read your meticulous comments does not mean that they are indifferent to your opinion or uninterested in learning how to write. It's more likely that your detailed criticism makes them so uncomfortable that they want to escape from it. Think about how *you* reacted the last time someone criticized your work, however constructive the criticism might have been. Your students are probably even more sensitive.

You have to evaluate your students' papers, of course, and point out their problems, but overwhelming them with negative feedback probably won't help. The NCTE booklet *Classroom Practices: How to Handle the Paper Load* and William Irmsher's book *Teaching Expository Writing* (New York: Holt, 1979) make good suggestions about ways to grade papers constructively. For now, try to remember that the quality of your composition teaching in not necessarily related to the amount of time you spend grading papers. You can be an excellent writing teacher without making yourself a composition slave.

ANALYZING YOUR AUDIENCE

As a novice composition teacher, you probably wonder how you should begin your class. Like any good rhetorician, you should start by analyzing your audience. An early writing sample will give you specific information about your students, but you can almost certainly make other reasonable assumptions before you even go into class.

First, most of your students have done little sustained writing; moreover, many of them live in a culture in which they don't know anybody who writes and in which writing is not valued. In another sense, however, they realize that books and magazines are powerful forces and that much of the work of the world is accomplished by people producing and exchanging written material.

They do have a reverence for the printed word, but they think the ability to write is rare and mysterious. Such attitudes make them enormously insecure about their own writing.

Second, many of your students hate and fear writing in a way that is almost incomprehensible to an English teacher, a person who by definition possesses high verbal skills. As Mina Shaughnessy puts it, "The student lacks confidence in himself in academic situations and fears that writing will not only expose but magnify his inadequacies." Students like these—and they are by no means all minorities or from disadvantaged homes—have probably been criticized for "bad" grammar and spelling every time they have written anything. Moreover, nobody seemed interested in what they had to say, only in what they did wrong. It is as if you tried to make a dancer out of someone by forcing him to perform and then ridiculing him every time he stumbled or missed a step. One or two highly motivated and stubborn people might become dancers that way, but most of your students would do almost anything to avoid such pain and humiliation.

Yet these people who are so insecure with the written word can manage language effectively in their everyday lives, and the person who is trying to teach them to write should assume that they have the ability to learn. What they need is motivation, encouragement, and confidence. That last ingredient—confidence—is the most essential, for, as Shaughnessy points out, "Writing is an act of confidence." Students will write competently only when they develop confidence in their ability to express themselves and trust that they have a reader who is interested in something besides their errors. Not that errors don't matter—they do, and students know it. But teachers who concentrate on errors will discover that their students will resort to the most elementary subjects and sentence patterns in hope of avoiding error. As their confidence declines, so does their willingness to risk working with serious ideas and complex structures.

MOTIVATION: HELPING YOUR STUDENTS GET STARTED

A popular way to help your students start writing is to ask them to practice *free* writing, that is, ask them to write anything that comes into their heads for ten minutes at the beginning of a class period. Peter Elbow's *Writing Without Teachers*, 25th anniversary edition (New York: Oxford UP, 1998), explains the method very well. He recommends that students write for a specified length of time without ever lifting their pens from the paper. They should write anything that comes into their heads, repeating the same sentence several times if that is all they can think of. The teacher may or may not look at this kind of writing; if the students seem to need to show it to a reader, the teacher can read it but *not* correct it or make any judgmental comments.

The purpose behind this kind of writing is to propel students into the actual motor activity of writing, to help overcome their blocks and fears. Once they begin to put down something—anything—and just keep going, they will find that they really can get words down on paper, words that make sense. And they will also find that the act of writing itself helps them generate ideas. When they know that they are not going to be graded or judged, they are more apt to concentrate on expressing themselves because they will not be inhibited from writing by the fear of making a mistake. It may take a while to convince them that you really are not looking for mistakes in free writing. But if you encourage them to use free writing as a stretching exercise, they may use it to warm up for longer pieces of writing.

Keeping a journal is another way to help your students get started. A journal is not the same thing as a diary. It is not a place for students to record daily appointments and activities; it is a place to reflect on ideas and insights that may prove useful later on. Because such a "source book" may help you interpret your students' writing processes, you may want to collect these journals periodically to see what your students are thinking. You should respond in some way to these journal entries—commenting on an idea or asking a question—but you should not criticize or correct the writing. A journal is a place for your students to try out ideas and for you to establish a dialogue with them about their writing.

Having your students keep a journal accomplishes three things. First, and perhaps most important, students believe that you are truly interested in what they have to say and want to communicate with them about it. Second, students discover that they actually can find things in their personal experience that are worth writing about and that can be used to illustrate and support public writing. Third, you can learn something about a student's normal writing, what he or she sounds like when not trying to impress someone or put up a protective wall of vague, abstract jargon.

You will need to approach motivation for writing regular assignments from several angles. One is economic. Today's college students are pragmatic. Aware that their education is no longer free, they want their money's worth. If you can convince them that learning to write will bring them direct and tangible benefits, they will probably be willing to spend the time and effort necessary to master the skill. And despite their contact with a culture that seems to depend on the telephone, television, and the Internet for communication, you should be able to convince them that the person who cannot put together an orderly and lucid piece of prose cannot survive in many professions, or, in fact, even get into them. For example, engineers and businesspeople have to write reports and proposals, nurses and emergency medical technicians have to write reports, lawyers have to write briefs, and social workers have to write case studies. So although your students may not see much writing going on in their immediate world, few people in positions of responsibility can avoid doing it. If you can get an admired professional to come to your class and talk about the part that writing plays in his or her field, you can reinforce your sales talk with direct evidence.

The kinds of writing assignments you give also affect motivation because students will work harder at their writing if they are interested in the topic. It's worth your while, then, to try to find out what their interests are and tailor some of your assignments to those interests. The writing assignments in *The Riverside Reader* invite students to use their personal experience either as the subject of their essays or as a way to write about their readings or some social issue. These assignments also try to move beyond the classroom, suggesting possible purposes, contexts, and audiences in the world outside school.

As you use these assignments or work with your students to formulate others, you may want to consult William Irmscher's criteria for a successful writing assignment:

1. A good assignment should have purpose. Students should believe that they are writing what someone might want or need to read.
2. A good assignment should allow students to draw on experiences that they have had or know about.
3. A good assignment should allow students to write about the specific and immediate rather than the abstract and theoretical. For example, instead of asking a student to write an article for the student newspaper on discrimination against handicapped students, suggest that she write from the point of view of a person in a wheelchair.
4. A good assignment should pose a hypothetical situation within a student's grasp. For instance, asking a student to imagine that she is running for president of the United States makes little sense; asking her to imagine that she is running for student representative to the university council would work much better.
5. An assignment should encourage a student to write by stimulating thought and providing a focus—a purpose—for the writing. An assignment shouldn't be a strictly-for-form exercise that bores both student and teacher.

Finally, we have to recognize that a major source of motivation for all student writers is the teacher's *genuine* response to what they write. Most students won't try very hard unless they believe that the teacher really cares and really wants them to become better writers. Now, a genuine response on your part doesn't mean that you have to love your students or involve yourself in their lives; it means that you have to take an interest in *what* they write and make them believe that it is important to communicate with you. You have to build up your own ethical appeal and overcome the stereotyped image of English teachers as police officers engaged in a constant hunt for errors. Many researchers working in composition believe that most students get the message that content doesn't matter; they can turn out any kind of garbage as long as it's correct, so why should they bother to write better papers? Shaughnessy puts it this way:

> This emphasis upon propriety in the interest not of communication but of status has narrowed and debased the teaching of writing, encouraging at least two tendencies in teachers—a tendency to view the work of their students microscopically, with an eye for forms but with little interest in what was being said, and a tendency to develop a repugnance for error that has made erring students feel like pariahs and allowed teachers of mediocre talents too many easy victories. (113)

You need to give students *real* feedback, not predictable or routine responses, if you expect them to make an effort. And when you run out of time to give them the kind of feedback they need, you can transfer part of the responsibility to their fellow students by using peer editing and group conferences.

ERRORS

Sooner or later, of course, your feedback on student writing is going to have to include comments about errors and suggestions for getting rid of them. Just when you should start making such suggestions depends on several considerations: how severe and pervasive the errors are, how insecure and sensitive your students are about their writing, the kinds of papers they are writing, how long it takes you to gain your students' confidence, and what kinds of expectations the other people they may be writing for have of them. There is no question that gross errors prejudice a writer's audience, and for this reason the composition teacher who doesn't eventually try to improve students' grammar and mechanics is being unrealistic and, ultimately, unfair to them. But try to wait until your students have relaxed a little about their writing and become convinced that your chief interest is in helping them, not in punishing them for mistakes. If possible, it would probably be better not to mark mistakes on their first two or three paragraphs or short papers.

But as Mike Rose points out, error is where education begins. Rather than using errors to find fault, however, use them as a method for working out teaching strategies. Read your students' essays carefully, analyzing the kinds of problems most of your students are having. Your students' writing samples will probably be more complex and mature than you had expected, but try to pinpoint one or two basic problems, such as overgeneralization or failure to follow through on the initial commitment, and talk about those problems in class. Try to demonstrate what Shaughnessy calls the "intelligence" of their mistakes. In an individual conference or class discussion, examine a piece of student writing that illustrates a "logical" pattern of error or an unexpected rupture in a pattern of correctness. That is, what is it about a particular sentence structure that causes a student to make the same kind of error over and over again? What logic is she using to be consistently incorrect? Or what is it about a particular idea or passage that causes a student who had always composed a sentence structure correctly to suddenly lapse into error? Does the difficulty of the idea he is trying to express force him to stretch his syntactical control beyond its normal limits? Such questions reconstruct the discussion of error so that it becomes a problem to solve rather than a sign of deficiency.

PLANNING

One of the major problems you will face as a writing teacher is to persuade your students to plan their writing. For many reasons, most of them don't see any value in extensive planning as part of the writing process. They have always written their papers at the last minute, seemingly unable to make their brains work until they are faced with a crisis. All writers—students, teachers, and professional writers—have, on occasion, used such excuses, but students seem more adept at avoidance behavior than those who have learned the value of planning.

To help students grasp the benefits of planning, set up an assignment schedule that requires them to submit a written prospectus (or abstract of what they tend to write) and, later, a complete, readable first draft. Be sure they keep copies of the work they submit. Look over their planning documents, particularly the first draft, and make one or two suggestions for improvement. Don't grade it. Simply return their work and ask them to revise. You will have to be hard-hearted about their getting drafts in on time, but this is the only way you will be able to comment on their papers and allow for revision before the final draft is due.

Your responsibility in this planning process is to help your students discover a purpose, audience, and strategy for their essays. You may be tempted to take over—to tell them what to do and how to do it. You should resist this role if possible, giving your students authority over their own text. A more valuable role for you in the planning process is as reader (rather than critic). What questions does the paper raise that it doesn't answer? What would you like to know more about? What did the writer do particularly well? What sections of the text confused or misled you? Your tasks are to free your students to plan their own papers and, at the same time, to inform them of the constraints they must adhere to if they choose a particular purpose, audience, or strategy.

DEADLINES

New teachers sometimes feel they are being too authoritarian and rigid if they insist that students meet deadlines and penalize them substantially for later papers. If you feel that way and want to try a more flexible approach, depending on student maturity, self-reliance, and motivation, by all means try it. With some students you may have success. Many experienced teachers, however, find that students, particularly 18- or 19-year-old freshmen, will do just about what you expect them to do. If you make it clear that papers are due on the assigned date whether the student is in class or not, most of them will get their papers in on that date. And you will find that grading and returning a set of papers goes much more smoothly if you don't have late ones dribbling in. You can temper the strictness of such a policy by allowing one penalty-free late paper during the term; such an escape clause will take care of most emergencies. It is also a good idea to write out an explicit statement of policy on all important matters and distribute it the first week in the semester. Having such a policy to refer to later can save you grief and misunderstandings.

CONFERENCES

Part of the traditional wisdom about teaching composition has always been that an instructor should have as many conferences as possible with each student because direct face-to-face contact provides the maximum feedback and one can explain more in person than in any marginal comment. Group conferences among students, especially about planning, are generally valuable. But you need to look carefully at how much you are really accomplishing with conferences and do some pedagogical cost accounting about the time you are investing.

For one thing, shy students often simply do not respond to a conference situation. They detest being called in to sit uncomfortably close to their teacher and have to explain what they were trying to do in their writing. You don't get much more from them than an occasional, "yes, ma'am" or "I don't know," and they are so eager to get away that they really don't listen. Talking to a solid B or C student who is satisfied with his or her grade and not willing to put any more time or effort into a paper to improve it can also be a great waste of time. And conferences with the very good student often turn into rap sessions.

Two kinds of students benefit enough from conferences to warrant the time they require. The first are highly motivated students who, regardless of the grades they are making, truly want to improve their writing. They may come in to confer every time you hand a paper back, want explicit advice, and be open to criticisms and suggestions. This kind of student deserves all the time you can afford to give.

The other kind of student who needs a great deal of individual attention and almost must have it if he or she is to get any benefit from the course is the borderline C−/D student who is hovering on the edge of disaster and doesn't seem to absorb class discussion about ways to improve writing. This kind of student is particularly apt to need help with planning and continual bolstering to keep up his or her confidence. This student might also need specific explanations about developing an idea. Such students must be pressured into coming in as often as possible because it is virtually impossible to give them enough help through marginal comments.

Obviously, working with these students at each end of the continuum will take up the five or six hours a week that the average teacher can afford to dedicate strictly to conferences. Of course you will also want to talk with any other student who voluntarily comes in to get help with a paper, but you should hoard your conference time for that comparatively small number of students who seem to be really benefiting from it. If you do not, you will exhaust yourself with talking and still have most of your grading left to do.

GRADING

Of all the activities connected with the teaching of writing, grading must surely be the most complex and troublesome. It poses a multitude of problems—ethical, political, and psychological, as well as pedagogical—and all too often it can take a disproportionate amount of a composition teacher's energy and time. This problem has no easy solutions, but you may feel more comfortable about the issues involved if you read what some professionals have to say. As a start, look at Paul Diederich's NCTE pamphlet, *Measuring Growth in English,* Chapter 4 of Shaughnessy's *Errors and Expectations,* and Chapter 6 of James Moffett's *Teaching the Universe of Discourse.* Reading them probably won't make grading any easier, but it should help you sort out your priorities and understand some of the effects your grading may have on your students.

Of course, all teachers have to abide by the grading standards of their institutions, and you are probably not free to set up the system that seems best to you or to decide whether you should give grades at all. If, however, you are free to choose between assigning grades or using a system of pass/fail, credit/no credit, or satisfactory/unsatisfactory, you should probably give grades. It's painful and often forces you into decisions you don't want to make, but most seasoned teachers believe that for most students, grades are necessary. An occasional student, particularly a mature one, may be motivated to work at his or her writing solely by the feedback and reinforcement your comments provide, but most will not. Students want to know where their writing ranks in relation to that of others in the class, and they want to know what you consider an A paper and an F paper. Also, many of them are willing to make the changes that you suggest or put in extra time planning and revising only if you hold before them the incentive of a better grade. All their previous schooling has trained them to work for tangible rewards, and you are not likely to change that attitude by simply changing the rules.

You also need to realize that if students are getting pass/fail grades in their composition courses but letter grades in their other courses, the composition course will be the one that they will neglect when the pressure is on. After all, they will reason, why spend five or six hours writing a paper to receive a "pass" when working only an hour or two would probably get them the same grade? They have to set priorities about how to spend their time, and they do their own kind of cost accounting. Another problem that you will almost inevitably face is setting a workable definition of a failing paper. That could cause you more anguish than giving grades.

But having made that case *for* grades, remember to give students some "no-fault" essays. Try *not* to give grades on the first few writing tasks. Rely only on comments until your students have done enough work in and out of class to establish some workable criteria for good writing. It is both cruel and unproductive to give a batch of D's and F's before the students have any idea of what you value in writing. You probably will not have too much difficulty deciding at what point you should begin giving actual grades; two or three weeks into the term, your students will be asking for them.

Whether you are giving comments only or comments and grades, ask yourself from the very beginning what you are trying to achieve with your grading. The answers to that question are necessarily complex, but unless you find some specific answers and establish some priorities, you will find that you are grading generally, which exhausts you and does not really help your students. If you try to mark and comment on everything noteworthy in every paper, you will never make it through the dozens of sets of papers you receive during a term, and you will write so much that most students will stop trying to follow your corrections and suggestions.

Each teacher has his or her own set of values about writing, and no one can tell you precisely which items of usage or mechanics or structure you should put high on your list. After reading the literature about teaching composition, one can extract a body of opinion on practices and priorities that gives the novice teacher some useful guidelines for grading: first, respond to content; second, reinforce what has been done well; third, make specific suggestions for improvement; fourth, stress what is effective, not what is "right" or "wrong"; fifth, choose a few of the most troublesome grammar and usage problems to work on in a set of papers rather than try to comment on all errors at one time.

Responding to Content

It is crucial that you respond to the content of students' papers. Of course you will want to respond as impartially and objectively as you can to get them to write honest papers, but if you ignore content and focus on form and surface features, you will quickly lose your credibility with your students. They will see your responses to their work as canned and impersonal, and in turn they will give you canned and impersonal papers. Then you will have created that situation in which, as William Coles says in his article "Freshman English: The Circle of Unbelief," both student and teacher think that the other one cares nothing about real writing.

You can overcome what seems to be English teachers' natural impulse to start marking errors as soon as they begin to read by simply not allowing yourself to put anything on the paper the first time you read it. Do your students the courtesy you would any other writer: read first to see what they have to say. Then make your first responses to *what* is being said and how well the writer says it. Then treat errors as interference with the communication, not as the communication itself. Remember that errors are the accidents of communication; they're important, but unless they're really egregious, they're not central. Also, you'll find that you will probably notice fewer errors on the second reading.

It's also useful to keep in mind that the more ambitious a student's purpose in writing, the more he or she tries to do, the more likely errors are to crop up in the writing. That phenomenon characterizes all attempts to expand skills. For example, you are more likely to make mistakes in speaking French if you try to have a real conversation with a Parisian than if you confine yourself to using simple expressions from a phrase book. And if you focus on students' mistakes and don't reinforce their attempts to express complex ideas, they'll quit trying.

Reinforcing What Is Done Well

Positive reinforcement helps students far more than negative comments. They pay attention to the good things you write and seem to learn from them. Your positive comments should be more than a "good work" at the end of the paper. You need to be specific about what you like in the papers; for example, bracket a sentence and say, "Good strong sentence," or write beside a paragraph, "Good example" or "Good anecdote." Then in your end comment, point out the specific strengths of the paper.

Copy and distribute really good papers to the class and ask students to analyze what specific qualities contributed to the papers' success. It seems to encourage most students to see that others in their class are becoming good writers and producing papers that are interesting and vividly written. If you analyze the good qualities of only professional writing, students may not pay much attention because such writing seems beyond their capacities, but reading a good student paper gives them a reasonable goal to shoot for.

Making Specific Suggestions for Improvement

When you do point out problems in student papers, ask yourself if your criticism is clear and if you have given the students some idea of how to solve their problems. In "Responding to Student Writing" (*College Composition and Communication*, May 1982), Nancy Sommers says that "most teachers' comments are not text-specific and could be interchanged, rubber-stamped, from paper to paper." Too often students are confused more than they are helped. For example, the notations "awkward," "vague," and "poor word choice" are not in themselves helpful; you need to explain what you mean. And to write "sentence structure" in the margin is almost useless. Maybe the student is trying to do too much in one sentence; maybe the sentence needs to be rearranged or combined with another one; perhaps the sentence is overloaded with nouns and prepositional phrases. Whatever the problem, the student will not write a better sentence simply by trying again if he or she doesn't understand your criticism. Organizational problems are particularly puzzling to students, and often students don't understand why their paragraphs are confusing. You need to suggest specific solutions, such as downshifting from an opening sentence or using a better mode of development, such as cause and effect or comparison.

In summary, ask yourself whether a student will have a substantially better paper if he or she takes your suggestions. Would the grade be better, and would the writer know *why* it is better? If not, you're not accomplishing much with your grading.

Stressing Effect, Not Correctness

Most rhetoricians today believe that you can make judgments about what is good or bad in writing only in terms of the writer's purpose. English teachers should believe in this maxim, preach it, and grade by it. Student writers should learn that the question for them to ask is not "Did I do it right?" but "Does it work?" The chances are that if they think about their writing from that viewpoint, they will make an effort to eliminate grammatical lapses and misspellings that distract or annoy their audience. Your students may also begin to realize how much a deviation from generally accepted usage costs them (see Chapter 1 in Shaughnessy) and that you are pointing out errors not because they offend you but because you want the student to understand how they interfere with communication. And they should realize that platitudes, jargon, unsupported generalities, and ambiguity interfere with communication as much as, if not more than, subject-verb disagreement or sentence fragments.

Of course, in most classroom writing situations, the teacher acts as stand-in for the real audience, and the student is inevitably aware of that. Your job is to defuse the tension and insecurity that knowledge causes by working hard to take the viewpoint of an actual audience and criticize only when the audience would criticize. For instance, does a student's failure to distinguish between *who* and *whom* or *lie* or *lay* really make any difference with most audiences? Almost certainly it does not, but writing *He done it* or *I can't hardly* probably does, and the student should be notified of that through grading comments and penalties.

Focusing on Specific Grading Problems

Many teachers like to limit the number of problems they tackle in one set of papers and try to resolve them before going on to others, reasoning that if they attach all their students' problems at one time, they will bog down in their grading and the students will become so discouraged that they will quit trying. Whether you want to take this approach about mechanics depends on the kind of students you have. If they are what Shaughnessy calls "basic writers," students with a poor grasp of even the rudiments of composition, you certainly should limit your goals. If, however, your students write fairly decent standard English, you may believe that you can point out most of the problems in usage and mechanics that are detracting from the effect they want to achieve and still not intimidate them unduly. After one or two sets of papers, you ought to be able to make a judgment about which and how many writing "accidents" you want to handle at one sitting.

However you choose to handle surface elements of your students' writing—and *surface* doesn't mean they're unimportant—you definitely need to set priorities about content for each paper assignment. If your students are writing autobiographies or statements of goals to accompany scholarship or professional applications, you should grade primarily on how well they present themselves and analyze their audiences, de-emphasizing smoothness, sentence variety, and so on. If they are writing arguments to present before a city council or a zoning board, you should grade on how well they gather and present their evidence, not on vigorous language. Discuss the purpose of the writing assignment with your students before they write, and promise to grade them *primarily* on how well they achieve that purpose. Other considerations enter in, of course, but don't let them distort your focus.

SETTING STANDARDS

Grading compositions is inevitably subjective, but it doesn't need to be nearly as subjective as students seem to think it is. Every teacher who hopes to get honest writing from his or her students is going to have to convince them that they will not be graded on their opinions or their personalities—the teacher does indeed have standards that can be defined. It is a good idea to write out those standards at the beginning of the term and to keep referring to them as you grade and return papers. They are necessarily relative, varying from one institution to another and from one teacher to another. Nevertheless, if you don't give your students some explanation of criteria, you can't expect them to understand your evaluations.

You may be able to adapt these criteria for your students.

F paper: Unsatisfactory. It has three or more of these characteristics: It shows no sense of audience or purpose. It does not make a commitment to the reader early in the paper. It is poorly organized, with ideas so jumbled that it is difficult to follow. The points it makes are primarily generalizations, not adequately supported with specific examples or details. It is marred by serious errors in punctuation or usage. Language is used inaccurately. It does not meet the requirements stipulated for the paper.

D paper: A below-standard paper. It shows a poor sense of audience and purpose. The commitment to the reader is vague or buried; the content is largely unsupported generalities. Points are inadequately developed, and there are few specifics or concrete examples. It is poorly organized and difficult to follow. There are enough errors in usage and punctuation to distract the reader seriously. Language is used inaccurately.

C paper: A satisfactory paper that makes a routine response to the assignment. It shows some sense of audience and purpose. It makes a commitment to the reader and attempts to meet that commitment. It is adequately organized so that the reader can follow it. Generalizations are supported with specifics. There are few distracting errors in usage, punctuation, or spelling. Language is used correctly.

B paper: A good paper that more than meets the assignment. It shows a strong sense of audience and purpose. The writer makes a clear commitment to the reader. The scope of the paper is narrow enough to be treated adequately. Generalizations are supported, and specific examples are used. Language is sometimes used colorfully or imaginatively. The writer's voice or personality comes through. It has very few errors.

A paper: An excellent paper that gives a strong sense of the writer's voice and holds the reader's interest. The writer seems always to keep in mind the audience and purpose. The commitment is clear and fully met. The paper is well organized, with good transitions, and the writer supports generalizations effectively, using vivid details and vivid examples. The writer keeps the scope of the paper narrow enough to handle. Language is vigorous. The writer has taken some risks and gotten away from formulas.

You can consult the appendix of Diederich's *Measuring Growth in English* for a fuller description of the characteristics of what he considers to be a high, medium, and low level of performance on the various components of writing assignments. But his criteria and those just cited may seem too strict for your group of students. If so, you will have to adapt your standards to suit your circumstances. Also, sooner or later you will believe that you have to reward students for effort and improvement, and positive comments without better grades will eventually wear thin. But you shouldn't deceive your students into thinking that all of them will be able to write A and B papers if they just try hard enough. For some of them, that is like saying they can be seven feet tall if they try.

Although you may find it useful to start out by giving students these rather abstract statements about standards, you need to reinforce the descriptions with concrete examples as soon as possible. Actually showing them student papers that fall into each category will be more convincing than generalizing, but you will have to work out a method that does not humiliate or punish any student in your class. You can use anonymous examples from another class if you are sure they cannot be identified, or keep papers from a previous year to use as examples. If you can find no suitable examples *without hurting someone*, you may have to create some typical papers. You may want to reserve the right to duplicate and distribute the first A paper you read in the term so that your students can see what an outstanding essay looks like.

COPING WITH ALL THOSE PAPERS

If you have more than fifty or sixty composition students who write a paper every week, or even every two weeks, and you have any other important responsibilities, you will find it almost impossible to grade all those papers all the time. Yet the one proven method of helping people improve their writing is to give them quality feedback and responses that help them develop their skills. This dilemma has no good solution, but you will have to find some workable alternatives to meticulous, individualized grading of every paper if you are going to survive. One frequently recommended method is to transfer some of the responsibility to the student's peers by having students edit and comment on one another's papers. You can then comment on and assign a grade to a paper only after students have gotten the benefit of response and advice from classmates.

Another compromise method is to edit and fully comment on only every second or third paper a student writes, but to give a grade and a general comment to the other papers. You could supplement this by duplicating or making a transparency of one sample paper from each assignment (with permission, of course) and editing it in class with the students' help. That procedure would give all student insights into the options available to them for that paper and into what kinds of rhetorical strategies worked and what problems arose. Another survival strategy is to grade only for certain things on each set of papers and let other problems go. Impress on students, however, that they are responsible for all the components covered in the course.

None of these methods can take the place of the kind of careful and personal attention you can give every paper when you have only a few students. The ideal would be a combination of group conferences for planning and first-draft editing and subsequent careful grading by the instructor followed by postwriting analysis from the class. Lacking that—and most of us do—you will have to juggle and experiment and have members of the class help each other as much as possible. And do keep reading the professional journals to see what other teachers are trying—often you will get some real help.

Grading becomes a little easier as you gain experience, but not much. You learn more about how to respond to students' writing in useful ways. But for most of us, as we learn to know our students, the personal element begins to creep in and to interfere in our judgments. It is always illuminating to notice how critical and thorough new teachers are in the practice grading sessions during preterm orientation and then to see the kinds of grades they actually give students in their classes as the term progresses and they develop a friendly relationship with their classes. But if papers are switched so that these teachers are grading students they don't know, the become strict again. It is a good corrective to arrange such a switch with another teacher at least once during a term; you will find out whether you are really doing for your students what you abstractly think the whole staff should be doing when they teach composition.

In the long run you cannot afford to be sentimental about grading. Anyone who takes seriously Neil Postman's statement that an important goal in the teaching of English is "helping students to manage their lives more effectively by increasing their control over language" should try not to see grading as a political or social act. It is a teaching tool that must be used sensitively and with an awareness of consequences. If you fail to grade constructively because of guilt, sympathy, or weakness, you really defraud the students. If, by giving undeserved grades, you gloss over incompetencies for which a student will be penalized when he or she leaves your class, you have done that student a serious disservice.

SUPPLEMENTAL READING ON TEACHING WRITING

The following bibliography lists books and articles on all aspects of rhetoric and composition:

Horner, Winifred Byron, ed. *The Present State of Scholarship in Historical and Contemporary Rhetoric.* Rev. ed. Columbia: U of Missouri P, 1990.

Lindemann, Erika. *Longman Bibliography of Composition and Rhetoric, Vol. 2, 1986.* New York: Longman, 1988.

McClelland, Ben W., and Timothy R. Donovan. *Perspectives on Research and Scholarship in Composition.* New York: MLA, 1985.

Moran, Michael G., and Ronald F. Lunsford. *Research in Composition and Rhetoric: A Bibliographic Sourcebook.* Westport, Conn.: Greenwood, 1990.

Tate, Gary, ed. *Teaching Composition: Twelve Bibliographical Essays.* Fort Worth: Texas Christian UP, 1987.

Descriptive Analyses
of the Essays and Short Stories

Narration and Description

THE STRATEGIES

Although the narrative and descriptive essays are often given as separate assignments in composition courses, they are combined in this first section so that teachers can present expressive writing and still reserve time for the many forms of informative and argumentative writing. This choice is tricky because it confirms the folk wisdom about expressive writing and rhetorical difficulty. According to custom, students can write narratives first because they are already familiar with storytelling and can organize a personal experience according to simple chronology. Similarly, students can write descriptive essays early because they can use their senses to discover details that can then be arranged according to spatial patterns.

Teachers can find considerable support for such conventional wisdom in their students' writing, which often seems more fluent when it focuses on personal narrative or describes something familiar. But teachers are also aware that narration is not restricted to expressive writing—historical narratives are informative and persuasive—and that the best personal narratives require the sophisticated use of pacing and point of view. Similarly, they know that description includes technical descriptions that are almost exclusively informative and that the most effective personal descriptions depend on the deft selection of evocative and telling detail.

Combining the two strategies into one assignment has an internal logic. Most narratives (telling what happened) are fleshed out by description (showing what something looked and felt like). And most descriptions are propelled by a strong narrative line. You may want to examine these propositions by discussing the way the two methods are presented in the section introduction and illustrated by the sample paragraph. Like the lesson in Kingston's paragraph, events occur in time and space. Thus writers must identify the central *conflict* in their essay, arrange the events in a sequence, and select those details that render a vivid picture of the events as they unfold. Most important, writers need to identify their purpose in re-creating the story for an audience. Such a discussion should help your students understand how strategies such as *plot, pace,* and *point of view* shape and sharpen the point of a narrative and descriptive essay.

THE READINGS

The six essays in this section illustrate these strategies in action. Helen Prejean opens her essay by describing the odd sensation of seeing Susan Sarandon acting in her stead in the film version of *Dead Man Walking,* and then she describes her own emotional response to the situations Sarandon re-created. George Orwell's essay proposes a theory about real impulses of imperialism and then illustrates that theory with a dramatic revelation of his role in shooting an elephant. Both essays establish narration and description as a means of proof and reveal how writers use pace to build anticipation and manipulate point of view.

Jill McCorkle's remembrance about a summer event that forever changed her understanding of her parents as people is an analytical narrative, similar to Prejean's and Orwell's in intent, but much more nostalgic in tone. The "story" in her essay presents a memorable sketch of childhood in the middle of the twentieth century, but it is also a coming-of-age story, in which the narrator is confronted, not with her own sexuality, but that of her parents.

Judith Ortiz Cofer uses narration to introduce and exemplify the points she is making in a larger analysis of stereotypes of Puerto Rican women. The stories in her text illustrate the kinds of prejudices she has faced as a Latina.

Andre Dubus' essay "Digging" is an elegiac text, mourning both the loss of his right leg in an automobile accident (although he doesn't tell readers that) and his father. He writes with careful attention to description so that his readers can learn the same lessons from his experience that he did.

Alice Adams' "Truth or Consequences" presents the essence of narration and description—an adult recounting a specific yet universal childhood experience. A frame story that mixes details of past and present, it subtly embodies themes opposing stereotyping that are common among all of the readings in this section of the text.

THE VISUAL TEXT

Marjane Satrapi's cartoon "The Veil" tells the story of the implementation of laws regarding women's dress following the Islamic Revolution. While holy men and politicians on both sides of the issue debate whether veiling women and girls results in their safety or restriction, the school-girls shown in Satrapi's drawing complain that the dress code is an imposition on them physically and emotionally; they are encumbered and rendered indistinguishable from one another by it. However, the playful adaptations that the girls make of their veils reveal the indomitable spirits of the young women beneath those garments.

THE WRITING

The writing assignments that conclude this section ask students to experiment with these strategies in their own essays. As students plan their first drafts, you should encourage them to see the relationship between two lines of action: (1) the events as they happened in real time and space, and (2) the events as they might be arranged and presented in an expressive way. Ask them to consider how certain events in their essay will have to be telescoped or expanded to dramatize the narrator's conflict or point of view. Once they have plotted the story line, they will be ready to write.

Each writing assignment sends students back to one of the essays for advice, evidence, and stimulation. For example, assignment 2 suggests that students explore a personal experience in which they had to perform an unpleasant deed (Orwell, Prejean), assignment 3 asks students to chronicle their own experiences with storytelling (McCorkle), assignment 4 asks students to parallel surrounding and familial cultural events (Cofer), and assignment 6 invites students to offer their own proof of the adage that "seeing is believing" (Dubus, Adams).

ANDRE DUBUS "Digging"

Purpose

It is impossible for the middle-aged Andre Dubus to write now to his father, who lay on his deathbed when Dubus was still a Marine Captain, so the writer eulogizes him with this tribute that describes his father's role in helping him achieve manhood. Extrinsically, the narrator of this book chapter and his father had little in common. Introduced as "my ruddy, broad-chested father," who had "sired a sensitive boy," the father hands his son over to a construction foreman with the command that he "make a man of him." The boy nearly fails as a manual laborer: his back and palms burn, he sees black spots before his eyes, vomits his breakfast, and sleeps through his lunch hour. That afternoon, his father benevolently appears above the trench where he is digging. The narrator thinks his father has come to take him home, where he will quietly accept his son's inadequacy; instead, his father buys him a sandwich and a pith helmet and takes him back to the job. A co-worker predicts, "You going to be all right now," when the helmeted boy returns, and the author admits that he was, although he claims he still doesn't know why. The calm assurance of the narrator's father seems to have helped the narrator to persevere as much as the pith helmet did.

In spite of his meek appearance, which "[drew] bullies to [him]," the boy admits to "a dual life" in which he often appears distracted but is mentally "riding a horse and shooting bad men." When his father suggests that it is time for him to get a job, Dubus cannot tell him that he does not want to work. He won't say that he doesn't want to wear the pith helmet his father chooses for him. He can't tell his mother and sister how ruined and despondent he feels after his first day on the job. In truth, the narrator wanted someone to make a man of him. Prior to enduring his summer of harsh physical labor, he feels "ashamed" and "incompetent," and remarks that he "did not believe [he] was as good at being a boy as other boys were." He says that he has written this chapter because he knows, "It is time to thank my father for wanting me to work and telling me I had to work and getting the job for me and buying me lunch and a pith helmet . . . ."

Audience

The tone of Dubus' chapter is nostalgic. He writes for other men his age who might recall a similar turning point in their own lives, and to young adult men who are or soon will be facing such a moment of truth themselves. Most of his readers would not relish the opportunity to dig a ditch with a pickax and a shovel any more than Dubus did at sixteen. The revelations that he was "shy" and "lived a life no one could see" pique his readers' interest. Not only is it time for Dubus to thank his father, but it is also time for him to tell what he would not reveal to his family or his coworkers during that difficult summer. His reader is his willing listener.

Many of Dubus' readers will heavily identify with his respectfully tacit conflicts with his talkative and manly father, especially where matters of race are concerned. The boy notices immediately that he has been assigned to work with black men, and he responds to their cheerful greetings in kind. At lunchtime on his first day on the job, he chooses to sit under a tree with his fellow black workers, rather than retreat with the white workers to "another shaded place." He says of his fellow trench-diggers that he "felt that we were friends," and "comrades," a transport that eventually extends to "all the black men at work." There is a hint of guilt in his revelation that at the end of the day, his coworkers "went to the colored section of town" while he went home to cocktail hour in a genteel home "where vases held flowers, and things were clean, and [the family's] manners were good." Dubus also expresses outrage that the black laborers were paid an "unjust" wage. The narrator's father refers to his son's compatriots as "nigras," an archaic usage that should be addressed in class discussion. It is as much an outdated relic as the drugstore lunch counter that the father visits with his son or the salt tablets kept by the water cooler at the job site in the outmoded belief that taking salt would help restore the electrolytes lost to excessive perspiration.

Strategy

The pace of this narration draws readers in and helps them empathize with the boy's predicament. The long opening description of the father who worked his way up as a civil engineer, read literary magazines, and gave up hunting for golf is part of the text's elegiac tone. It also shows that his actions on the day of his son's first job were probably prudent and loving. Describing the first morning of the job itself takes up half of the chapter. Readers are taken down into the three-foot trench under the hot sun. They are invited to feel the weight of the pickax in their backs, legs, arms, and shoulders until they empathize with the narrator's nausea and despair.

Most readers want, as the boy does, that he be taken home and cared for by his mother after the first morning's work. Dubus helps his audience learn the same lesson he did from the incident. His description of what would have happened on that fateful day, had his father surrendered and taken him home, helps readers appreciate what a defining moment it was when his father sent him back to work. In the end, it was the narrator's father, not the job foreman, who made a man of him.

JILL MCCORKLE "The Mullet Girls"

Purpose

In this memoir, Jill McCorkle narrates a seemingly innocuous incident that "took only a few minutes" but galvanized her burgeoning awareness of her own sexuality, and, more alarmingly, that of her parents as well. Thirteen years old at the time, the storyteller is still torn between the childish activity of fishing with her father and the tandem adolescent pursuits of garnering a tan and attracting admiring looks from boys. When the story opens, she is playing cards with her male cousins, who regard her and her sister in a decidedly unromantic way and bait them to say the phrase "the ace of spades," to accentuate their southern accents. Outwardly, at least, the narrator is still a child, laughed at by those boys. She describes her fishhook baiting prowess of the recent past, bragging that once her bait was been sufficiently skewered on a hook, she would wipe "the blood and goo on the butt of [her] swimsuit." However, during the summer in question, she has begun to wear "bikinis." Styles of women's swimwear provide tangible symbols of the incipient struggle in the narrator's mind and body. Her mother cautions her against looking like the girls at the shabby tourist area nearby who went about with "breasts spilling from tight bathing suits." The "mullet girls" who come to call on her father are attired in "skimpy outfits," while her mother's set wears "suits that hid[e] all evidence that children had ever sprung from their bodies." This is a coming-of-age story that Freud would endorse; a girl's own sexuality is awakened when she realizes that others see her father as a man.

"The Mullet Girls" is an especially apt nickname for the women who call on the storyteller's father, as it also invokes, although anachronistically, a particular hairstyle that denotes their class and culture. Ostensibly, they have come to the family beach house to offer the narrator's father some mullet, fish that they promised to share if they caught any. Their appearance and attitude, however, leave little doubt in the narrator's mind about what the women are really fishing for. When they approach the screen door and one calls "Johnny! Oh Johnny," his daughter recoils, explaining that she "did not like the sound of his name coming out of her mouth." Instantaneously she realizes that her father is a sexual being, and she feels fear that he will abandon the family. She wants to shield herself and her mother from this reality. The oxymoronic adolescent urge to protect her mother from adult reality occurs again in the story when a teenage boy looks at her "that way," and she is secretly pleased by the attention but embarrassed that it is her mother who points it out to her.

Audience

Subtle clues in the text reveal elements of characterization designed to help readers identify with the narrator and her family. They are Southerners with accents that sound like *The Andy Griffith Show* and amuse their cousins from the "Northern" state of Maryland. The Mullet Girls, however, speak with the truly funny accents, those that make "the folks from Mayberry sound like British royalty by comparison." We learn that the narrator's family are quite ordinary Americans, not the summer home set, and that their beach house, which was narrowly spared by a hurricane a few years earlier, is on loan from a friend of the narrator's father who pays but "seventy odd cents a year" in property tax for it. The area is not as touristy as Ocean Drive or Myrtle Beach, but is in a seedy part of South Carolina's waterfront, where one can "get married, get a drink or two, buy some fireworks, get a divorce and still be home in time for the 11 o'clock news." Even readers who are not familiar with the area can get a good mental picture of it.

McCorkle is apparently a baby-boomer, and her references to popular culture of the '50s and '60s endear her to that audience and establish the cultural setting for the piece. The children watch *The Andy Griffith Show* (precursor to *Mayberry RFD*), and the father drinks Falstaff beer from the beach house refrigerator because the Playmate Cooler has yet to be invented. Most telling however, is the narrator's fear that her father would run off with Julie Andrews, whom he found "pretty" in the then newly released movie *The Sound of Music*. Readers who have seen that movie will realize that the chaste governess who marries her widowed employer after observing his affection for his large brood of exceptionally talented children is hardly the siren the narrator dreads. However innocent or slight the father's attraction to Julie Andrews, it demonstrates that he is not likely to be lured away by the Mullet Girls.

Strategy

McCorkle constructs a conflict for her story around the child's fear that her father will run off with the Mullet Girls by narrating how she protects her mother from the same dread. The mother's questions about the strange visitors are innocuous enough, but the child imagines "a flush to her cheeks" that may well be concealed by sunburn. She reassures her apparently unconcerned mother that the women were "old looking. Coarse. Rough and worn out" and that they "smelled fishy." The mother's reply, that "Something's fishy" does not incite the merriment she expected from her daughter. After twenty years of marriage, the narrator's mother finds the Mullet Girls' overtures laughable, as do the other family members.

The father's character is built and reinforced throughout the narrative, so that the reader is really not surprised by his indifference to the Mullet Girl's real or implied offers. His tenderness toward his daughters, the way he wraps his beer cans to keep them cold as well as to encourage his youngest daughter to believe they contain bait, and his fishing from a lawn chair that was a Father's Day gift all paint a picture of a devoted family man. When the narrator reveals that her father suffers from depression but is candid, even philosophical about it, readers can guess that his genial relationship with the Mullet Girls was nothing more than friendly fishing talk. Of course he introduces his pathetic mermaids to his family and accepts their gift with "Southern kindness." However, as readers, we have known since he released his "spiney sharp-toothed" catch with a hook embedded in its mouth and sent it back to find its disappointed fish wife that the narrator's father is a man whose thoughts and passions never stray far from home.

JUDITH ORTIZ COFER "The Myth of the Latin Woman: I Just Met a Girl Named Maria"

Purpose

Cofer, who is an accomplished poet and novelist, says that in her travels around the United States to give readings, she tries through modeling and storytelling, to change the negative stereotyping of Latin American women that prevails in our culture. This chapter from her book *The Latin Deli* extends that crusade into print. She demonstrates the confusion that results when the members of one culture judge those of another by their own idiosyncratic standards. Her example about Hispanic schoolgirls trying to dress for "Career Day" shows how unreasonable it is to ask people of color to conform to white American values. Her attempts to act British in London convince her that "the Island" travels with those who leave Puerto Rico; one should not attempt to abandon her own identity.

Cofer's purpose is to prove that cultural stereotypes are damaging and wrong. She argues that "some people" who don't bother to look past one's "Hispanic appearance" misjudge the dress, demeanor, and potential of Latinas. Acknowledging her own good fortune and the providence of her parents who gave her a good education and "a stronger footing in the mainstream culture," Cofer speaks for her many Hispanic *campaneras* who lack the social standing or language skills to speak for themselves. To subtly reinforce her thesis, she paints unstereotypical portraits, such as the "Chinese priest" who performed a Spanish mass in New Jersey, the female Italian American business-school student, and the Chicana Ph.D. student; her essay ends with a quotation from one of her own poems about "Latin women [who] pray in Spanish to an Anglo God/with a Jewish heritage . . . ."

Audience

Writing specifically for "those who should know better," but still succumb to the urge to "put others 'in their place,'" Cofer recounts embarrassments she has suffered as the object of cultural stereotyping. She wants to curb the behavior of the patronizing man who sang to her on a British bus, or the obnoxious one in a "classy metropolitan hotel," the boy who expected her to "'mature early,'" and the woman at a poetry reading who mistook the Latina poet for a waitress. Cofer tries to correct stereotypes about Latin American women by educating her audience. It is "culture clash" that causes her Italian American friend to observe that Puerto Rican girls' jewelry looks like they are "wearing 'everything at once.'" Cofer describes the tropical heat, colorful environment, and strict Catholic morality that pervade Puerto Rico as a way of explaining styles of dress common to Latinas.

Cofer's observation that what is called a "party" in the United States is really just "a marathon conversation in hushed tones" draws a sharp contrast between herself and her audience. Assuming that her readers have not visited Puerto Rico, she describes the *piropos*, or provocative poems that young men recite impromptu to women on the streets of the island. Their outrageous but never obscene poems contrast sharply with the "dirty song" invented by the man in a tuxedo who embarrasses Cofer and her colleague in their hotel. This book chapter is an answer to that man's daughter who expected the women to "laugh along" with her father's inappropriate performance.

Strategy

Narratives exemplify and strengthen every point in Cofer's arguments against stereotyping Latin American women. The story of the young man who regaled Cofer with "an Irish tenor's rendition of 'Maria' from *West Side Story*," introduces the essay's theme. Recounting how she "agonized" over what to wear to school on "Career Day" proves that "it is custom . . . not chromosomes" that prompt Puerto Rican girls to opt for "tight skirts and jingling bracelets." Cofer's indignation at the behavior of the boy who escorted her to her first formal dance underscores the fact that Latinas are not promiscuous, as the young man thought. The middle-aged man who delights his companions by taunting Cofer as "Evita," sharply demonstrates that race does not automatically determine one's social class, even though the man would not similarly objectify a "white woman." The narrative about the woman at the poetry reading who unwittingly orders a cup of coffee from the poet she has come to hear underscores Cofer's point that Latinas are not simply "menials," to be relegated to jobs as domestics. Cofer's best strategy, however, is an ethical one. She is a Latin American woman who defies stereotypes by speaking out against them.

HELEN PREJEAN "Memories of a Dead Man Walking"

Purpose

Sister Helen Prejean is perhaps America's most outspoken opponent of the death penalty; in keeping with that crusade, this essay offers a narrative about the experience of watching her book being made into a movie, and a fervent argument in support of the United Nations Declaration of Human Rights. Prejean summarizes the Declaration for her audience, explaining that it calls for prisoners to be granted "two very basic human rights . . . the right not to be tortured, the right not to be killed." Prejean's moving story of her experiences as spiritual advisor to convicted murderer Patrick Sonnier is laced with facts about the death penalty and its victims in America, along with the astute observation that "The essential torture of the death penalty is not finally the physical method" of execution, but the anticipation and dread that causes condemned human beings to "die a thousand times before they die."

Audience

Many readers of this commentary will have seen the movie *Dead Man Walking* and know immediately which scenes Prejeans alludes to in her narrative. Beyond certifying that the filmmakers "got certain scenes right," Prejean wants to make certain that her readers understand the autobiographical nature of the film, including the suffering of its narrator (depicted by actress Susan Sarandon) when she clutches "the crucifix around her neck, praying 'Please God, don' let him fall apart.'" Readers know that the nun is simultaneously asking for strength for herself. Just as viewers of the film and readers of this narrative are "sucked in" to the intertwined plights of Sister Prejean and her death-row pen pal, the real life Prejean reveals that watching the filming of *Dead Man Walking* "sucked [her] back into the original scene, the white-hot fire of what actually happened." Even though the filmmakers "shot each scene ten or more times," Prejean says it was like living through the depicted events again each time.

Since most of Prejean's audience is familiar with the movie about her experiences in the Louisiana death house in 1984, she offers insights that go back further and deeper than the movie's rendering of her story. She answers critics of the film (and the book that inspired it) who said that a nun should not defend a murderer. For filmgoers who did not read the book, Prejean explains how she became involved with convicted killer Patrick Sonnier in the first place. Prejean speaks directly to her detractors, who quote Bible verses such as "an eye for an eye," and dismisses what she calls "'biblical quarterbacking'" as sophistry. Conceding "Religion is tricky business," Prejean denounces "people wanting to practice vengeance and have God agree with them."

Strategy

Prejean enlightens her audience about the inequities of the death penalty in America. Although she says "everybody who lives on this planet and has at least one eye open knows that only poor people get selected for death row," she knows this is news to some of her readers. She also reveals, in her colloquial way, that there is "a greased track to prison and death row" from the projects where she volunteers. Furthermore, Prejean reveals racial inequity in the enforcement of the death penalty in the United States, claiming that government execution is "almost exclusively reserved for those who killed whites." As one who has been inside the death house and received the last, loving words of a convicted killer, Prejean believes she has a duty to let other Americans know what happens in the name of justice.

The narrator's admissions that she was "scared out of [her] mind," "in over [her] head," and unaware that an inmate's spiritual advisor witnesses his execution explains how a fairly ordinary citizen was drawn into the death-house drama. A nun who has dedicated her life to serving the poor, Prejean uses her ethos and naiveté to make her story and her arguments hit home with readers. She opens with the scene where Susan Sarandon prays for strength in the women's room of the death house, and in the middle of her essay she returns to the real-life inspiration for that scene, explaining that "in the women's room, just a few hours before the execution. . . God and I met . . . and it was like a circle of light." Although she had not realized initially that she would be the one who could prevent Patrick Sonnier from dying alone, she claims that God gave her the strength to support him to the end.

Although Prejean confirms that "the movie got this scene right," in some places it seems she is writing to make sure that its audience understands that Patrick Sonnier was "a human being" who was "fully alive" and that he "died with dignity." She wants the viewers of the film to know how very real both her life and Sonnier's life were. Actor Sean Penn, who played "Matthew Poncelet," the character who represented Sonnier in the film version of the story, was "executed" on a Hollywood set, surrounded by admirers and technicians. The gritty reality of the death penalty is better described by Prejean when she reveals, "At the end I was amazed at how ordinary Patrick Sonnier's last moments were."

GEORGE ORWELL "Shooting an Elephant"

Purpose

In addition to presenting a suspenseful story, Orwell's classic essay "Shooting an Elephant" offers political commentary whose purpose it to prove the ironic thesis that imperialistic forces are, ultimately, controlled by the peoples they oppress. Orwell's relationship to the "natives" in the story is analogous, he maintains, to Great Britain's role in Burma. It is "those two thousand Burmans" who followed the narrator who made him shoot. They wanted a spectacle; they expected it. The police officer had as much as promised to kill the elephant, he realized, when he sent an orderly to borrow an elephant rifle. In addition, he could not let the crowd laugh as he was trampled by the elephant, and since he was afraid to do the honorable thing (to go within "twenty-five yards of the elephant and test his behavior"), he believed he had no choice other than to shoot, especially since showing fear in front of the Burmans would discredit all white men in the East. Therefore, the narrator admits that he killed the elephant "solely to avoid looking a fool." The essay suggests that greater stakes than elephants are lost when a government believes it knows what is best for remote subjects. Orwell says that "when the white man turns tyrant it is his own freedom that he destroys."

Audience

Orwell wrote this essay in 1936 for an "antifascist" periodical called *New Writing* whose readers probably agreed with the author that imperialism was ideologically corrupt. In fact, many readers might have mistrusted Orwell because of his service in the Indian imperial police, executing British rule in Burma; therefore, he is eager to quell any such misgivings. He admits in his second paragraph that "I had already made up my mind that imperialism was an evil thing. . . ."

Writing in the first person point of view, Orwell assures the audience that he is a reasonable, open-minded, honorable character. His explanation of why he shot the elephant is laced with statements such as "I knew with perfect certainty that I ought not shoot him," "I did not in the least want to shoot him," and "But I did not want to shoot the elephant." Orwell seems aware of his readers' political consciences, expecting them to side with the Indian elephant owner, who believed the beast should not have been shot. Orwell, in fact, agrees and counts himself lucky that the "coolie" was killed—making him, if not morally right, at least legally correct.

Because the audience for this essay is mostly Englishmen, the crowd of Burmans who press the issue is compared with an English crowd. Also, most of the story's readers have no experience with elephants or Eastern culture; therefore Orwell outlines the usual procedure for handling an elephant whose attack of "must" is due and explains that his "old .44 Winchester" is much too small to kill an elephant, but that an elephant gun aimed at the animal's ear will do the trick.

Strategy

Like the crowd that follows the police officer on his fateful elephant hunt, readers of the essay believe, almost from the start of the expedition, that he will shoot the animal. Clues lead Orwell to the elephant (destroyed hut, killed cow, devoured fruit stalls, damaged rubbish van, and slaughtered man), and Orwell's arguments lead his readers to the conclusion that the elephant must be shot. Details develop the tension in the essay. The description of the dead coolie, partially skinned, dragged through mud, and left dead in a crucified position, with his "teeth bared and grinning with an expression on unendurable agony," lends a grim immediacy to the problem. In contrast, the elephant, when he is found, completes a pastoral scene. Orwell describes the giant animal with subjective detail, calling him "grandmotherly" as he feeds on grass just eight yards from the road where the crowd gathers.

The death of the elephant is majestic compared to the coolie's demise. At first shot, he does not drop, and when he finally does fall, he seems to rise for a moment. The great change that comes over the dying elephant causes the narrator to regret his action even more and to try to hasten the end of the elephant's suffering and his own, first by pouring bullets into the elephant and finally by going away where he could witness no more. It takes the elephant half an hour to die, a short time compared with the duration of the narrator's remorse. Orwell's details and pacing are as persuasive as his arguments in this essay. The elephant could have been spared, but the police officer had no choice. Although he fired the rifle, the crowd decided the animal's fate, but, ultimately, it was imperialism that killed the elephant.

ALICE ADAMS "Truth or Consequences"

Purpose

Emily Ames, the protagonist in Alice Adams' short story, "Truth or Consequences" learns to look beyond stereotypes in judging people. The teasing engaged in by Emily and her classmates does not acknowledge the human feelings of the "truck children" at their school. When her friends begin calling her "Emily Jones" and pretending that "'Emily would like to kiss Car Jones!'" the narrator confesses that "in all of this new excitement, the person I thought of least was the source of it all: Car Jones." Proud of having been exempted from a year of schooling herself, she easily dismisses Carstair Jones as one of the "several overgrown children" who are often "expelled from . . . class . . . for some new acts of rebelliousness." Like her peers, Emily believes that all of the country children are unkempt, unconcerned with studies, and the offspring of illiterates. A product of her environment, Emily has adopted the middle-class, "middle-South," middle-of-the-century stance that Car Jones and others like him are "'abnormal'" or "'different'" people.

As the lives of Emily Ames and Carstair Jones unfold, the two become more alike. Both are dissatisfied with the mores and social roles their culture demands. Car Jones demands to be tested and is placed in high school. He attends the local university, and his family moves into town. While a college student, his sexual exploits with the "most popular senior in [the] high school" become almost legendary, and a play that he has written is performed by the college dramatic society. At the height of his academic achievement, Carstair Jones turns down membership in a prestigious campus fraternity. Later in life, his name graces the society pages and gossip columns of newspapers as he marries "a famous former movie star" and acquires a sort of celebrity.

The proper Emily Ames, well-to-do daughter of a deceased banker and niece of a college professor, lives through "three marriages to increasingly 'rich and prominent' men, . . . three children, and as many abortions." She confesses that she hasn't "counted [her] lovers," and she reveals that she was "once raped, by someone to whom [she] was married." Her life has not turned out as simply or happily as she expected. Emily realizes that Car Jones appears to have achieved more fame and satisfaction in life than she has, in spite of his humble and her promising beginnings. Married to a prominent surgeon, and probably to all outward appearances content and successful, Emily wonders at the story's conclusion whether Car "could be as haunted as [she is] by everything that ever happened" in their lives. She has learned to distrust appearances. Just as Car Jones was more complex than the stereotype of a "truck child," his life must now be more complicated than the typical, carefree image of celebrity persons.

Audience

Adams' story is set in the southern United States in the middle part of the twentieth century, although it was not published until 1982. She includes details and explanations that communicate the social structure of her small town, and its social mores to contemporary readers. The story's narrator, Emily, enumerates Hilton's three social classes of that time period: "At the scale's top were the professors and their families. Next were the townspeople. . . . Country people were the bottom group." Shedding more light on the town's attitude, she explains that Negroes might have been in a fourth social class, but "they were so separate. . . . They were in effect invisible." Adams seems to expect that her audience is more enlightened and worldly than the citizens of Hilton. She does not translate Charlotte Ames' French idiom, which means literally, "good student," when Emily's mother refers to the proper suitor, Harry McGinnis, as one of the *bien élevé* Southern boys."

The social mores of the time and place are communicated by example. The gallant Harry McGinnis takes Emily "to a lot of Saturday movies" where they "clammily [hold] hands . . . for the rest of that spring, and into the summer." However, Car Jones creates a scandal when he is reputed to have "'gone all the way'—to have 'done it'" with a local girl. The older narrator, who casually mentions her lovers and abortions, takes pains to re-create these more restrained customs and quaint euphemisms from her past, reminding readers that cultural expectations change with time and locale.

Strategy

This historical narrative story is set within the frame of a contemporary narrative. The adult narrator has happened upon "a gossip column" reporting that "a man named Carstair Jones . . . married a famous former movie star." The adult Emily then recalls her childhood interactions with a "truck child" named Car Jones, who must surely be the same person. Adams' flashback plot allows her to interweave herself and Car as childhood and adult characters in her story, thus gradually revealing their separate but similar fates. Both felt like outsiders as children, she because of monetary wealth and scholastic success and he from an apparent lack of those valued traits. Both adults have gained a measure of outward "success" through fortuitous marriages.

Adams uses evocative description to engage her readers in the story. She chooses universal images to encourage her audience to imagine the schoolyard where the "truth or consequences" game occurs, listing "the huge polished steel frames for the creaking swings, the big green splintery seesaws, the rickety slides" and naming the activities of the children: hopscotch, jumping rope, and talking and giggling for the girls; and football or baseball for the boys. Similarly, she catalogs the elements of "Southern spring," the "opulence" of which includes a "profusion of flowering shrubs and trees . . . riotous flower beds . . . lush lawns, . . . rows of brilliant iris, the flowering quince and dogwood trees, crepe myrtle, wisteria vines."

The pace of the story engages readers as well. The plot moves slowly until the schoolyard game links Emily and Car together. The story's title names the action that is most crucial to its plot and thesis. The childhood game of "truth or consequences" has consequences of its own. Emily's friends' playful insinuations that she is going to kiss Car Jones come true in a disturbing way. After that, everything happens more quickly. The retelling of the story, which occurs in the last few pages in which the adult Emily tries to re-envision Car Jones' childhood, telling it from a differently biased point of view, is very brief in comparison with her first telling of the story's events. In the last analysis, the *consequences* of her and Carstair Jones' lives provide a glimpse at the *truth*.

Process Analysis

THE STRATEGIES

The process-analysis essay is an elementary but essential writing strategy. Most teachers prefer to teach it as the first expository form because all students have had experience giving and following directions and because composition students can use the skills that they have already studied in narration and description to explain the stages in a process. Like the chronology of events and the pattern of details, the stages in a process provide a plan for the process-analysis essay. Indeed, most students suspect that if they write about a process that has established stages— "how to fix a flat tire"—the essay will write itself. Students soon discover that drafting a set of clear and logical directions is not as simple as it looks.

The chief advantage of teaching the process-analysis essay is that the class can often *test* written instructions against the process they propose to explain. For example, ask a few students to analyze a common procedure—finding a book in the library or typing a paper on a word processor. If they omit steps, reverse steps, or fail to explain the use of basic tools, your other students should be able to detect the error, thus learning how defective instructions do not produce the intended results.

Such demonstrations will prepare students to understand the purpose of the information contained in the introduction to this section. Writers must examine their purpose and audience to understand *why* they are analyzing a process and *whom* they are analyzing it for. The sample paragraph from Henry Petroski's "The Book on the Bookshelf" makes a painstaking analysis of the seemingly simple problem of replacing a book back on a bookshelf after its space seems to have changed dimensions.

THE READINGS

Each essay in this section illustrates the use of these essential strategies. Barbara Ehrenreich describes a process that most readers have attempted: cleaning a house. The specific methods that she learns as a professional "Maid" will strike her audience as inadequate precisely because they have already learned better habits. Similarly, P.J. O'Rourke describes the common task of driving a car, complicated by the hazards and customs of the Third World.

Nikki Giovanni focuses on an entirely internal process—how black students can develop the attitude and actions that will help them succeed at predominantly white colleges. Giovanni offers straightforward advice and backs it up with logical rationale.

Julia Alvarez plumbs the depth of a writers' composing process by exposing the contents of her *curiosidades* file. She shows how the things that catch her notice eventually are transformed into characters or incidents in her fiction and poetry.

Serena Nanda provides excellent examples of how this writing strategy can be used to explain complex sociological processes. She counteracts the American notion that romantic love should be the basis for matchmaking by exploring the positive and negative aspects of arranged marriage in India.

Elizabeth Winthrop's story about simple processes exemplifies the more complex process of maturation. Although her protagonist, Emily, learns to tie fishing flies and pierce her ears, emancipation from an oppressive family situation is her ultimate achievement.

THE VISUAL TEXT

James Stevenson's comic flow chart showing how many steps it takes to change a light bulb demonstrates a rather serious point about process analysis: some processes necessitate additional projects. Notice that in the cartoon, the "installation of a new bulb" generates a secondary process that starts with "removal of obsolete item." Of course, everyone knows how to change a light bulb. The myriad jokes on the topic are predicated on the simplicity of that task. However, it might surprise students to discover how many steps are involved in the other relatively simple operations suggested by the writing assignments associated with the visual text.

THE WRITING

The writing assignments for process analysis encourage students to discover, outline, and test the steps in several kinds of procedures. For example, assignments 1 and 2 ask students to analyze some physical process (how to solve a mechanical or artistic problem) or to complete a personal project (how to compose a research paper). Assignments 3 and 4 invite students to discover, outline, and evaluate specific aspects of the process analyses they have read (Nanda's exploration of arranged marriage). Finally, assignments 5 and 6 ask students to look to the works by O'Rourke and Winthrop as models when they write an analysis of some event that could serve as a cultural metaphor.

BARBARA EHRENREICH "Scrubbing in Maine"

Purpose

Going beyond *Working,* Studs Terkel's landmark 1974 sociological study, Barbara Ehrenreich actually takes on a series of low-wage jobs around the United States as research for her book *Nickled and Dimed: On (Not) Getting By in America.* In this essay, Ehrenreich finds that working as a housecleaner is not as "correct" as it appears in the BBC series *Upstairs, Downstairs,* or even as orderly and "serene" as it seems in her employer's training videos. The Maids, the national franchise Ehrenreich works for, tends to dehumanize its employees. Its policy of moving workers around prevents them from forming "sticky and possibly guilt-ridden relationships" with customers. Its "disturbing" training videos equate workers with their tools, and it requires that workers spend "only so many minutes per house," precluding the opportunity to sit "down with a tall glass of water" after a particularly exhausting task. For little more than minimum wage, this mostly female workforce is driven to provide "cosmetic touches," to clients' homes the way their employer prescribes it (but not actually to "clean" them).

As the title of Ehrenreich's book suggests, she is arguing that employers are swindling low-wage earners. Ehrenreich reports that an independent housecleaner is "likely to earn . . . up to $15 per hour." On the other hand, she and her cohorts at The Maids are paid just "$6.65 for each hour [they] work," while the company nets "$25 per person-hour." Granted, the company furnishes its workers with uniforms, cleaning supplies, and cars, but the inequity is still appalling. Ehrenreich charges the company with preying on those who have few options, noting that it is impossible to work for The Maids if one doesn't have a car and must "arrive straight from welfare or . . . the bus station." At the company, Ehrenreich discovers that her coworkers have settled for a lower standard of living than many Americans would, subsisting on pizza and Jell-O shots or residing with a boyfriend and his mother. *Nickled and Dimed* attempts to speak for those who have quietly resigned themselves to NOT *Getting By in America.*

Audience

Most everyone has some experience with attempting to clean house. Ehrenreich draws on her mother's lessons in cleaning a bathroom, using "Niagara-like quantities" of water to demonstrate how far from common sense The Maids' approach to housekeeping is. "Germs are never mentioned" in the training videos that Ehrenreich watches, and, like most readers, Ehrenreich is haunted by the "possibility of transporting bacteria, by rag or by hand, from bathroom to kitchen or even from one house to the next" using the methods espoused by the company. Instead of real cleaning, The Maids instructs employees to "Fluff up throw pillows" or fold the loose ends of toilet paper and paper towels as they're done in hotel bathrooms. One of the cleaning companies to which Ehrenreich applied indicated that it did not like to hire employees who had formerly worked in the business because they were "resistant to learning the company's system"; presumably that means *unlearning* how to properly clean a house.

The audience for this essay has likely seen or heard of the British television series *Upstairs, Downstairs,* about the antics of the nineteenth-century English serving class. Ehrenreich expects her readers to draw a parallel between those workers' "egotistical masters" and Ted, the franchise owner and boss who is her employer. When he pops in to proudly announce that the activities on the training video were "figured out with a stopwatch," he doesn't seem to understand, as the readers of the essay do, that this over-regulation and mechanization of human activity is demeaning. When the inventor of the special vacuum cleaner that The Maids use announces that, when properly strapped in, its user *becomes* the vacuum cleaner, the transformation of worker to machine is complete. Thus, Ehrenreich finds ironic comfort in Ted's pronouncement that "'Cleaning fluids are less expensive than your time,'" or, as she explains: "in the hierarchy of the company's values I rank above Windex."

Strategy

Ehrenreich's book is about the difference between the way affluent Americans see the nation's working class and the reality of their lives. Behind the "glowing" uniforms and the "attractive," "serene," "obedient," "possibly Hispanic" model in the films are the real housecleaners whose personal habits are marshaled by "a special code of decorum." The real maids "run" to their cars to head out for work and "run" to the doors of the houses they are to clean because of Ted's draconian "time limits." There is clearly a schism between the reality of work life for The Maids employees and that portrayed in their training films. Ehrenreich wonders if the maid in the films is "an actual maid" and whether the home in the films is "someone's actual dwelling." Even the setting for the films is stylized, romanticized, and "perfectly characterless and pristine even before the model maid sets to work." In the end, Ehrenreich is not just criticizing bosses like Ted, but customers who unwittingly perpetuate such unfair systems as those that companies like Ted's administer.

At the outset of her experience with The Maids, Ehrenreich makes a play on words with the title of the BBC show about service staff, saying that she had "no idea, of course, just how far down these stairs will take me." In her first day out with a cleaning team, she says she discovers that "life is nothing like the movies, at least not if the movie is *Dusting.*" The training films, though, have already taught the new recruit about the fundamentally unsanitary cleaning methods practiced by The Maids. Her revelation on the job, then, is about the individual lives of her coworkers, who must perform physically strenuous tasks without sufficient nourishment. The sacrifices of her fellow maids don't even pay off in financial gain, as Ehrenreich learns that one of her coworkers doesn't have 89 cents to spare for a soda. Although Ehrenreich can't impose her mother's standards of cleanliness on The Maids' employees, she does end up wishing she could "force" an undernourished coworker to drink a glass of milk with "mommylike" influence.

P.J. O'ROURKE "Third World Driving Hints and Tips"

Purpose

Sometimes a process-analysis essay does not mean to provide directions or reliable information at all, but is simply a venue for entertainment. Such is the case with P. J. O'Rourke's pseudo-cautionary breakdown of rules for driving in Third World countries. As he indicates in the essay's opening paragraph, O'Rourke's work as a journalist has put him behind the wheel in such diverse driving conditions as the roads (or what passes for them) in Mexico, Lebanon, the Philippines, Cyprus, El Salvador, Africa, and Italy. Presumably, he also has driving credentials from New York, Baltimore, and Ohio, but those don't suit his comic "Americans Abroad" purpose in this essay. However, since what he is describing is largely the frustration of drivers who encounter ruts, confusing traffic signs, impatient fellow motorists, police and other roadblocks, wildlife, and traffic accidents, one needn't have traveled much beyond his or her own driveway to identify with much of what O'Rourke finds to complain about.

As early as his first sentence, in which O'Rourke carelessly classifies Italy as a Third World country, his real purpose—entertainment (not driving instruction)—is revealed. Transferring the classic comic timing of stand-up comedians in the tradition of Henny Youngman to paper, O'Rourke communicates familiar repetitions and comedic intonations to his readers. For example, after explaining that attempting to drive fast on rutted lanes will "result in disaster," O'Rourke says that driving slowly in the same circumstances "will also result in disaster." This sort of humor is best-suited to a nightclub act, but O'Rourke applies it to a topic that is not typical nightclub fare, so his readers must mentally supply their own laugh tracks and rim shots to the text.

Audience

Because O'Rourke is lampooning his subject, he can afford to poke fun at his ostensible audience, too. In pretending to offer useful advice to Third World tourists, O'Rourke acts like he thinks his readers will be Americans with "Hertz #1 Club cards" who can afford to "throw big wads of American money at everyone." In reality, the audience for this essay is fans who first discovered O'Rourke's irreverent style on the pages of *Rolling Stone* or *Atlantic Monthly*, or possibly even in the mid-twentieth-century underground newspaper *Harry*. Such readers are as unlikely to exchange their office chairs or subway benches for the driver's seats of cars imperiled by Third World driving conditions as are the hypothetical moneyed travelers addressed in the essay. However, they might enjoy picturing the unlikely pairing of such adventure-seekers with recalcitrant goats and furious foreign constables.

A tongue-in-cheek essay written in English is unlikely to find its way into the hands of the "natives" described by O'Rourke; if it did most would find themselves as unflatteringly presented as the privileged American class he pretends to address. The humor of this piece depends partly on its audience's temporary suspension of empathy with those "natives." A reader who is apt to counter that O'Rourke's facetious method of converting kilometers to miles represents typical American arrogance, or that chickens are precious in certain countries because they represent the difference between prosperity and starvation, takes life too seriously to appreciate O'Rourke's sense of humor. Far from lampooning the inhabitants of Third World countries, O'Rourke is actually poking fun at Americans, including himself, who feel inconvenienced by the poverty that envelops the less fortunate nations that they are compelled or inclined to visit.

Probably the audience that would best receive O'Rourke's work is comprised of fellow news correspondents who have found themselves in the backseats of rickety taxis endangered by the perils he describes. However, since American drivers also confront frustrations on roadways at home ("Road Rage" is ample evidence of that!), O'Rourke's essay does suggest a process by which any driver can cope with problems that arise: humor. His quips that certain road signs look like the symbols on "Boy Scout merit badges," that there is a direct correlation between the number of white crosses lining a curve and its danger for drivers, and his definition of a car horn as an "'Egyptian Brake Pedal'" will strike different chords with all drivers. In spite of writing about driving conditions in countries most of his readers will never visit, O'Rourke's strategy of using familiar images to describe foreign conditions makes it applicable to his readers' lives.

Strategy

O'Rourke's essay demonstrates one of the most complex uses of humor: to win sympathy. After joking about road conditions, speed limits, traffic signals, irate fellow motorists, roadblocks, and the proclivity of various animals to run from or toward traffic, the author introduces the sobering observation that "Third Worlders are remarkably fond of their chickens and their children," and warns that "If you hit one or both, they may survive. But you will not." Fierce protection of their children underscores the humanity of people. O'Rourke acknowledges through this detail that the lives of people in genuinely underprivileged nations is not so funny for those who aren't just driving through.

NIKKI GIOVANNI "Campus Racism 101"

Purpose

Outspoken poet, educator, and activist Nikki Giovanni addresses black students at predominantly white colleges in her book *Racism 101*. In this excerpt from that text she argues that black students should not use racism as an excuse for abandoning their dreams of a college education, and she offers a formula for success in school. At the heart of her process analysis is an admonition to black students to maintain self-control. She reasons that American blacks will inevitably interact with whites, and "the only question is, will you be in some control of yourself and your actions, or will you be controlled by others?" She advocates self-control on the part of black students as the best method of containing racism and its attendant explosive emotions.

Giovanni reminds black students to remember why they came to college, encouraging them with the promise that "four years of college gives you an opportunity not only to lift yourself but to serve your people effectively." The alternatives she cites to peacefully discouraging campus racism (low-paying jobs, unemployment, military service, and prison) are not personally fulfilling or culturally uplifting. She advises students to see themselves as individuals "worthy of respect, and make everyone else deal with you the same way."

As a black professor at a predominantly white school, Giovanni offers compelling reasons why blacks should participate in interracial education. Her own reasons for choosing to teach at Virginia Tech range from the mere fact of the school's existence, to a need to minister to its black students—a desire to "not allow white students to go through higher education without interacting with Blacks in authoritative positions," and the recognition that integration is necessary because "predominantly Black colleges cannot accommodate the numbers of Black students who want and need an education." Her own commitment to succeeding in a predominantly white educational environment is summed up in her definition of *tenure*: "I have a teaching position for life. . . ."

Audience

Although students of all races will find good advice for achieving success in college and dealing with peers of differing backgrounds, Giovanni's essay is addressed primarily toward black students enrolled in predominantly white colleges. Gradually, her opening paragraph reveals her intended audience as the examples she toys with become increasingly pointed toward black would-be college dropouts. Her final hypothetical cartoon shows students leaving school because they "want to be white." In her conclusion, she addresses these students directly, reminding them that education is a private goal; they must not let racism deter them. She cautions her audience against taking "the racial world on [their] shoulders," reminding them that "Your job is not to educate white people; it is to obtain an education."

Strategy

Giovanni establishes her straightforward, authoritative tone early in the essay by posing hypothetical questions (such as "Is it difficult to attend a predominantly white college?") and answering them with wit and surprising candor. Her strategy is to give advice plainly, offering a process analysis of academic achievement for minority students. The steps in her process are arranged chronologically, as well as being prioritized by order of importance. Therefore, she begins with the first, most basic step: "*Go to class.*" This is necessary to complete the second step ("*Meet your professors*"), which, in turn, facilitates the following one ("*Do assignments on time*"), and so on. The last task in her series of steps, "*Participate in some campus activity*" is so-placed because it should come *after* academic obligations are met and because it is the least pressing, although still important, of the elements of the process she outlines.

Another strategy Giovanni employs to plainly issue her advice is the modeling of appropriate behaviors through a series of sample questions and answers. Notice that the responses she suggests are informative but not deferential. For instance she suggests that the age-old question, "Why do all the black people sit together in the dining hall?" simply be turned around, and that black students ask in return, "Why do all the white students sit together?" Reversing the inference subtly confronts the questioner. Giovanni urges her black readers to use their visibility in predominantly white schools to educate fellow students and faculty.

JULIA ALVAREZ "Grounds for Fiction"

Purpose

Showing people how to find ideas to write about is a way of prompting people to begin telling their own stories. An accomplished novelist and poet, Julia Alvarez provides her followers with a window into her own creative process that both satisfies their curiosity about the origins of some of her published works and encourages them to emulate her practices in their own writing. She traces elements in her novels and poems to such stimuli as a letter found in the trash, an article in a medical journal, a question reprinted in an old housekeeping magazine, small-town gossip, newspaper articles, errant facts from nonfiction, and a handwritten memoir from her father. Each of these was kept in her yellow pocket folder labeled *curiosidades,* or curiosities, which are the commonplaces Alvarez has collected. She advises her readers to start similar idea files for themselves and exhorts them to follow Henry James' advice, "to be someone on whom nothing is lost." Her message is that life is filled with subjects to write about, and would-be readers need to be attuned to them.

Alvarez is convinced that everyone's natural curiosity drives him or her to be a writer. She contradicts the popular wisdom that authors write what they know best with the opinion of writer Marcie Hershman, who said, "We write what we need to know." Alvarez believes that writers are motivated by discovery, as well as by "the whole Scheherazade issue" of needing to tell stories. Scheherazade is the heroine of the ancient collection of tales, *The Arabian Nights,* who marries the vengeful king and stops his pattern of taking and murdering a new wife each day by weaving fascinating tales and withholding their endings until the next day has passed. Alvarez argues that storytelling is a mode of self-preservation, a survival tactic that was denied Adolfo Gonzales when he was committed to an Oregon mental hospital because no one could understand his unique Indian dialect.

Audience

Ostensibly prompted by the requests of audience members at public readings who approach Alvarez with ideas for stories they hope she will write, this essay explains to those hopefuls why no one can tell someone else's stories. Instead, she suggests that her readers who, in the words of poet W. H. Auden, "like hanging around words listening to what they say" might follow her example and begin compiling a file of potential stories waiting to be told. The essay, then, is largely a set of examples designed to show her listeners and readers how ideas are discovered and nurtured into full-blown texts over time.

Alvarez assumes that her audience is largely made up of active readers. Her casual allusions to Wallace Stevens as "a vice president of Hartford insurance Company," to the first line of William Carlos Williams' "The Red Wheelbarrow" show that she expects that her audience is well read. She also supposes that they are familiar with a fair number of her own works, quoting snatches from poems that her audience might recall in total or mentioning the Mirabal sisters, who fought against Dominican Republic dictator Rafael Leonidas Trujillo and were brutally assassinated by his henchmen in 1960. Their story is the basis for Alvarez's book *In the Time of Butterflies.*

Strategy

Ironically, Alvarez writes a very brief paragraph to outline the "hours and weeks and months and years" she spend writing a piece of fiction. Even for an accomplished and prolific writer such as Alvarez, the process by which text is composed remains a "mystery (or madness)." She has set herself a difficult task: to describe a process that can't be observed or logically broken down into prescriptive steps. Its final stage must be performed by someone else: a lawyer who checks to see if anything she has written is libelous, or a family member who sees shades of himself or herself in one of her characters.

Alvarez focuses instead on the tangible parts of a writer's task: the scraps of paper in her yellow folder, "most of which have been in [her] folder for years." She describes some of the artifacts that suggest to her "the seed of a plot that might turn into a novel or a query that might needle an essay out . . . ," but she cannot say how she determined that each had "an aura" about it, or how she was attracted to that idea or story and not another. In retrospect she can describe the process by which certain artifacts wove their way into her work. An angry letter rescued from someone else's garbage provides the voice of her character Marie Beaudry. An Indiana house-wife's trepidation at cutting yard goods married itself with the love of words to become Alvarez's poem "Naming the Fabrics." A long-held fascination and desire to write about the Mirabal sisters took root when her father described meeting one of the last men to see the sisters alive. In an irony as inexplicable as composition itself, the spark from her father's letter ignited Alvarez's mind to produce the book she wrote nine years later.

SERENA NANDA "Arranging a Marriage in India"

Purpose

A common theme in process-analysis essays that provide information is that the process in question is much more intricate than it first appears. That is true of "Arranging a Marriage in India," as Serena Nanda learns that what she "had thought would be an easy matter [turns] out to be quite complicated." Initially, she assumed that she could efficiently help her friend find a perfect mate for her eligible son during her year's stay in India. When Nanda returns to the United States, her friend seems "no further along in finding a suitable match for her son," although Nanda has learned a great deal about the complexity of arranging a marriage. She also learns to be patient with the Indian way of choosing a mate, and that effort pays off two years later when she succeeds in finding a wife for her friend's son.

Before taking the opportunity to discuss arranged marriage with single, young Indians, Nanda considered the practice "oppressive." However, Sita, an eligible Indian bride, convinces the American author that the practice is not so unreasonable as it might seem. Nanda discloses her "second thoughts on the matter." Because brides become part of their husband's households, it is essential that the whole family find a mate who will fit comfortably into their lifestyle. The essay presents Sita's arguments that the wisdom and experience of her parents is valuable in choosing a mate, arranged marriage allows young people to focus on personal development rather than popularity with the opposite sex, and it provides a newly married couple with the excitement of learning about one another—all factors that contribute to the low divorce rate in India. In her essay's postscript, however, Nanda also describes more sinister reasons for the infrequency of divorce among Indians: social stigmatism and "dowry deaths." This process analysis is designed to curb the knee-jerk response that romantic Westerners often exhibit toward the concept of arranged marriage.

Audience

An American anthropologist writing for American readers, Nanda asks the kinds of questions a Westerner would pose about her subject. For example, she assumes that arranged marriage might mean that Indian women "don't . . . care who [they marry]," or that they are missing the fun of dating. Sita's calm responses demonstrate that these are not concerns shared by her Indian counterparts. Nanda herself acknowledges that her research embodied "more curiosity than tact," and she writes about delicate issues that Indians would almost certainly not tell an audience of strangers. Indians probably would avoid talking about this subject among themselves as frankly as Nanda presents it. The author is an investigator conducting cross-cultural research to enlighten her compatriots.

Throughout the process of finding a mate for her friend's son, Nanda makes the sort of mistakes that a Westerner would. She is impatient with the exacting and critical role of her friend, and she is quick to assume that a proposed match is a good one without considering all of its ramifications. For instance, she does not understand the liabilities of the boy's former military career or his short stature and dark skin. Nanda must keep "pressing for . . . explanation[s]" when her friend rejects potential brides. One comes from a family with so many daughters that they might not be able to afford an elegant wedding, and the potential bride's married older sister also wants to visit home too much. Another young woman is well educated but too independent-minded to fit into the family; she takes the bus out and about Bombay on her own, and she is of a slightly higher social caste, which may cause problems in the future. The last rejected candidate is "fat and wears glasses." None of these attributes is likely to be a serious liability to a sincere American suitor, so Nanda takes pains to explain why each results in a failure to make the match.

Strategy

Nanda's essay chronicles the exacting and sometimes tedious task of arranging a marriage. Happily, it concludes in the wedding of her friend's son, but it demonstrates that many considerations are involved between the time that parents decide to seek a mate for their child and the surrender of a daughter to her husband's family. The steps of the process are illustrated through narratives of failed and successful matches. The importance of issues that are foreign to Nanda's American readers, such as caste and dowry, is demonstrated through stories of failed matchmaking attempts. The essay's postscript, which describes the abuse some Indian women face when the match has been uneven, emphasizes the weight of matchmaking decisions.

Comparing an unfamiliar concept with a well-known one is a good way to help readers understand new information, and Nanda presents the unfamiliar Indian rituals alongside American customs. Her discussions with Sita in the essay's opening, counteract American prejudice against arranged marriage by making it appear more reasonable and successful than dating many potential mates or marrying for romantic love. It is not until the essay's postscript, when the audience has had a chance to see how well-arranged marriage can work, that Nanda exposes the dark side of the Indian tradition. Following an "accident" or "suicide," the boy's family might crank up the whole process again, trying to choose a "suitable" bride for themselves.

ELIZABETH WINTHROP "The Golden Darters"

Purpose

Elizabeth Winthrop's short story, "The Golden Darters" deals with many processes. Although it deals overtly with the process of tying fishing flies and obliquely with the processes of smoking, leg shaving, and ear piercing, it is mostly concerned with the processes of maturation and emancipation. It about an adolescent girl's efforts to free herself from an irascible, dominant, quick-tempered father.

Emily, the story's narrator, describes herself as "a cautious, secretive child," who "could not bear to have people watch [her] doing things." Such a temperament is alien to her "large, thick-boned" father, a man with "sweeping gestures, a robust laugh, and a sudden terrifying temper." The father sets up his fly-tying operation in a corner of their summer cottage living room, working in full view of his wife, two sons, and timid daughter. He naps on the lawn "for all the swimmers and boaters to see," although this behavior embarrasses his retiring wife.

When her father insists that Emily, who is allowed to closely observe the patriarch at his hobby because she doesn't "bounce" as her brothers would, receive instruction in the delicate art of fly tying, she is reluctant. Emily is shy and afraid of arousing her father's anger, but most importantly, she does not share in his enthusiasm for fly tying and, ultimately, luring "a rainbow trout out of his quiet pool." Differences between father and daughter are further emphasized by the opposite effects the process of fly tying has on the two characters. The father is tying flies to relax and pass the time needed to mend his back following surgery. Emily, conversely, finds her father's hobby tedious with little opportunity to rest her "aching spine against the chair."

At first, Emily finds it difficult to escape her father's insistence that she join him in his newfound hobby. However, by the end of July, when her young friends have arrived at their lakeside homes, she is beginning to separate herself from her family's expectations. The twelve-year-old narrator consents to having her ears pierced, even though her mother has forbidden it until she is college-aged. When the shy Emily acts boldly, wearing as earrings the golden darters she has tied with her father and pulling her hair up so that the adapted fishing lures make her look "free and different and dangerous," she has escaped her parents' control. Her mother objects that the earrings make her "look cheap," and her disappointed father remarks distastefully, "that is not the purpose for which the flies were intended." However, when Emily's father turns off the light, so that she "couldn't see his face anymore," readers sense a small victory for the story's struggling protagonist.

Audience

Everyone struggles with defining his or her own identity as separate from parents and family, and in that respect, most readers will readily understand Emily's plight. Winthrop paints the family in her story with broad strokes, making it essentially like many households in America. The father is overbearing; the mother, although she tries to defend her daughter from her husband's demands, is often absent, leaving the room whenever a potentially tense situation arises. The energetic brothers seem relieved that their father prefers to control their sister with his attention. In short, they are an average middle-class family, straight out of twentieth-century middle America.

Winthrop uses a comparison between a familiar and an unfamiliar object when she tells readers that the fly-tying instruction manual "read like a cookbook," saying "things like, 'Cut off a bunch of yellowtail.'" She also describes the "golden darter," the fly that takes on new significance at the story's end, explaining that it is "A big flashy fly, the kind that imitates a small fish as it moves underwater." While her readers are likely to be familiar with family dynamics and the emancipation process, they are less apt to know about fly tying.

Strategy

What passes at first for attention to the process of fly tying in Winthrop's story is, in fact, the careful creation of the picture of Emily's father. He has forbidden the maid from coming near his fly-tying station, he self-centeredly announces "the completion of" each "latest project to the family," and the narrator finds it unlikely that her father would use "thread and bobbins," needles, feathers—the "tools normally associated with woman's work." As details of the father, his hobby, and its elements ranged upon his work table accrue throughout the story, readers are prepared to fully imagine the story's final scene involving the anxious mother, the disapproving father amid his trappings, and the bouncy daughter.

The two processes overtly described in the story, tying fishing flies and piercing ears, are described with comparable attention to detail. The author seems to assume that her audience would not be entirely familiar with either procedure. Readers learn that one begins tying a fly by clamping a clean hook in a vice, adding feathers, wrapping thread about the body and cementing a head in place. Securing the slippery feathers to the tiny hook is the most precarious of these steps, and it is the point in the process where Emily makes mistakes. Similarly, Winthrop tells her audience the major steps in ear piercing: numbing the ear lobes with ice cubes, sterilizing a needle, stabbing it through the lobe, inserting stud earrings, twisting them and swabbing the wound with alcohol to avoid (or to treat, in Emily's case) infection. Ironically, the most difficult steps in each process involve using sewing needles for other than their strictly intended purpose.

Comparison and Contrast

THE STRATEGIES

In some ways, the comparison-and-contrast essay is the most functional of all the expository forms. It is so fundamental to our thinking processes that students are asked to make comparisons in virtually every college class: this novel versus that novel, this historical cause with that historical cause, this scientific theory with that scientific theory. Of course, the whole college experience is a matter of making comparisons: this class versus that class, this major versus that major, this career versus that career. Because students constantly face the problem of comparisons, they see the logic in learning a systematic procedure for discovering, organizing, presenting, and evaluating alternatives.

To teach the comparison-and-contrast essay you must illustrate the two basic strategies for gathering and presenting information on two subjects—the divided and the alternating pattern. The introduction to this section describes these two strategies, but it also encourages your students to compare them and to consider how each one can assist them in composing an essay with a specific purpose for a specific audience. They should learn the strengths and weaknesses of each strategy and then assess the difficulty of their subject, the knowledge of their audience, and the purpose of their essay before they select a strategy. They may decide to experiment with each strategy (to see how a pattern affects the meaning of their essay), or they may decide to combine patterns (to underscore the complexity and importance of their subject).

Whatever their decision, they must remind themselves that the mere presentation of information in an organized pattern does not make a successful comparison-and-contrast essay. Comparisons must be made for some purpose—to assert a thesis or to arrive at a conclusion about the items being analyzed. Such is the case even when a comparison is made in the restricted space of a paragraph. Notice that David McCullough begins his paragraph with a broad assertion (FDR and Truman "were men of exceptional determination") and then restricts that assertion to a more specific topic ("Truman was more of a listener. . . ." or "Roosevelt loved the subtleties of human relations").

THE READINGS

Similarly, the readings in this section illustrate how the various patterns of comparison-and-contrast essays can be used to argue a thesis. Mark Twain's "Two Views of the River" provides a short but memorable example of the divided pattern to demonstrate how knowledge changes perception. All the information on the first subject—the poetic (impressionistic) view of the river—is presented in one unit. Then all the information on the second subject—the practical (nautical) view of the river is presented in a second unit. Twain draws his conclusions about these two views at the end.

In contrast, Sarah Vowell's essay on "Cowboys v. Mounties" and Paco Underhill's examination of male and female shoppers illustrate how the alternating pattern can be used to good effect in a long essay. Because both writers use many points of comparison and because their subjects might appear similar on the surface, Vowell and Underhill use a point-by-point pattern to demonstrate subtle but important differences between their subjects.

Ann Roiphe compares two complex subjects. She compares her parents' marriage with her first marriage as a basis for discussing the complicated motives for and outcomes of divorce. Both experiences support her thesis that divorce is a necessary social construct.

Laura Bohanen contrasts two cultures' differing responses to a Shakespearean plot, and Witi Ihimaera uses comparison-and-contrast strategies to weave a funny and poignant story about a young Maori man in New Zealand who is pressured by his friends and family to adopt the social graces of white society while in attendance at a government ball. In the process, both writers discover that contrast is not necessarily a bad thing in culture.

THE VISUAL TEXT

Don Hong-Oai's classical-looking Asian landscape painting makes a comparison between the silhouettes of gibbon monkeys at play and the Chinese characters depicting that verb. His visual text suggests the concrete history of ideographs (word pictures) as he facetiously suggests how those letters might have been inspired originally. As the old saw goes, not only is a picture equivalent to a thousand words, but also many words look or sound like what they mean in English, too. Students might want to closely examine a word like "drop" to show how it is visually related to its denotative meaning.

THE WRITING

The writing assignments suggest that students try out all the strategies of the comparison-and-contrast essay. For example, assignments 1 and 2 encourage students to look for similarities and differences in items in the same class—the same place viewed from two points in time and the same person viewed from the perspective of two different cultures or communities. The first assignment suggests Twain's divided pattern as a model; the second suggests Underhill's alternating pattern as an illustrative example. Assignment 3 invites students to analyze differences between the environments (what distinguishes between "dorm" and "home" talk). Assignments 4 and 5 invite students to see the same event from two points of view (as different people, cultures, or media would represent them), and assignment 6 asks them to compare and contrast two sides of a controversial issue (as Vowell does).

MARK TWAIN "Two Views of the River"

Purpose

Twain's purpose in comparing his "Two Views of the River" is to contrast the bliss of ignorance with the wariness that comes with experience. This essay, a strict comparison and contrast, juxtaposes descriptions of the same section of the river as viewed by the same man. The difference, which is the focus of the topic, lies not in the river, but in its observer: Twain, first as a young apprentice and later as an experienced riverboat pilot.

Each description of the river is presented in its entirety and appears to be a complete picture. Twain's memory of the early scene is a painstakingly detailed romantic tableau of the river at sunset. He compares the many hues of the "boiling, tumbling rings" that enliven the surface of the water with the tints in an opal. His second view of the river, based on conjecture, is built upon the same elements as the first, but the pilot's expertise allows him to expose the dangers inherent in the scene. Thus, besides natural beauty, the opal-tinted rings signify "a dissolving bar and a changing channel." The awe of the apprentice is replaced by the caution of the older pilot. This essay laments the sacrifice of naive appreciation to the rote calculation of expertise. Twain seems to believe that he has lost more than he has gained in learning his trade, especially since naïveté is absolutely irretrievable.

Audience

Twain anticipates that his audience will be familiar with just one of the attitudes he compares: the poetic response to the river at sunset. Nearly everyone has marveled at the beauty of nature, and most readers have seen a river or other body of water at sunset. Therefore, Twain begins with the familiar; presenting the apprentice's view first, he uses that common ground as a reference point for his technical description of the river. He does not expect that his readers want to learn to navigate the Mississippi, nor would most want to be robbed of their blissful appreciation of the river's beauty. Twain's audience is likely to answer his final question as he would, that education at the expense of wonder is no gain.

Strategy

A striking fanciful comparison between riverboat pilots and physicians, both of whom sacrifice appreciation of beauty to professional understanding, concludes the essay, but the best evidence supporting Twain's thesis is a strict comparison and contrast, organized around a divided strategy. The essay is short enough for readers to remember the separately presented experiences. Arranged in this fashion, the essay achieves the effect of re-creating Twain's early view of the river before he describes the disillusioning second, repeating key words and phrases including, "floating log," "slanting mark," "tumbling [rings]," "silver [streak]," and "dead tree."

Twain also lists his points of comparison in the same order in both descriptions in order to facilitate comparisons. The points of comparison are listed in the order in which they appear to the narrator. Close, low objects appear before distant, high ones. The river is presented first in visual terms. Red, gold, black, ruddy colors, and silver dominate the scene. In the second view of the river, its beauty is obscured by danger signals, such as wind, rising water, a hidden reef, a troublesome shoal, a snag.

The riverboat pilot's naïve awe of the river is forever replaced by his knowledge of its dangers. Any reader who doubts Twain's assertion that the majesty of the river "could never be restored to [him] while [he] lived" need only reread the first paragraph of the essay while trying to forget the second.

SARAH VOWELL "Cowboys v. Mounties"

Purpose

Although Sarah Vowell's essay is a paean to our neighbor to the north, it also pays tribute to the exhilarating spirit of the American West—not to our history of genocide, but to most everything else that is romantically linked to the Wild West. In extolling the virtues of Canada and its citizens, Vowell uses a comparison-and-contrast strategy to show that the fundamental differences between the United States and Canada do not necessarily make one country morally superior to the other. The United States, represented by the image of the Marlboro Man, and Canada, embodied by its "old fashioned, red serge [suited]" Mounties, seem to present a contrast between the shoot-before-you-think mentality of the cowboy and the excessive planning and forethought that went into the preemptive creation of the North-West Mounted Police, now the Royal Canadian Mounted Police. In comparing the spirits of these neighboring countries, Vowell seems to be encouraging her compatriots (on both sides of the "medicine line") to emulate the prevailing Canadian "knack for loving their country without resorting to swagger or hate."

Unlike the violent and revolutionary history of the United States' war for independence from Britain, Canada's sovereignty was achieved through "polite meetings taking place in nice rooms." During Canada's succession, government leaders made tea in china cups instead of by the barrel in the Boston harbor. Vowell reports that Ian Brown of the Canadian Broadcast Company said his country's history ". . . isn't inspiring," and that a Canadian history textbook referred to its separation from Britain as a "'modestly spectacular resolution of their various ambitions and problems.'" One purpose of Vowell's essay then, is to assert that Canada's peaceful history is inspiring and that the historic stance of "one law for everyone" is admirable, especially since Canada's human-rights record strongly enforces it. This stands in contrast to the "big to-do about all men being created equal" that Americans espouse but often have difficulty carrying out.

Audience

Recognizing that what comedian Jon Stewart said most people think about Canada ("'We don't.'") is true, Vowell uses humor to keep her readers attuned. She expects that her audience is familiar with Canadian comedy exports Martin Short, Eugene Levy, the Kids in the Hall, and *Saturday Night Live* producer Lorne Michaels. Emulating those comedians, she suggests that, lacking America's proliferation of firearms, Canadian killers are tossing hair dryers in bathtubs as murder weapons. Her anticipated audience is young and liberal, just the sort who would find her crack about conservative presidential candidate Pat Buchanan as a Nazi admirer funny. The levity of the piece makes its history lesson and admiration for a neighboring country palatable for residents of the States.

Beginning with the provocative sentence, "Canada haunts me," Vowell tries to educate her audience and explain her own fascination with "dispatches from the Maritimes and Guelph." She wants her readers to get beyond the "hockey obsession" most U.S. citizens have about Canadians and appreciate the deliberate, pacifist culture that makes her "feel Canadian." Striking, however, is Vowell's use of the term "American" to describe the people of the United States; since Canada is also in North America, its residents are technically "Americans," too. This suggests that Vowell's audience is largely from the fifty states. When she says that a Mountie's conviction that "you need conformity" hurt her ears, she is siding, in the end, with her fellow Yankees.

Strategy

All of the differences between the United States and Canada are not superficial or funny, of course, and Vowell uses the concept of our national border as "the medicine line" to illuminate the serious side of her subject. Canada's answer to the United States' "violent, costly Indian wars" is presented as hopeful, but flawed. The preemptive creation of the Mounties may have led to conformist thinking in present-day Canadians, and the northern country's attempts to live by the motto of "one law for everyone" created an unintentional haven for Native Americans, which was sorely tested when Sitting Bull and his band proved "difficult" and were sent back down to the United States, over the objections of Mountie Major James Walsh. The "complications" surrounding Sitting Bull that make Walsh Vowell's "favorite Mountie" also demonstrate that neither the United States nor Canada's approach to westward expansion was superior.

Although Vowell uses Pierre Berton's observations about the difference between the weather of the two countries to ground her comparison and contrast, she also says point-blank that the chief difference between the two "all comes down to guns." The two points are inextricably linked in Berton's scenario, as he finds it hard to imagine a gun duel in weather so cold "'that the slightest touch of flesh would take the skin off'" the shooter's thumbs. Clearly, it is more than the murder rate that differentiates Canada from its North American neighbors, and the widely divergent images of Dudley Do-Right and the Marlboro Man, with their contrasting clothing, histories, and ideologies evoke that well.

PACO UNDERHILL "Shop Like a Man"

Purpose

Because his consulting firm, Envirosell, tracks consumers to determine their shopping habits and preferences, Paco Underhill knows more about merchandising than the most seasoned bargain hunter. Goods and the way they are displayed lure most people into stores, and Underhill and his colleagues are making detached judgments about product placement, packaging, and promotion. His objective analysis of cultural shopping behaviors provides retailers with sound strategies for marketing, and gives his readers insights into why they buy the way they do. As this essay reveals, Underhill's company has conducted research in how Americans shop in places as diverse as grocery aisles and cosmetics departments, and he has discovered that men and women shop very differently from one another. Although the essay is called "Shop Like a Man," it shows that women tend to look more thoroughly at goods, ask more questions, and buy fewer things that aren't on their lists—all of which seem like the attributes of a skillful shopper. However, Underhill argues, if more stores catered to the way men shop, men would be the ideal "potential source of profits."

Underhill reveals that men shop differently than women, but that most retail environments cater to women more explicitly than to men. He argues that the cultural tide is turning; men stay single longer and shop for themselves more as a result. Once married, men are much more likely than they used to be to put the baby in a stroller and go get the groceries—or the lingerie. Although men are discouraged easily if they don't see what they're looking for, they are also readily open to a suggestive sale and culturally predisposed to prove their virility and live up to their image as providers by pulling out their wallets at the cash register. The typical shopping experience, then, still intimidates and alienates the rapidly growing portion of the population most likely to buy it if it fits and do so quickly.

Underhill's twenty years of experience in the anthropology of shopping qualifies him to go beyond "the conventional wisdom on male shoppers . . . that they don't especially like to do it." He demonstrates how "the entire shopping experience . . . is generally geared toward the female shopper," and shows how this is changing as more men enter the marketplace as consumers. Through copious observation of videotaped shopping interactions, customer surveys, and focus group meetings, Underhill has created a science of retailing with compelling statistical evidence. Seventeen percent of men who frequent computer stores go there more than once a week. "Sixty-five percent of male shoppers who tried [an article of clothing] on bought it." Seventy-two percent of men look at price tags while considering an object in a store. Men shop quickly, they don't ask questions, and they like the power of paying. On the other hand, female shoppers spend nearly twice as much time in a store when accompanied by another woman as when they shop with a man, but they purchase only 25 percent of the clothing they try on.

Audience

Everyone shops, be it on the Internet, in consignment shops, grocery and convenience stores, or in the boutiques of Neiman Marcus and Saks Fifth Avenue. Underhill's article, ostensibly aimed at retailers, can teach much to the average shopper as well. The result of Underhill's research should make shopping more informative and convenient for men and women. For example, he reveals that men like copious information about products; they want access to information such as which cell phone package is most comprehensive, how a sofa is made, or which glassware is used to serve each libation. According to Underhill, we can thank male shoppers for being told the wattage of microwave ovens and vacuum cleaners, or being given the option to purchase "butch" looking stainless-steel kitchen appliances. Household products with masculine names such as "Hefty Bags," "Bold" detergent, and "Bounty" paper towels are similarly targeted toward the male shopper. Underhill and his colleagues take a hard look at what most shoppers simply take for granted: what products are available, how they are named and packaged, where they are placed, and why different people are drawn to them.

Strategy

Examples are the rhetorical strength of this essay. They validate the wealth of statistics Underhill offers. Because Envirosell's methods include the observation of shoppers, they generate a wealth of concrete information. Underhill's grocery store anecdotes alone are memorable and convincing: a father who lets his daughter eat animal crackers while perched on his shoulders, showering him with crumbs, or the dad who rips the top off a box of cereal and hands it to his sons, knowing it will be consumed before he reaches the checkout counter. Underhill conjures up images of a father who won't shop for jeans because he can't maneuver the stroller he is pushing down that aisle, or the husband who pantomimes pulling a beer from an imaginary tap into a glass on display. The essay describes a man shopping for underwear who suddenly "reached around, grabbed a handful of his waistband, pulled it out and craned his neck so he could learn—finally!—what size shorts he wears."

Underhill offers retailers two alternatives for pacifying the male shopper. Facetiously, he suggests passive restraint—creating a barber-shop-like atmosphere in a corner of the store, but then admits that other shoppers don't want to see "six lumpy guys in windbreakers slumped in BarcaLoungers watching TV." More seriously, he suggests that companies can attract and sell to men by providing in-depth information about products in print brochures and signs, grouping products that men are interested in together in one area of stores, and naming and packaging products so that they have more masculine appeal. As Underhill notes, sex roles are constantly in flux; men shop more than they used to, and women are single longer (and again) more often than in generations past. Merchandising to attract the new male shopper just might appeal to the new female shopper as well.

ANNE ROIPHE "A Tale of Two Divorces"

Purpose

By comparing and contrasting her parents' marriage with her own, Anne Roiphe shows the benefits for society of liberal divorce laws. She portrays her mother, an heiress, as being "fearful of horses, dogs, cats, cars, water, balls that were hit over nets," and so forth to explain why her mother never sought the divorce she occasionally threatened and certainly needed for her own sanity. Roiphe claims that, at age twenty-seven, she "married a man whom [she] thought was just the opposite of [her] father." Learned patterns are well ingrained in the human psyche, however, and she eventually came to see that her husband was "more like her father than not," and that she, like her mother, "had no faith, no confidence, no sense that [she] could fly too." Unlike her mother, she divorced her husband, realizing that her "divorce was related to her [mother's] undivorce," and that leaving her husband was necessary to spare her daughter from having a maternal role model who would lead her to "perpetual grief and [the] thought of herself as . . . unworthy of the ordinary moments of affection and connection." She shows how divorce, as well as the lack of it when it is actually necessary, can be equally destructive to children.

Roiphe argues that "in twentieth-century America we place so much emphasis on romance that we barely note the other essentials of marriage that include economics and child rearing." Her father married her mother because "she was his American dream"; he "loathed poverty," and so he married for money. Her own husband was unable to hold their child because "he was either too drunk, out of the house, closed into his head" or neurotically obsessed with his own success, yet she had married him out of romantic notions about his being an artist. She says women often marry for the wrong reasons, and she argues that they are not "in need of the perfect orgasm," but require, instead, "a body to spoon with in bed, a story that [couples] could tell together. . . ." Now that her own children are of marriageable age, Roiphe sees the institution with a mother's protective vision. She hopes that her own stories will encourage others to marry for the right reasons or divorce if that is the right thing to do.

Audience

Almost everyone in America has been touched by divorce, and Roiphe recognizes that her story is interchangeable with those of many of her readers. She asserts that all divorce stories sound the same, and yet each is as "unique as a human face." That is certainly the case in comparing her own divorce with the one her parents should have sought. Roiphe knows that the two divorces she describes will sound familiar to her readers. Originally published in a collection called *Women on Divorce: A Bedside Companion*, this essay is most likely to be in the hands of recently divorced women or those summoning the courage to ask for divorces. Therefore, she is free to examine the institution mainly from a woman's point of view.

Roiphe also marshals forces against the political right who bemoan America's escalating divorce rate, saying that she listens "with tongue in check to all the terrible tales of what divorce has done to the American family." Her own situation and her mother's suggest that divorce can be the best alternative for some women and their children. She gives some credence to the argument that the so-called corruption of family values may cause children to be lost and wounded, but she counters that many things can damage the psyches of the young, such as the death or untreated depression of a parent, addictions, or economic problems within the family. She argues that divorce is best avoided by making a good marriage in the first place, something that everyone is not able to do.

Strategy

Comparison-and-contrast strategies work very well in this essay to show how the seemingly sharply differing stories of Roiphe's own marriage and that of her parents were fundamentally the same. She describes the contrasting backgrounds of her parents in order to show why their marriage was such a disaster, and she gives details from her parents' daily miseries. Her father told his wife "she was unbeautiful," he stayed out in bars, had relationships with other women, lost money, and somehow convinced her that no other man would have her if she left him. Roiphe's marriage was several years along when she noticed that her "husband was handsome and thought [her] plain, . . . poor and thought [her] a meal ticket, . . . dwarfed of spirit and couldn't imagine another soul beside himself," a husband who "had other women" and "went on binges and used up all [their] money." This essay is built around two fundamentally comparable marriages with one sharp contrast: Roiphe was able to leave her husband, and her mother was not.

Roiphe surmises that her decisive action saved her daughter from a fate similar to her own, but the outcome of her divorce is contrasted with the effect divorce has had on her stepdaughter. Even now, as a married woman and mother herself, Roiphe's stepdaughter trembles and tenses as she speaks of her parents' divorce. Her reactions cause Roiphe to admit that "divorce is never nice." Nevertheless, she argues that divorce must always be available and that each person must weigh his or her options carefully. Roiphe remembers herself at seven, sitting on the edge of her mother's bath after expressing the desire that her parents stay married to one another. "'God,'" her mother responds, "'Help me.'" Roiphe responds that her mother "had asked the wrong person." Neither her young daughter nor God could help Roiphe's mother at that point; she had to make the choice to help herself.

LAURA BOHANNAN "Shakespeare in the Bush"

Purpose

When an English scholar tells Bohannan that Americans "misinterpret the universal [in Shakespeare's works] by misunderstanding the particular," she counters that "human nature is pretty much the same the world over," and argues that "the plot and motivation of [Shakespeare's] greater tragedies would always be clear everywhere." After three months of studying a copy of *Hamlet* while visiting an African homestead on the Tiv during rainy season, Bohannan is even further convinced that "*Hamlet* had only one possible interpretation, and that one universally obvious." Then she attempts to tell the story to a group of African tribesmen. Convinced that by explaining or changing "some details of custom" she can adequately convey Shakespeare's classic tale of tragic revenge, she sets out to relate the "one possible interpretation" to her African audience. As she embarks on the story, Bohannan thinks that this is her "chance to prove *Hamlet* universally intelligible."

The tribesmen insist that Bohannan "explain what [they] do not understand" as they have done for her in telling their own stories. Consequently, they interrupt frequently to re-tell aspects of the story that don't ring true in their own culture. By the time Bohannon has finished narrating the plot of Hamlet, the men have recast it as a story about witches, Claudius' honorable protection of his brother's wife, Laertes' murder of Ophelia in order to sell her body, Polonious' failures as a hunter, and Claudius' plot to kill Laertes. Hamlet, the hero of the English play, is judged to be out-of-line by the African audience for avenging his father's murder, mistrusting an omen from his father, and setting up Rosencrantz and Gildenstern's murder. The essay thus refutes Bohannan's initial belief that the meaning of Shakespeare's work is universally agreed upon.

Audience

Bohannan's essay displays a double awareness of audience: she must translate concepts from Shakespeare to African tribal culture, and she must relate African tribal norms to her British and American readers. Her telling of Hamlet includes many substitutions, such as *chief* for *King*, *omen* for *ghost*, *age mates* for *school friends*, *machetes* for *swords*, and *beer* for *wine*. Ironically, Bohannan, who is an anthropologist and scholar visiting the tribe, attempts to translate the concept of "scholar" but fails because her word choice suggests "witch." She quickly learns that, while she can usually adapt specific words to fit African ideas, she cannot escape the differences in cultural norms between Shakespeare's England and the contemporary Vit. She is frustrated because she could not have anticipated the men's objections to Hamlet's behavior nor the twisted motives that they ascribe to Laertes and Claudius to make the story logical by their standards. She admits that, with that audience, "Hamlet was clearly out of [her] hands."

This comparison of Shakespeare as understood by Anglican and African audiences depends on Bohannan's audience's knowledge of Shakespeare's text and its popular interpretations. Aware that most of her readers are not familiar with life in a modern African homestead, Bohannan interjects definitions and explanations into her essay. She tells her readers that in an elder's hut, "important people shouldn't ladle beer themselves." She explains the men's disapproval of her reading in her tent since "looking at paper" in their culture means poring over bills and receipts. She intrepidly defines *zombies* as "dead bod[ies] the witches had animated to sacrifice and eat." Dialogue in the essay reveals that African chiefs take many wives so that they can offer beer and food to many guests without levying taxes on their people.

Strategy

Bohannan uses dialogue to show the differences in cultural assumptions between herself and her audience. Generally, the Africans ascribe much more to witches than she realized. First, her audience argues that Hamlet is "bewitched" since everyone knows that "only witchcraft can make anyone mad, unless, of course, one sees the beings that lurk in the forest." This revelation is so unique that Bohannan switches from storyteller to anthropologist/observer and takes out her notebook to record the Africans' concept of "madness." Ophelia's madness is similarly dismissed when the tribesmen tell Bohannan that "the girl . . . not only went mad, she was drowned. Only witches can make people drown." By reporting these conversations as they occurred, Bohannan invites readers to experience the humor and frustration she found in the situation.

The punch line of the story comes when the tribesmen and Bohannan echo one another with similar thoughts. An old man in the hut says, "People are the same everywhere," but he is defending his interpretation that the story is the predictable plot of "the great-chief who wished to kill Hamlet." Like the English colleague who informed Bohannan that Americans "have difficulty with Shakespeare," the tribesmen tell her, "the elders of your country have never told you what the story really means." The tribesmen also believe there is only one correct reading of Hamlet—theirs.

WITI IHIMAERA "His First Ball"

Purpose

Comparing and contrasting the two dominant cultures in New Zealand is one of Witi Ihimaera's purposes in writing this story. The Maori people are the indigenous inhabitants of the island, and the Pakeha are the European immigrants and their descendents. When Tuta, a Maori, receives an invitation from the wife of the Governor-General to attend a state ball as a representative of his coworkers, he is offered a chance to see how the other half lives. His family and friends are intrigued by his opportunity, but Tuta himself remains skeptical. The many preparations he must make to be schooled in Pakeha manners show the differences between the cultures; dress, table manners, dance, and social graces among the elite white citizens differ sharply with Tuta's habits. Some readers will be familiar with Pakeha writer Katherine Mansfield's story about a similar incident, and they will be able to compare the two stories to further understand the differences between the cultures.

Documenting Maori culture and making sure that it is recorded in the literature of his native land is one of Ihimaera's life goals. He created Tuta to show the habits and customs of working-class Maori in contemporary New Zealand. He also wants to show the independence and pride of his people. Tuta rejects the Pakeha, especially after they demean him with their patronizing attentions at the ball. Although their manners are supposedly superior to those of Tuta and his friends, the Pakeha behave badly in this story, ridiculing Tuta's name and his ignorance of their expensive hors d'oeuvres.

Indirectly, the story champions those cast out as "others" everywhere in the world. Ihimaera's message is that there will always be "others." That is why Joyce appears in the end of the story and tells Tuta, "Before you . . . it was me." She has been excluded because she is "six feet six at least." Tuta and Joyce's ultimate response to the ball show that outsiders who cannot join the elite can nevertheless "beat them if [they] want to" by simply refusing to play the game.

Audience

The story alludes to George Bernard Shaw's play *Pygmalion* (or its musical version, *My Fair Lady*) when Ihimaera notes that "Mrs. Simmons felt quite sure that Professor Higgins didn't have it *this* bad." This literary convention suggests that the author is not writing for fellow Maoris but rather for whites, particularly people of European descent. Notice, too, that Ihimaera describes the habits Tuta must unlearn, such as preferring to wear purple, keeping his hair long, shuffling his feet, drinking beer, and "hot rock" dancing, but assumes that his readers are familiar with the social graces Tuta must quickly acquire.

Tuta and Joyce are the most likeable people at the ball. When they agree to stop mimicking the "beautiful people" at the party, they also have the most fun. Ihimaera's audience undoubtedly includes readers who find themselves inside and outside the elite set. He explains that conformity should not be the goal of a diverse society. Tuta decides to truly represent his mother, "Mrs. Simmons, Desiree Dawn, and the boys—Crazy Joe, Blackjack and Bigfoot" by behaving as a true Maori citizen at the ball. He thinks that outsiders will have to enter society "on their own terms . . . as the real people they [are] and not as carbon copies of the people already on the inside." This message is directed at the socially elite and inferior alike.

Strategy

Tuta is a touchstone for readers throughout the story. When his coworkers, friends, and family members get excited about his invitation to the ball, he remains skeptical and reluctant to go along with the scheme. His first response is that the invitation must be a joke being played on him by one of his friends; in the end he learns that it is a joke being played on him by society, especially by those who mock him at the ball. Throughout the story, Tuta remains unimpressed by high society and its impractical concerns. He wonders why the meals at balls are served in courses when it makes more sense to "just stick all the kai on the table at once." His well-grounded responses foreshadow his realization at the ball that fitting in should not entail acting like his oppressors.

Everyone in his circle who tries to prepare Tuta for the ball must go against his or her own grain in doing so. Tuta's mother, who assumes the invitation is a summons to court, asks her son, "Oh Tuta, what have you done?" Nevertheless, she cautions him to make polite conversation at the ball. Mrs. Simmons betrays her own Maori roots when she speaks in her own lingo to someone at the Government House on the telephone. Tuta's drag-queen friends attempt to teach him to dance differently than they normally would. His friends who drive him to the ball can't find a suitable limousine, so they festoon a Jaguar as if it is being used in a wedding. It is no wonder that Tuta has little objection to dancing with Joyce, in spite of her unusual height; Desiree Dawn, a "six-foot transvestite," had coached him to dance at the ball. He is most at home among outcasts.

Division and Classification

THE STRATEGIES

The classification essay is a valuable expository form because it provides students with a procedure for sorting and analyzing large quantities of information. It is also valuable because it uses the strategies studied in process analysis and comparison and contrast even as it anticipates some of the skills that will be examined in definition. Division, often the first step in classifying a subject, is similar to analysis in that it breaks something into smaller parts. Once these parts (or categories) have been established, they can be distinguished from one another by using the techniques of comparison and contrast. In the classification essay, such techniques become more complicated, however, because to classify effectively, writers must analyze at least three categories. To establish each category, writers must define its unique properties so that it will not overlap with the others.

The classification essay, like the previous writing strategies, can be seen as a way of organizing and presenting information. That is, narration is organized by the chronology of events, description by the evocation of the senses, process analysis by the sequence of steps, and comparison by the divided or alternating patterns. In subsequent (and more sophisticated) forms—definition, cause and effect, argument—the writer must create the organizational pattern. But as the introduction to this section points out, the classification essay follows a fairly recognizable form. Some beginning writers see this format as little more than an outline: divide subject into categories, arrange categories in sequence, define each category by differentiating it from the other categories, and illustrate it with examples. More experienced writers see this formula like a poet sees the rhyme scheme for a sonnet—a structure that encourages endless variations. For a brief example of how this pattern can be integrated into graceful writing, ask your students to examine Gareth Tucker's "Gentlemen! Start Your Engines."

THE READINGS

The essays in this section illustrate all the essential thinking and organizing strategies writers use when they try to classify—and by extension clarify—a subject. James H. Austin presents a thorough and exhaustive list of categories of chance, including at least one that readers may not have thought about before, to demonstrate that luck is not a totally random phenomenon. Mary Mebane's discussion of "Shades of Black" provides not only a categorization of skin tones, but also one of responses to them. Hers is a very complex essay that branches out to incorporate several classification systems as part of the analysis it provides.

The essays by Garry Wills and James H. Austin, although very different in tone and purpose, are classical division-and-classification texts. Each writer defines his subject, lists the categories he will describe, and provides examples illustrative of each type. Both authors use a parallel structure in inventing and defining their categories. Wills' system, however, is very complex, and the categories do overlap some out of necessity.

Philip Lopate's and James Q. Wilson's division-and-classification essays demonstrate the usefulness of that writing strategy, even when it is impossible to provide an exhaustive list of the categories involved. Lopate's classification of "Modern Friendships" examines his own preference for having many good friends instead of one best friend, and Wilson's "Democracy for All?" explains why worldwide democracy in the twenty-first century is unlikely.

Flannery O'Connor's "Revelation" *reveals* the degree to which all of us spend our lives classifying everything in the universe—especially other people. Ruby Turpin spends much of the early portion of the story outlining her system and judging other people by its criteria. But once she is hit in the eye by a book on *Human Development*, she discovers the ironies in her system. Indeed, she discovers to her horror and to the reader's amusement that "the last shall be first."

THE VISUAL TEXT

Roz Chast foregoes the usual meteorological classifications of clouds (e.g., cumulus, cirrus, and stratus) to make her own humorous list of cloud types. Because her purpose is to entertain, and the persona she adopts in her cartoons is always a bit confused and irrational (perhaps even paranoid), the system she devises is not mutually exclusive or exhaustive. Chast classifies clouds by their motives, a personification that is at once preposterous and thought provoking. After all, we have all been stuck under a "Sigmund" cloud before.

THE WRITING

The writing assignments assume that all students are natural classifiers: they classify restaurants, music, dates, teachers, jobs, virtually everything they encounter in their daily lives. For that reason, they could choose any subject—humorous or serious—for a classification essay. The assignments listed in the book emerge from the readings. Assignment 1 encourages students to construct a scheme for analyzing something trivial like trash, junk, or inanimate objects. Assignment 2 presents a variation on Wills' essay by suggesting that students explain the punishments for various classifications of murder.

Assignment 3 asks students to analyze a system that uses power positively, and to answer, in effect, the negative power system outlined by Mebane. Assignment 4 asks students to apply Austin's findings to their own experience. The final two assignments invite students to further divide of one of Lopate's categories (5), or apply Wilson's point of view about inequality of wealth and power in society (6).

JAMES H. AUSTIN "Four Kinds of Chance"

Purpose

Chance is often thought of "as something fortuitous that happens unpredictably without discernable human intention," but Austin's purpose in "Four Kinds of Chance" is to show that individuals can influence some kinds of chance. His division and classification demonstrates that "chance plays several distinct roles when humans react creatively with one another and with their environment." The four kinds of chance identified by Austin are closely related to each other yet profoundly different in the type of intelligence, receptivity, and participation their recipients must exhibit. Chance I and II, for example, depend upon the inevitable occurrence of blind luck, but Chance III is not passive; it comes only to those who think and act, thereby increasing their ability to utilize fortuitous circumstances.

Austin groups his three kinds of chance, characterized by luck, exploration, and sagacity, as variations on serendipity, which he defines as "the facility for encountering unexpected good luck," but *altamirage*, the fourth kind of chance established within Austin's classification system, is the result of tenacious preparations. It is of a "different domain" than the other kinds of chance; it involves the highly individual area of "the personality and its actions." Chance IV is "one-man-made," engaging "the invisible forces of chance we know exist yet cannot touch." Austin's purpose in differentiating Chance IV from the other kinds of good luck is to encourage readers to follow the example of de Sautuola, pursuing peculiar interests with passion and always inviting the favor of the illusive and magnificent *altamirage*.

Audience

Austin organizes his categories with his audience in mind, starting with the most familiar and ending with the least-known type of chance. This arrangement causes the discussion of types to get progressively longer and the author's tone to grow more formal as the essay develops. Austin's presentation of Chance I is contained in a single paragraph, comprised of a one-sentence definition and a hypothetical example involving cards at a bridge table. This first kind of chance does not require much elaboration, and Austin speaks directly to his audience, addressing readers as *you*, because everyone is subject to blind luck and already has some experience with it.

The other forms of chance require various levels of involvement or preparation, so Austin provides successively more concrete examples to illustrate them. He does not assume that all his readers have experience with the higher forms of chance. Each category is progressively more complex; each requires more human intervention and is more difficult to define or distinguish from other categories. Therefore, each requires a more detailed example. Chance II is illustrated by the epigrammatic philosophy of automobile mogul Charles Kettering. Chance III is exemplified by the scientific experiment and process that lead Alexander Fleming to the discovery of penicillin, but the first three categories are merely background on Austin's real discovery. Half the essay describes Don Marcelino de Sautuola's discovery of cave paintings at Altamira and defines Chance IV within this category because of the revelation Austin wants to deliver to his audience: chance is susceptible to "subtle personal prompting." Readers of this essay can act to improve their chances of receiving good luck.

Strategy

Austin's strategy involves arranging his four categories in an emphatic order to build evidence for his thesis that chance is affected by human intervention. His first category involves "blind luck," which occurs naturally as a matter of mathematical probability without any human interference. Chance II requires only action, a relentless collision with fate that is bound to produce some good luck. What Louis Pasteur called "the prepared mind" is the prerequisite for Chance III, and ability to recognize and use good fortune when it serendipitously arises. *Altamirage*, or Chance IV, is the result of a life well spent. Peculiar to the individual, it occurs as the culmination of a series of unintentional but passionately executed activities.

Austin cites authorities to verify each of his more complex categories; he quotes Kettering, Pasteur, and Disraeli. He also makes frequent use of comparisons to describe his abstract subjects. Thus, Chance II is likened with stirring up a pot, and IV is described as sharing qualities with a mirage. Because the differences between his categories are subtle, Austin groups them together, explaining that Chance I and II require only minimal human involvement and that two of the first three classes of chance are variations of serendipity. These subdivisions emphasize the singularity of Chance IV, a discovery that may result from *altamirage*—the culmination of Austin's own interest and creative pursuit of chance.

MARY MEBANE "Shades of Black"

Purpose

The relationship between color and power in America is widely acknowledged, but the subtle gradations of shade among African Americans examined in Mebane's essay are not often discussed openly in print. Mebane reveals that some of the most overt prejudice against blacks comes from within members of their own race. She argues that vestiges of "the segregated world," where "power was thought of in negative terms" and "the concept of power as a force for good . . . was not in evidence," remain in African American culture where lighter-skinned blacks often assume dominance over their darker-skinned counterparts. Mebane recounts examples of lighter-skinned blacks making damaging assumptions about "black black" women, such as the college English instructor who informs her of her high verbal score on a placement exam. Although the instructor doesn't say so, Mebane realizes that the light-skinned teacher is wondering "How could this black-skinned girl score higher on the verbal [examination] than some of the students who've had more advantages than she?"

More disturbing, however, is the tendency Mebane isolates of oppressed peoples to identify with their oppressors, adopting and enforcing the very codes that hold them down. She cites the example of a schoolteacher who "was just as black as she could be," but who remained "a strict enforcer" of the culture's skin tone "standards." Among black males, particularly college-educated men, prejudice against dark-skinned women is apparent, according to Mebane. But her most alarming evidence of the painful ramifications of categorizing people by skin tones are the black black women who accept the stereotype and fall prey to "total self-rejection." These women, Mebane says, think of themselves as " . . . black, . . . ugly, . . . nobody" and adopt the stance that they "will perform on the level" that society has "assigned" to them. Mebane, herself a dark-skinned black woman, pleads with African American men and women to reject the cultural standard of dismissing black black persons as less intelligent or less attractive.

Audience

This essay is of interest to a wide variety of readers, many of whom will want to take the opportunity to confront their own skin tone prejudices. However, Mebane's primary audience for this piece seems to be black readers, those who can identify with the examples she gives from primarily black school settings, and whose attitudes she directly confronts. Her opening statements about "gross abuses of authority" in the "segregated world" define her audience as black readers. The essay confronts the attitudes of light-skinned black women, dark-skinned black women, teachers in primarily black schools, black black African American men, college-educated black men, uneducated black men, and, finally, black black women themselves. She is attempting to change the assumptions and behaviors of all of these groups of people.

Mebane examines the problem of skin tone prejudice historically. She wonders whether "African men recently transported to the New World considered . . .African women beautiful in comparison with Native American Indian women or immigrant European women," and she suggests that discovering the cultural turning point when African men turned their "interest away from black black women" would "prove to be an interesting topic for researchers." She notes that during the 1960s, when " black had become beautiful," skin tone became a less overt "handicap" for black black women, and explains that today, when she meets college-educated black men, she tries to "gauge" their ages. According to Mebane, college-educated black males born before 1945 retain prejudice that is not as severe among their younger counterparts.

Strategy

Several classification systems organize this essay. For instance, Mebane explains that "social class and color were the primary criteria used in determining [students'] status on the campus" at the university she attended. She outlines the campus social structure, which included "first . . . the children of doctors, lawyers, and college teachers," then the offspring of "public-school teachers, businessmen, and anybody else who had access to . . . money, " and, finally there were the children "of the working class," who comprised "the bulk of the student population." Black people are classified by skin tones throughout the essay; shades of black identified by Mebane include "black black," "caramel-brown," "light brown," "reddish yellow," "light skinned," and that shade that "was indistinguishable in color from . . . white."

Mebane also classifies responses to dark-skinned black women. Among African American men, she notes that college-educated individuals born before 1945 seem to hold black black women in the lowest esteem, followed by uneducated black men of the same generation. Younger college-educated black males respond to her more favorably, but "oddly enough" it is "the lighter-skinned black male" who does not "seem to feel so much prejudice toward the black black woman."

The most poignant classification system described in the essay is the manifestations of color prejudice among dark-skinned African American women. Some adopt the attitude that "they are nothing but 'sex machines,'" and spend their lives practicing and boasting about their "supposedly superior sexual performance." Others "swing all the way across to intense religiosity," working in "the more traditional Southern Churches—Baptist and Methodist," or become "leaders and ministers" in the "evangelical Holiness sects." A third group devotes their lives to "excellence in a career," and, according to Mebane, most of these black black women become teachers. All of these responses to skin tone prejudice are methods of compensating for society's scorn. Sexuality, religiosity, or career excellence become, for these women, "their sole reason for being and for esteeming themselves." Readers will easily infer that Mebane herself belongs to the last of these classifications of black black women.

PHILLIP LOPATE "Modern Friendships"

Purpose

As Lopate notes in his introduction, the topic of friendship is such a perennial favorite among essay writers that each wants to prove himself on the topic. In this essay, though, Lopate asserts that he has a legitimate reason for adding to the body of work on the topic: the nature of friendship has changed in modern times. He concedes that "Aristotle and Cicero, Seneca and Montaigne, Bacon and Samuel Johnson, Hazlitt, Emerson, and Lamb" have all chipped away at the topic, and he quotes five of these nine authors in the course of his own examination of friendship. He agrees in part with each of the predecessors he cites and offers evidence from their work to strengthen his own positions, but he also quibbles with their suppositions, reinterpreting each with a modern twist.

Lopate hopes to disabuse his readers of the notion that having a "best friend" is essential, or even wise. He argues that modern relationships require pluralistic friendships. Because it is impossible to see completely "eye to eye" with another person, Lopate suggests that a best friendship puts too much burden on participants to reach consensus. He also notes that we have a tendency to want to "improve" our friends, making them more punctual, personable, or perspicuous, and so we should simply choose a variety of friends, each with qualities we would hope to find in an ideal best friend. Believing that "friends can't be your family," Lopate answers the "question that has vexed many commentators" including Aristotle and Cicero, when he says that a coterie of friends is best. Interestingly, Lopate reveals in the essay that he is a "bachelor" who must "fight to overcome the feeling that [he is] being 'replaced' by the spouse" whenever one of his friends marries. Readers might wonder if his "serial friendship" theory would hold, should he meet someone he wanted to marry.

Audience

Although Lopate expects that his readers will recognize the prominence of the nine essayists he names who have written notably on the topic of friendship before him, he does not expect that his readers will know exactly what each has said. He tactfully brings his audience up to speed on the subject by summarizing Aristotle's three types of friendship, quoting from Cicero's treatise on the topic, judging Montaigne's thoughts on friendship "a bit high hat," and enlarging upon Emerson's notion of friendship as conversation. Each time he introduces a new subject, he quotes from some of the writers he has acknowledged as his predecessors.

Noting that "the personal essay is itself an attempt to establish a friendship on the page between writer and reader," Lopate reveals that he likes to have his friends function as confidantes who remain focused on their conversations. Naturally, then, he confides in his readers, telling us that a memorable experience from his childhood involved being cuddled by his younger sister and that he once "found [himself] in a state of emotional despair," and having "exhausted [his] hopes of finding love or success," he actually "felt suicidal." Lopate defines the "Friendship Scene" as "a flow of shared confidences, recognitions, humor, advice, speculation, even wisdom," all of which occur in the pages of his essay.

Strategy

A variety of classification systems form the structure of this essay. At first, Lopate classifies the types of friendships that occur as human beings grow into adults: "basic" or "family" friendships like the one he enjoyed but outgrew with his sister, possessive grade-school friendships like the one that ended when he slept "with [his] best friend's girl," and the pluralistic friendships that result when one abandons the "Best Friend expectation." He also classifies the problems to which modern pluralistic friendships fall prey: the "need for consensus" that he experienced with an unnamed female friend, clashes of character, the infrequency of face-to-face meetings with friends due to "tight schedules," and conflicts with controlling or married friends. Finally, he lists the qualities "that characterize the best friendships": "rapport, affection, need, habit, and forgiveness," saying that the greatest of these is forgiveness.

Lopate ends his examination of modern friendship with three specific examples from his own experience. He tells about Richard, a "dear old friend," who, nonetheless, is embarrassed by his friend's "confessional talk," and Charlie, who "is often very distracted" during the first half-hour of any meeting, but eventually settles down to listen to "virtually anything" and responds with "candor." It is Michael, however, whom Lopate describes as "a close writer friend" who seems to embody all that he is looking for in a friend: he is frank and intent, telling Lopate about a friend who is dying of AIDS and listening to Lopate's concerns about his father's poor health. It is with Michael that Lopate can "[dwell] long enough in the shared privacies of [their] psyches." To the reader, it may seem like Michael would be a candidate for "best friend" if Lopate believed in that sort of thing.

JAMES Q. WILSON "Democracy for All?"

Purpose

The beginning of the twenty-first century is an optimistic time for democracy, and James Q. Wilson poses a timely and interesting question in this essay, asking "whether the world might become democratic." It an attempt to determine the likelihood of such a possibility, Wilson classifies the conditions necessary to foster and sustain democracy as it has been developed in relatively recent history. Such analysis is not simple; as Wilson points out, it is easier to explain why the twentieth century was an era of genocide than to understand why it also fostered the growth of democracy worldwide. The philosophical movement of people from a village mentality, in which all "others" are the enemy, to the inclusive sort of society that is run by "votes cast by strangers" is difficult to trace.

By looking at successful democracies in the world today, Wilson is able to isolate four characteristics that are common to most. These are physical isolation, individual property ownership, homogeneous population, and reliance on democratic traditions—none of which can be effected overnight. In most cases, these criteria are out of reach for flat, land-locked, nondemocratic countries whose populations are diverse (e.g., "China or Russia or in much of Africa or the Middle East"). Furthermore, Wilson points out that legislating democracy through a written constitution has not worked very well in the past, and, although religion is sometimes successful in building tolerance between diverse peoples, it has just as often failed. For these reasons Wilson believes that democracy can come to much of the world by one of two means: military conquest (which he deems unlikely) or economic globalization. He jokes that "In the face of widespread knowledge about what efficiency can achieve, nondemocratic governments will have to scramble to maintain inefficiency." In other words, Wilson is arguing that the Internet, which is "making it clear to everybody in every nation just where one can buy the best goods at the lowest prices," will succeed in promoting democracy where geography, ideology, economics, and ethnicity have failed.

Audience

Writing for the political magazine *Commentary*, Wilson envisions a mature, well-educated audience who are already informed about cultural and historical matters. His references to landmark twentieth-century matters, such as the World Wars and the democratization of Germany and Japan, as well as his allusions to politics in Africa and South America, suggest that he is not teaching a lesson about history, but making a specific point for readers who have lived through these historical events. Take heart, though, because even readers who are not quite (or even close to) ninety years of age can learn from Wilson's ideas about what fosters democracy, and among those readers will be the survivors who can determine the accuracy of the predictions of Wilson and his friend.

In fact, by identifying the Internet as the most viable impetus in worldwide democratization in the future, Wilson engages and challenges younger readers to make it happen. His response to his friend's prediction about China, wondering whether it will *still* be democratic in 2033, presents a clear mandate for the architects of Internet commerce to build a virtual political realm that sustains the worldwide democracy it will foster. Wilson's conclusion, that in nourishing our own democracy "we may hope that others will acquire something equally worthy of nurturance," speaks of the global, Internet society as much as of the physical American democracy.

Strategy

Wilson uses the division-and-classification strategy to break down the complex and nebulous factors that sustain democracy into just four essential elements. Of these, he looks most closely at the one over which all governments have the most immediate control: ownership of private property. It is no coincidence that this is also the chief difference between democracy and its competing political ideologies, such as communism and socialism. Using England as his historical example, Wilson shows how clans, or individual property ownership rights, cut down on disputes (and therefore laws) concerning real estate, commerce, and domestic matters. He notes that in feudal England, "a man had to own land before starting a family" because individual property ownership was considered the cornerstone of social responsibility. According to Wilson, the ownership of land in England, America, Canada, Australia, and New Zealand "laid the groundwork for democratic rule."

Of course, countries can't move mountains and oceans or change their history if they wish to become democracies. However, Wilson does offer some hope that countries whose natural conditions are not conducive to democracy can thrive as such anyway. Switzerland stands as a beacon of promise to the world. The Swiss have "managed to create a democracy out of an alliance among French, German, and Italian speakers who were divided almost equally between Protestants and Catholics." Noting that America, Canada, and New Zealand are thriving democracies that lack the traditional homogeneity he has identified among successful democratic nations, Wilson explains that those countries' political aims were forged when their populations were less diverse. However, even as the United States of America has become more ethnically, racially, religiously, and socially diverse, it has continued to become, perhaps, the most successful experiment in democracy of all time—proving that, all classifications and analyses aside, the evolution of a successful democracy is a "happy accident."

GARY WILLS "The Dramaturgy of Death"

Purpose

Gary Wills' readers will have to agree that the history of capital punishment is one of exaggerated brutality after reading that in 1570 the Turkish general Lala Mustafa Pasha had an enemy "mutilated (nose and ears cut off), dragged around the city walls, dangled from a ship's mast, tied naked to a post, skinned alive, beheaded, and quartered (his four limbs cut off)." And that was just the beginning of Marcantonio Bragadin's execution. Wills uses a division-and-classification strategy to systematically refute historical and contemporary arguments for murder by the state and to show the fallacies behind each that makes them contradictory. The first section of his essay, in which he presents profuse examples from classical culture to Jeffersonian America, contains some vivid and repulsive evidence that the rationales for the death penalty have been, in effect, a license for physical, psychological, and even spiritual torture.

A well-prepared opponent of the death penalty, Wills uses his research findings to show that, in Western mythology and history, the ultimate punishment has often been abused, both in executing persons most citizens would not think of prosecuting today and by using means that are far too brutal for contemporary public taste. The immorality of the death penalty is also illustrated by Plato's legal code, which prescribed the death penalty for a slave who killed a free man, but not for the reverse. Thomas Jefferson authored the Virginia statute that denied a white woman who bore a black child from protection under the law, leaving her abandoned and likely to die. Readers will be shocked to learn that one of the fathers of modern thought and a framer of the Constitution was a zealous advocate of capital punishment. Will's numerous examples of state executions of dead men, where corpses were propped up, drawn and quartered, beheaded, or otherwise desecrated, dramatically illustrates the senselessness of public executions.

Audience

Since many of his readers believe that the death penalty is an effective deterrent to crime, Wills focuses much of his essay on debunking that position. He argues that parts of the United States where the death penalty is carried out are, not coincidentally, the highest crime areas, and that countries without the death penalty enjoy lower crime rates. The death penalty is most often invoked to punish crimes of passion, and Wills argues that criminals acting in anger, revenge, or under the influence of controlled substances do not act rationally, so logical stratagems such as deterrence bear little influence, if any, on their behavior. Wills points out the irony that families of victims are often invited to witness executions, when it is the company that criminals keep that is more likely in need of deterrence. Modern American execution rituals offer "free legal aid . . . family visits. . . reading . . . TV. . . a last meal. . . a last request, religious attendance, guaranteed burial, a swift and nearly painless death" all shut away from the public eye. This, Wills maintains, is scarcely the way to use capital punishment for deterrence. He lists prominent politicians, including Dianne Feinstein, Andrew Young, and Hillary Clinton, who have shifted their positions to endorse capital punishment as a deterrent, to demonstrate that the pedagogical value of the death penalty is simply a myth that political figures hide behind when they want to look tough on crime.

The final defense of the death penalty classified by Wills is "closure," or the need for survivors to see retribution enacted in order to put terrible events behind them. He tries to expose the "buzzword" closure as a cover-up for more base motives. For example, he says that the "unmarried mother of Jesse Jackson's child sued Reverend Jackson, . . . not about anything so crass as money," but for "'closure.'" In the same way, politicians called for the execution of Timothy McVeigh for closure when they really wanted revenge and the approval of their constituents. Real closure, Wills argues, comes from moving on with one's life, not focusing energy and attention on crimes, courts, and criminals. An execution is a very violent denouement.

Strategy

Wills divides his refutation of support for the death penalty into four parts: The Rationale, Public Execution, Deterrence, and Closure. His first section is further divided into fourteen historical modes and manners of execution. His classification system is incomplete because, as Nietzsche has already noted, the practice of capital punishment did not emerge from a "single or consistent theory of its intent or effect." The history of murdering criminals is built upon "a tangle of overlapping yet conflicting urges," and many of them were "fitted out with later rationalizations," which makes the logic of the subject difficult to trace or classify.

The breadth of research supporting Wills' arguments is impressive. He supplies examples from his reading of Greek mythology and ancient history as well as the public statements of many contemporary political figures. He describes the biblical story that "Bible-quoting fundamentalists" have ignored; in John 8:3-11 an execution for adultery is interrupted by Jesus. Wills' strongest evidence is leveled against the notion that capital punishment is an effective deterrent of crime. He contradicts the "'gut feelings'" of former Massachusetts governor William Weld and former Florida governor Bob Graham with ample statistical evidence. Drawing upon recent surveys of "present and former presidents of the most prestigious criminological societies" in 1995 and a survey of police chiefs and sheriffs conducted by Peter D. Hart Research Associates in the same year, Wills shows that people most closely connected with the capture and punishment of criminals have very little faith that executions reduce crime. The incorporation of secondary sources in this essay is masterful; it contains stories from mythology and history, statistical data, and quotations from past and present political figures. Wills hammers home his point that the tradition of capital punishment is built on contradictions and falsehoods when he quotes President George W. Bush as saying that Jesus is his favorite philosopher. As governor of Texas, Bush oversaw 152 state executions. Like all of the other contradictory and overlapping notions about the death penalty, this one is also likely to go unresolved.

FLANNERY O'CONNOR "Revelation"

Purpose

The action in O'Connor's story "Revelation" teaches Ruby Turpin the most basic tenet of human worth, that all people, white or black, poor or rich, sullen or jovial, religious or insane, are fundamentally equal—in the eyes of God. Even Ruby's imagined consultation with Jesus, in which he takes her aside and explains, "There's only two places available for you. You can either be a nigger or white-trash," acknowledges that the soul is independent of earthly identity. The soul, in this case, is Ruby's own, and her game of "what if" recognizes that her superior status in life results from the grace of Jesus, whom she, ironically, imagines speaking in the discriminatory terms of "nigger" and "white-trash." She praises Jesus for making her "a respectable, hard-working, church-going woman" (albeit a fat one) and for giving her a good disposition.

In spite of her obsession with categorizing people and trying to establish a hierarchy among classes of humans, Ruby considers herself unbigoted in her magnanimousness. She muses that "to help anybody out that needed it [is] her philosophy of life. She never [spares] herself when she [finds] somebody in need, whether they [are] white or black, trash or decent." Ruby's thoughts reveal her fundamental prejudices; the purpose of O'Connor's story is to expose the deep-rooted bigotry that motivates some of society's most pious citizens.

The story is humorous. As fiction, its purpose is to entertain. Perhaps the most enjoyable scene in the story occurs when Ruby is repaid in kind for her false flattery. Ruby, who has complained that she is sure "tired of buttering up niggers," confesses humiliation, which she could not show her husband Claud, to the cotton pickers. The hyperbole of their response is pure comedy, as one black woman assures Ruby, "You the sweetest white lady I know," and another tops that with, "Stout as she can be and sweet. Jesus satisfied with her!"

Audience

O'Connor's audience sees through Ruby's hypocritical selflessness almost immediately when she makes a show of insisting that Claud take the only empty chair in the waiting room. Readers are struck, too, by Ruby's unnatural preoccupation with classifying her fellow human beings. O'Connor assumes her audience perceives religion and social equality much differently than Ruby does; the story's humor and plot depend on that. For instance, Ruby's superior, self-congratulatory attitude, at least in part, provokes Mary Grace's attack. As Ruby claims more and more moral high ground for herself, the girl's indignant responses escalate from simply looking up from her *Human Development* text to heaving the book and lunging at the throat of the source of her anger. Ruby, Claud, the doctor, others in the waiting room, and even the cotton pickers all ascribe Mary Grace's behavior to insanity, but O'Connor's readers are aware that the girl's disturbed response, although inappropriate, is intentionally directed at Ruby.

Readers of the story can adopt different points of view, unlike Ruby, who is too well satisfied with her own perceptions to consider the focus or validity of others'. Ironically, most all of the characters in the story perceive themselves to be better than some other group represented, and many assume that they are better than Ruby herself. The empty flattery of the cotton pickers and of Mary Grace's mother, who assures Ruby, "Oh, *you* aren't fat," implies a condoning superiority. The white trash woman's remarks indicate her grandiose self-perception, and even the casual demeanor of the pharmacy delivery boy is indicative of his self-centered world view. Only the common, aptly named Claud is self-deprecating in his comments and behavior.

Strategy

Division and classification order Ruby's world. She starts categorizing the people at the doctor's office immediately. They are variously old, stylish, white trash, common, and ugly. Ruby also assesses people's clothes and shoes as an indication of their social worth. "Without appearing to," O'Connor explains, "Mrs. Turpin always noticed people's feet." As this demonstrates, Ruby's categories are not mutually exclusive. She tries to place her system of social classes into an hierarchic order, beginning with "most colored people" at the "bottom of the heap" and "next to them— not above, just away from" are "white-trash," followed by "home-owners, then home-and-land owners," followed by "people with a lot of money and much bigger houses and much more land." But her system always fails her because she realizes that some rich people are entirely too "common," and some "good" people have lost their money, and some black people (such as the dentist who owns two red Lincolns, a swimming pool, and a farm) "own their homes and land as well."

It galls Ruby that the white-trash woman in the doctor's office does not recognize her place in this ill-conceived hierarchy; she believes that she is better than blacks and wants to "send all them niggers back to Africa." She thanks "Gawd" that she "ain't a lunatic." But she really angers Ruby when she presumes to place herself above the Turpins by announcing, "Two thangs I ain't going to do: love no niggers or scoot down no hog with no hose."

Three visionlike experiences comprise Ruby's lesson in human worth. The first is her old dream that usually follows her bedtime contemplations of social order. Its persecution imagery includes all the classes of people crowded in the same boxcar bound for a gas oven. This succeeds only in confusing Ruby, whose private caste system does not really begin to break down until *Human Development* hits her squarely in the head. Alone in the "pig parlor," she implores God to explain the significance of Mary Grace's epithet. She sees Claud's truck, ferrying the cotton pickers home in the "transparent intensity" of the evening light and imagines the truck smashed by a bigger truck, leaving "Claud's and the niggers' brains all over the road." This gruesome equality is possible in death. As the evening sky darkens, Ruby perceives a vision of what is to come. A streak of light appears to connect the field and heavens, conveying souls to afterlife. The souls are arranged according to earthly social groups, but they are without earthly attributes; "even their virtues [are] being burned away." Ruby's acceptance of this higher order is apparent as she walks back to her house, the voices of crickets, like the hallelujahs of the souls, in her ears. Perhaps her faith wasn't hypocritical after all.

Definition

THE STRATEGIES

Definition is one of the most important kinds of expository writing. Twenty-five hundred years ago Aristotle recognized it as one of the natural methods for expressing an idea or developing a point, and modern rhetoricians such as Richard Weaver still cite it as a particularly effective tool for argument. Often an extended definition is the basis for an entire philosophy or theory—Plato's *Republic* or Newman's *The Idea of a University*, for example—and writers frequently begin their essays with a proposition that is in essence a definition: "In many ways, Japan is still a feudal state." Such sentences are generative, inviting the writer to supply the evidence that illustrates the accuracy of the definition. But students usually don't realize that they are defining when they write this kind of sentence or when they analyze the characteristics or ingredients of something. By reading, responding, and assessing extended definitions they will learn to see how "the need to define one's terms" lurks behind many of their general assertions.

You may want to teach the definition essay by focusing on three points: (1) Why is the author defining? (2) What strategies does he or she use to define? (3) How might your students adopt those strategies for writing their own definitions? A good place to start is Joyce Carol Oates' paragraph defining romantic love. She starts with a negative definition, telling what romantic love is *not*, and then proceeds to describe what it *is*. She illuminates her discussion with the example of Diana, Princess of Wales, whose marriage to Prince Charles was not romantic, and whose life ended in a quest for romantic love. Jason Utesch's paragraph about personality demonstrates that such a common word is very difficult to define accurately.

THE READINGS

All of the writers in this section use definition primarily for informative purposes. Christopher M. Pizzi provides a definition of "doorways" that is part oral, part visual rhetoric. John Berendt's essay on "The Hoax" provides an entertaining, yet sincere, definition of his playful topic. Diane Ackerman attempts to quantify and describe a sensation that often defies language. William Langewiesche and Stephen Harrigan have complex purposes for their definitions. Langewiesche attempts to capture the magnitude of the 9/11 cleanup operation by defining the American ingenuity of the workers who accomplished it. Harrigan defines the essence of "tiger" to explain why Miguel, an eleven-year-old tiger in the Houston Zoo, suddenly and violently killed one of his caretakers on a peaceful morning in May.

Alice Walker's short story, "Everyday Use," is an excellent example of how the defining process works. Her characters each operate from their own definitions of African American culture. Maggie sees it as traditional skills and observances which have been handed down for her use, but her sister Dee thinks of her own heritage as a museum piece, which she must preserve without understanding.

Probably the most valuable lesson composition students can derive from these attempts at definition is to see the effectiveness of using concrete, familiar, and vivid examples to illustrate a point. Most beginning writers do not recognize the power of an example. They try to define with synonyms—usually adjectives and abstract nouns. Like the writers in this section, student writers can draw on personal and historical examples to clarify the meaning of their words.

THE VISUAL TEXT

Adbusters is known for its ironic and sardonic commentary on acquisitive culture and the Madison Avenue agencies that feed that desire. The photo included in the Definition section of the book raises provocative questions about how young people define themselves, both through the brand-name objects they buy and covet and the tattoos they choose to symbolize their desires and dreams for themselves. The photo at once trivializes the craze to be tattooed and to identify oneself with brands of automobiles, soft drinks, and blue jeans. The relative permanence of tattoos raises issues about how transient our desires are. Students might be encouraged to talk about how they have defined themselves at various stages of their lives and to examine whether they would regret having that self-perception or goal permanently affixed to their skin.

THE WRITING

The writing assignments at the end of this section encourage students to deal in specifics by drawing on a range of experience. The first two assignments ask students to follow the strategies in the essays—to define themselves through a special interest and a celebrity. Assignment 3 asks students to use Harrigan's technique—examining the behaviors of a specific breed of animal to analyze its temperament and typical actions. Assignment 4 suggests that students try to emulate Langewische's portrait of ingenuity as embodied by David Griffin by profiling someone they know who exemplifies a specific characteristic. Assignment 5 invites students to analyze and exemplify Berendt's analysis of the phenomena of "hoaxes" by determining why they enjoy something that is just plain fun. The last assignment urges students to call on their experience in other courses to define a concept such as "a good education."

CHRISTOPHER M. PIZZI "Doorways: A Visual Essay"

Purpose

Naturally, anyone who has visited civilization has a working knowledge of doorways. The purpose of Christopher M. Pizzi's essay is not to define doorways for the ignorant, but to draw readers' attention to the variety of doorways through which they blissfully pass on the way to destinations in or outside these ubiquitous portals. He asks readers to consider how they regard doorways: "As a place? As a threshold? Or simply as a way in or out?" Pizzi believes that every doorway presents a mystic moment of passage from one environment to the next—whether the doorway delivers us from nature to the comfort of "indoors," or to the foot of an impressive staircase that leads to an important room.

Audience

The doorway is what we seek when we approach a building. It is where we interact with the façade of the structure. Properly designed, it should hint at the transition from exterior to interior and prepare pedestrians for the space they are about to enter. It should reduce the scale of a massive structure down to an entrance that is small enough to be opened and closed by a single human being and welcoming to that person as well. Every doorway contains some common, functional elements, such as a "handle or knob," "a letter slot," "a peephole," a lock," and "a knocker or doorbell." Still, the variety of doorways, from the ancient and ornate to modern "aluminum and glass doors" that represent the standard "products from manufacturers' catalogues," warrant the attention of those who pass through them. They are simultaneously archetypal and individualistic.

The examples that Pizzi illustrates to accompany his meditation on doorways are located in the vicinity of Washington, D.C., or Jerusalem, Israel. Both of these cities are revered for their culturally significant architecture, and readers who have visited either city, or other cosmopolitan cities, will have a catalog of similar examples in mind. However, even small cities house a variety of doorways, exterior and interior. Consider the doors of churches, courtrooms, public libraries, schools, stores, and houses. Also, think about the gates of parks, cemeteries, and private lawns. Wherever readers live, they will be able to cite local examples of doorways that are intimidating, inviting, ornate or spare, and those that invite nature and sunlight in or shut them out. Pizzi invites his readers to consider the role that doorways play in their lives, and most readers will agree with Pizzi's pronouncement that revolving doors are "awkward and disorienting to move through." Regardless of where they live, readers will be able to think of doorways that intimidate or intrigue them.

Strategy

College students reading this essay are likely to have a wealth of examples on which to draw. Older instructional buildings contain doorways with such archaic elements as transoms, ornate hinges and other hardware, and frosted, beveled, or leaded-glass windows. By contrast, newer buildings are likely to divide space with doors that are more minimalist and serviceable, doors that may contain such modern elements as panic bars, invisible hinges, and tempered glass. Faculty might also want to extend discussion of this essay by explaining why they teach with their classroom doors open or closed.

Pizzi mixes verbal and visual rhetoric in this essay. The drawings that accompany the text foster a visual dialogue, offering competing views of classical, baroque, Georgian, Renaissance, Middle-eastern, and minimalist elements. The placement of the drawings throughout the essay invites conversation about the juxtaposed images and text. For example, the first two drawings show a nearly flush and deeply recessed doorway to illustrate the function of doorways as "archway," "passage," "wall," portal," "threshold" and "place."

The inherent simplicity of line drawing allows Pizzi to focus his reader/viewer's attention on the basic elements and details that define the essence of "doorway" in its various permutations. The contrast between wood, masonry, and glass materials used in each is suggested by the monochromatic pen-and-ink drawings. With the exception of Pizzi's rendering of the façade of the Renwick Gallery at the Smithsonian Institution, the doorways are shown divorced from the buildings that house them, focusing his audience's eyes on the details of the portal alone. The medium used to represent the doorways also reduces all to a common pen-and-ink denominator, facilitating comparisons. None outshines another, so that the viewer's attention is focused entirely on the architectural elements of each example. While photographs might have depicted the doorways discussed in more realistic detail, Pizzi achieves a heightened attention to elements by suggesting them with pen strokes and carefully controlling the shadowing of each drawing. After all, a camera sees everything in much the same way the human eye does, so Pizzi's purpose in getting his audience to see doorways differently is better served by showing them the way his eye sees them.

JOHN BERENDT "The Hoax"

Purpose

Berendt's admiration for a good hoax is evident from the first words of this essay. Obviously, he appreciates situations where an underling gets the best of a supposedly superior intellect or when a harmless prank tests the social graces of the most socially graceful. His opening example concerns a couple of undergraduate students who perpetuate a witty hoax upon two households of Beacon Hill socialites by posing as furniture movers and stealing a sofa from the rich to give to . . . another presumably wealthy couple. Also duped by the hoaxes Berendt recounts are "two of New York's most sophisticated households," who learned lessons about "snobbery, class, race, and sex"; Nazi Hermann Goring, who was deservedly parted from his money; and McGraw-Hill, the publisher who took a huge loss on its eagerness to publish the secrets of hermit Howard Hughes.

Wit distinguishes a hoax from a simple prank. Berendt explains that "the wit inherent in" the sofa-stealing caper "elevated it from the level of a prank to the more respectable realm of hoax. Talent plays an important role as well. Each of Berendt's examples demonstrates that a good hoax requires skills ranging from impersonation and acting to oil painting in the style of the old masters or carving a human form from the plasterlike mineral gypsum.

Audience

Berendt's article makes him something of a hoaxster himself, since his expertise on the subject and the widely inspiring range of his examples probably prompted some of his *Esquire* readers to perpetrate hoaxes on their own. Readers, who most likely share Berendt's admiration for a witty trick, would not lament the stolen sofa, misplaced hospitality, fraudulent "Vermeer" painting, squandered publisher's advance, or "embarrassed historian" reported in his essay. Most, in fact, would probably aspire to commit such daring and deserved acts.

Perhaps appealing to readers, too, is that all of the hoaxters in Berendt's examples is appear to benefit, at least for a while, from the act. The sofa is graciously relinquished, Van Meegeren demonstrates his painting skill as part of his defense against charges of being a Nazi, Clifford Irving spends his $100,000 publisher's advance before he is "convicted of fraud and sent to jail," and the Cardiff Giant nets "a farmer named Newell" a tidy sum before it is copied by the ultimate hoaxster, P. T. Barnum.

Strategy

Berendt's definition of a "hoax" is given in relation to the more widely practiced practical joke or "prank." He tells readers early in the essay that "to qualify as a hoax, a prank must have magic in it." The word *hoax*, he informs readers, "is derived from *hocus-pocus*, after all." Berendt's chief definition strategy is the example—the essay is a series of entertaining examples which illustrate the range and cleverness of celebrated hoaxes, from the inspiration behind John Guare's film *Six Degrees of Separation* to the classic example of "Orson Welles' lifelike 1938 radio broadcast of H. G. Wells's *War of the Worlds*" that "panicked millions of Americans, who were convinced that Martians had landed in New Jersey."

The example of humorist Robert Benchley as an undergraduate impersonating a furniture repairman in order to perpetuate a hoax upon a couple of Beacon Hill sofa owners and their neighbors provides a frame for the essay. Berendt builds suspense in his essay, which is otherwise without a central conflict, by informing readers that he will "get to [the outcome] of that story shortly," and then saving the punch line of that joke for his concluding sentence. Because the essay is brief, readers have no problem remembering its opening details when Berendt announces in his conclusion, "And as for Robert Benchley's game on Beacon Hill. . . ." Benchley, like Mr. Newell, who owned the original Cardiff Giant and got his "comeuppance" from P. T. Barnum's replica, is out-hoaxed by the gracious Beacon Hill sofa owners, who follow Benchley's bogus delivery with one of their own, giving "the sofa's slipcovers," and, effectively, the sofa, to its recipients.

DIANE ACKERMAN "Pain"

Purpose

As Diane Ackerman reveals in the conclusion of her essay, "Pain," Virginia Woolf noted in an essay that "English . . . has no words for the shiver and the headache . . . let a sufferer try to describe a pain in his head to a doctor and language at once runs dry." Ackerman agrees that "it is difficult to define pain," and yet, in this essay, she examines several kinds of pain and the contexts in which they are felt more and less acutely. Pain can be experienced directly, vicariously, or as "ghost" pains or referred pain. Its intensity may depend on how fearfully it is anticipated and what sorts of distractions occupy the person experiencing it. Ackerman demonstrates that our definition of pain encompasses every discomfort from the stinging of flesh in a candle flame to emotional distress. "Pain" is the word we use to describe a huge range of physical and emotional sensations, yet we have remarkably few specific words with which to elaborate upon that vague term.

Ackerman attempts to demonstrate that people have some control over pain, or their receptivity to it. She cites examples of soldiers and martyrs who endure unthinkable pain without anesthetic, injured soccer players who don't realize they have been hurt until the game is over, and other athletes who can "'clean and jerk' three hundred pounds" or "swim the English Channel" as evidence that pain is subjective and contextual. Add to that the ritual mutilations endured for tribal ceremonies or beauty treatments, and it is clear that many people who willingly subject themselves to pain display remarkable stamina in facing up to it. Contrast that with our culture's expectations about childbirth, and a whole array of pain-killing drugs and treatments come to mind. Ackerman explains that "the internal organs don't have many pain receptors (the skin is supposed to be the guard post)"; however, the mind seems to control the amount of pain a body can endure.

Pain is a constant in most people's lives; they either live with it or in fear of it. Most people lack Lawrence of Arabia's fortitude "not to mind" pain, a scene recalled by Ackerman in the opening of this essay. However, Ackerman's attention to pain does reveal some helpful advice for her readers. If pain is largely mental, then perhaps people can learn to overcome it by not thinking about it. We can pattern ourselves after the fakirs and "well-to-do business people" who walk on hot coals or the "women from other cultures" who "stop their work to in the fields to give birth" and then get back to work. We can focus on something other than pain to help us keep extending our physical limits and "evolving sharper ways to adapt to the environment." In short, pain, or more precisely the fear of it, is one of the hindrances to human advancement.

Ackerman concedes that pain is a powerful force. It makes husbands of pregnant wives "take to bed with childbirth pains" or amputees suffer the "tortuous, perverse, maddening" phantom limb syndrome. Pain is puzzling; patients can undergo brain surgery with only local anesthesia, but shrink the coronary arteries and the resulting angina pectoris is almost unbearable. Ackerman's later examples in the essay suggest that human beings will never truly conquer pain. Perhaps the reason we have so few words to describe it is its very mysteriousness.

Audience

Readers who are familiar with Peter O'Toole's greatest film role will have no trouble conjuring the image of "T.E. Lawrence holding his hand over a candle flame until the flesh starts to sizzle," but younger audience members may require some contextualizing information. The allusion to the 1962 classic film about the World War I hero will be lost on many college-age readers. However, Ackerman's brief sketch of the scene introduces her thesis that pain is a matter of mind over matter. The first two-thirds of the essay then catalog instances under which ordinary people withstand extraordinary pain and seem "not to mind." About the time that Ackerman has her audience convinced that they, too, can conquer pain with willpower, she introduces a series of examples that illustrate how capricious and beyond reason pain can be. She suggests that there is no simple way to vanquish pain, just as there is no simple way to define it.

Strategy

It would be impossible to write the complete "Natural History" of pain, so Ackerman chooses her examples from a wide range of cultures to demonstrate that "Pain has plagued us throughout the history of our species." Fascination with pain unifies people across time and cultures. Although it is possible to learn more about pain, its causes, sensations, and cures, a complete definition of pain will probably continue to elude us forever.

WILLIAM LANGEWIESCHE "American Ingenuity"

Purpose

The cleanup of the World Trade Center disaster site was accomplished astonishingly quickly amid the shock, despair, grief, and skepticism of the world's onlookers. In his essay "American Ingenuity" William Langewiesche focuses primarily on one man, David Griffin, who embodies the spirit and personal traits that were necessary to efficiently get that job done. Langewiesche reports that Griffin, who, with his father D.H., was making a more-than-comfortable living demolishing old buildings in North Carolina, was "drawn to the Trade Center site" because he had expertise to contribute and wanted to assist New Yorkers and the nation in getting back to normal. Essentially a "walk on" to the demolition team, Griffin loaded his family in his car and drove the nine hours to New York shortly after the Towers fell, propelled by a tandem sense of duty and adventure. Like most everyone who entered "the pit" containing the rubble of the Trade Center and the remains of its inhabitants, Griffin was willing to take risks. For instance, once it was ascertained that there was no safe way to bring down the ruins of the Marriott Hotel on the site, Griffin's men readily took on the dangerous task of climbing the compromised structure and cutting it down from the top. Langewiesche demonstrates that the cleanup of the disaster's aftermath took bravery, but it also required ingenuity in determining how to best remove a host of unstable building remnants from a job site of unthinkable scale and horror.

Langewiesche's focus is on native American intelligence, brawn, and wit. He chooses to interview David Griffin and his father because they exemplify those traits. Neither man has a college education. Griffin senior, Langewiesche reports, is "a ninth-grade drop-out" who worked his way up from various jobs in a cigarette factory and a junkyard to his present net worth of "about a quarter of a billion dollars." His son grew up "at wrecking sites from the age of two, sleeping in concrete culverts at night with laborers standing guard" as the family demolition business grew. Although David never attended college, he received a lifelong education in the technical side of building dismantling, and the character necessary to take on seemingly impossible tasks with modesty and self-assurance. That American pragmatism—and the tension between the college educated and the practically educated—is emphasized at the end of Langewiesche's story when another demolition worker, Pablo Lopez, dismisses the efforts of a naïve psychologist who tells him to "imagine a safe place." Working in the Trade Center pit amid twisted steel, pulverized concrete, and decaying body parts while the country is in the throes of an anthrax scare, Lopez suggests that "At least she could have said 'Imagine a steak house.'"

David Griffin takes on the dimensions of a folk hero in this essay. Although he is not afraid to get right in the middle of the pit, he is perennially attired in "immaculate golfing clothes." His I.D. badge hangs from a strap that says "I love Jesus." Like many Southerners, he calls his father "Daddy." An unabashed NASCAR fan, he takes a ribbing from the "sophisticated" New Yorkers around him. Yet he is sly; Griffin gains access to the Trade Center site by patiently awaiting the opportunity to slip past National Guardsmen after his attempt to bluff his way in by pretending to work for "Bovis" fails. On the job he is determined, persistent, pragmatic, and a bit of a daredevil. As demolition consultant for the whole site, he works close enough to the action to have been hit by the counterweight of a swinging excavator and knocked down a slope; Langewiesche says he might have been killed by the accident, but he checked with the site doctor and immediately reported back to work. Griffin never exhibits anger. He trusts his experience and intuition, defying risk and regulation to get the job done. In all of that, Langewiesche observes, Griffin exhibited "a lack of grandstanding" and "a way of making things seem simple."

Audience

This essay addresses a broad contingent of potential readers. In the aftermath of the 9/11 tragedy, everyone in the United States was exposed to news reports of the cleanup operation. As Langewiesche mentions, there were widespread allegations of safety violations on the job. The whole process was exposed to scrutiny and mired in controversy as some survivors wanted the skeletal remains of the Towers left in place. Langewiesche explains why regulations were necessarily violated, and his description of the danger in taking down the remains of the Marriott suggests why other pieces of twisted steel were unstable and had to be removed as well. He notes that "Outsiders believed that the constant danger—along with the presence of the dead—had to be getting to people." However, his portrait of David Griffin and the men who worked for him demonstrates that it was, indeed, American ingenuity that triumphed on that job site.

Strategy

Langewiesche's portrait of David Griffin helps his readers absorb the magnitude of the World Trade Center site cleanup. By focusing primarily on one person among many, he gives readers a clear understanding of the bravery, experience, and ingenuity required of everyone who worked the site. When he describes Griffin's confrontation with a DDC engineer who keeps blocking the necessarily dangerous work on the Marriott building, readers cheer for Griffin when he says, "'We're not going to *talk* it down. We gotta do *something*.'" Specific examples and dialogue help readers understand the frustrations and challenges the site presented to demolition experts.

Griffin's "gentlemanly manners" and southern drawl are well represented in the dialogue Langewiesche reports or invents in this essay. He shows Griffin's inner thoughts as well as his conversations with National Guardsmen, his father, site engineers, and his interviewer. When Griffin describes blasting away at the base of the ruins as "'shooting'" them, or precutting the internal structure of ruins as "juicing them up," readers gain an understanding of the dangerous methods required to complete the demolition of the buildings on the site and some insight into how David Griffin thinks and operates. In the end, Langewiesche's description of the cleanup of the Trade Center site is effective because it so intimately portrays the thoughts and actions of one of the men at the center of the pit.

STEPHEN HARRIGAN "The Tiger Is God"

Purpose

The immense power of a tiger is equaled only by the forceful instinctive drives that govern its behavior. Stephen Harrigan's definition of tigers, in his essay "The Tiger Is God," shows that tigers, in spite of the way they often appear in zoos and cartoons as oversized house cats, possess frightening strength, quickness, and a predisposition for murder. Miguel, the tiger from the Houston Zoo who killed his caretaker, Ricardo Tovar, in 1988, exemplifies the impulsive and dangerous traits that Harrigan outlines. All of the caretakers at the zoo, including Tovar, recognized the tiger's deadly potential. Harrigan says that none of the zoo's workers "regarded Miguel's aggressiveness as aberrant," and that they all "well understood . . . that tigers were supposed to be dangerous." After the attack that killed Tovar, zoo officials and the public eventually realized that Miguel "was just being a tiger." Harrigan theorizes that, in the mind of the tiger, the murder of his keeper "was merely a vignette"; he had no sinister motive in killing the man who had come to clean his habitat but was just doing what tigers do. Harrigan says "he had a predator's indifference to tragedy; he had killed without culpability."

Miguel, and other tigers in zoos, are kept in secure cages and habitats because the humans who associate with them know all too well the threats they pose. Harrigan reveals that "fatal zoo accidents occur more frequently than most people realize," and that two Siberian tigers, the same subspecies as Miguel, killed a Bronx Zoo employee three years before Tovar's death. He explains that Tovar was "well aware of Miguel's temperament" and took precautions to avoid sharing space with tigers. The Houston Zoo used a very sophisticated system of steel mesh holding cages with guillotine doors to separate the tigers from one another, as well as from human caretakers. Tovar was attacked through a wire-reinforced glass window, set in a steel door, in a cinderblock alcove between holding cages. Although some zoo workers had questioned the necessity of the window, no one had thought it posed a safety hazard until Tovar was dragged through it by the tiger. The zoo believed it had adequately gauged the tiger's deadly instincts and provided suitable protection for its employees. However, after Tovar was killed, the tigers were kept in their holding pens until the safety of the public could be certified. Even zoo experts could not be certain that they realized the cunning and deadly potential of the tigers in their care.

Audience

Many of Harrigan's readers have visited zoos themselves, and are familiar with the public side of a captive tiger's habitat. He describes the familiar environs for his audience briefly as a half-acre rectangle including "shrubs and trees," "fake boulders," "a water-filled moat," and a "backdrop" which appeared to be a "high rock wall seamed with stress fractures." He reveals that the plaster and cement scenery camouflages the holding cages and the alcove where Tovar was trapped by Miguel. Harrigan is aware of human beings' archetypal fear of tigers, and he calls the window through which Tovar was dragged "a portal through which mankind's most primeval terrors were allowed to pass unobstructed." Although visiting a zoo is generally safe, Harrigan reveals that tigers "grow more alert than most people would care to realize when children pass before their gaze." In short, any visitor to a tiger exhibit could trigger the instinctive impulses that Tovar did, but they would not be as vulnerable to tiger attack as he was.

Realizing that his readers probably only experience zoos as visitors, Harrigan answers many questions for them that the story of Tovar's attack and the zoo's response must raise. He tells his audience that the window through which the caretaker was dragged was "only slightly larger than an average television screen." Although experts believe the attack was not motivated by hunger, Harrigan reveals that the killing occurred on one of the tiger's "'fast' days," a Thursday or a Sunday, when food is withheld from tigers at the Houston Zoo to prevent them from "growing obese in confinement." He also explains that the "shooting team," which responded to fellow museum worker John Gilbert's call for help upon discovering the tragic scene, is "seldom convened," and does not kill animals unless they "pose an immediate threat to the public." However, following the killing of Tovar, the "zoo switchboard was jammed" with callers advocating for and against the capital punishment of Miguel. Harrigan explains that for zoo officials, the decision to preserve the tiger was "automatic."

Strategy

Harrigan begins his essay with a general description of the way tigers attack men. They usually strike from behind, break their victims' necks, and kill very swiftly. The details of Tovar's death, as they emerge throughout Harrigan's investigative report, conform to that pattern. Tovar's "primary cause of death was a broken neck." He was snatched from a blind spot, outside the range of vision permitted by the small window. Investigators theorize that Tovar was "grabbed . . . by the chest with one paw, crushed against the steel door," and quickly drawn through the window and "killed . . . outside." The scenario threatens to repeat itself, and tragedy is narrowly averted when John Gilbert, happening upon the scene moments later, is confronted with the "tiger's head suddenly appear[ing]" in the broken window frame. Gilbert flees, slamming and locking the second door between the tiger and the outside world, leaving Miguel to pick up his prey by the head and begin to drag it to safety, which is also characteristic predatory behavior.

The legendary prowess of the tiger as a hunter is revealed throughout Harrigan's essay. He reveals that Siberian tigers weigh as much as 450 pounds. They have "four long canine teeth—fangs," "keen, night-seeing eyes," and an "acute" sense of hearing. Tigers are natural predators, whose "mission on the earth is to kill," usually within "thirty-five to ninety seconds" of their initial strike against a victim. While only one percent of all tigers are "'dedicated man-eaters," seeking human beings as a steady diet, about a third would kill a human, given the opportunity. Harrigan also divulges a great irony about the most-dreaded tiger: although Siberian tigers are a powerful and deadly threat to human beings, the whole fragile subspecies is in grave danger, with fewer than 300 remaining in the worlds of the Soviet Far East.

ALICE WALKER "Everyday Use"

Purpose

The purpose behind Walker's short story "Everyday Use" is to remind readers that, by definition, heritage must be inherited. Dee (Wangero) is eager to claim an abstract ancestry but repudiates her family. She will not bring her friends to visit her mother and sister. She even rejects her name, ostensibly because it is a white woman's name, although Mrs. Johnson attributes it to her great-grandmother and can trace it within her family "back beyond the Civil War."

The story compares Mrs. Johnson's and her younger daughter Maggie's pragmatic definition of culture with the older daughter Dee (Wangero's) superficial interest in her family's way of life. For example, when pressed to prove the family history of the name *Dee*, Mrs. Johnson claims that she was not there before her sister Dicie "cropped up" with a variation of the name, so "why should I try to trace it that far back?" Her existence is Spartan; knowledge and things must have a use. In winter she sleeps in a flannel nightgown and wears overalls during the day. For Maggie, the daughter who lives at home, heritage is as real as memory and as tangible as the goods in the house. It is she who remembers the origin of the butter churn's dasher, reciting, "Aunt Dee's first husband, whittled the dash. . . . His name was Henry, but they called him Stash." She also actively preserves their culture. She can quilt, having learned the skill from Grandma Dee and Dicie (Big Dee).

Dee (Wangero) has none of her sister's or mother's skills, but is anxious to claim material objects that are fashionable symbols of African American heritage. She takes the top from her mother's churn with "milk [still] in its clabber" to use as "a centerpiece for the alcove table" and then takes the dasher, which she hopes to do "something artistic" with, probably unaware that she has destroyed the churn. She believes that her objectification of culture reflects a deeper appreciation of heritage than her mother and sister's "everyday use" of family artifacts.

Audience

Walker writes for a sympathetic audience. Although some readers will admire Dee's (Wangero's) quest for education, her escape from impoverished beginnings, and her appreciation of African American culture, Walker expects readers to empathize with the large, manly Mrs. Johnson. When Dee (Wangero) repeatedly photographs her mother, sister, and a cow in front of their house, Walker describes the action objectively, trusting that her readers will perceive the insensitivity of this act, that Dee (Wangero) regards her family members as little more than zoo animals or "natives" to be captured on Polaroid snapshots in their quaint, natural habitat.

After Mrs. Johnson refuses to give Dee (Wangero) Grandma Dee's quilts, Maggie smiles " real smile, not scared." When Dee (Wangero) and Hakim-a-barber leave, mother and daughter sit in their newly swept yard, dipping snuff and "just enjoying." This is a different scene than Mrs. Johnson predicts in the story's opening: "Maggie will be nervous until after her sister goes . . . ." Readers of this story are likely to rejoice that "*no* is a word the world . . . learned to say to" Dee (Wangero), and that Mrs. Johnson and Maggie are finally free of her intimidation.

Strategy

The underlying strategy organizing this story is an analysis of different definitions of African American heritage and culture. Mrs. Johnson and Maggie are frequently contrasted with Dee (Wangero). Maggie is plainly dressed, too thin, and scarred from a house fire, and her mother is overweight and unkempt, while Dee (Wangero) is light-skinned, full-figured, and flamboyantly arrayed in an African dress, long gold earrings, dangling bracelets, and sunglasses. Mrs. Johnson confesses that she could never make eye contact with a strange white man; Dee (Wangero) "would always look anyone in the eye. Hesitation was no part of her nature." Maggie is "not bright"; she stumbles at reading, and her mother has no education beyond the second grade, but Dee (Wangero) has gone to school in Augusta with money raised by her mother and the church. Maggie will marry the unpromising John Thomas, and Mrs. Johnson doesn't know whether Dee (Wangero) has "really gone and married" Hakim-a-barber.

The most significant difference between Dee (Wangero) and her mother and sister is their attitude toward heritage as demonstrated by their argument over the quilts. Mrs. Johnson and Maggie live their heritage, putting ancestral knowledge and objects to "everyday use," but Dee (Wangero) wants to display her cultural heritage "artistically" on a table.

Walker starts her story with a symbolic representation of the chronic tensions in the Johnson family. Foreshadowing her successful confrontation with her daughter, Mrs. Johnson dreams she is reunited with Dee (Wangero) on a television talk show, and she is just as her "daughter would want" her to be: thinner, with light skin and glistening hair. The description of the dream establishes the problem between Mrs. Johnson and her daughter and predicts a change in their relationship.

Small details enliven the story and make all three key characters realistic. Walker's humor surfaces frequently, for instance, when Dee (Wangero) exclaims over the old benches at her mother's dinner table: "You can feel the rump prints." Details also establish Dee (Wangero's) ungrateful superiority. She and Hakim-a-barber send "eye signals" over Mrs. Johnson's head, and when her mother reaches to touch her own quilts, Dee (Wangero) pulls them back. Walker's characterization of Dee (Wangero) suggests that, although her mother and sister offered her a great lesson in the proud and humble nature of heritage, she remains above learning it from them.

Cause and Effect

THE STRATEGIES

You should teach the cause-and-effect essay in your composition course for at least three reasons. First, cause-and-effect reasoning plays an important part in most people's everyday lives. It affects their budgets, their health, their personal relationships, and their political choices. College students, therefore, need to analyze and evaluate cause-and-effect writing to recognize when it has been done well and when it has been used to distort probabilities. Next, much of the writing students do in college and later in their professions is cause-and-effect writing. For that reason, they need to understand how to construct a cause-and-effect analysis. Finally, studying cause-and-effect writing can sharpen your students' thinking. Much sloppy thinking comes from people's tendency to oversimplify causal relationships. Students need to learn to avoid such common pitfalls so that their writing will stand up to criticism.

When teaching a cause-and-effect essay, you will probably want to emphasize these questions: What relationship is the author trying to establish and why? What strategies does he or she use to achieve effective results? How can students learn to assert cause-and-effect relationships and support them? You may want to test the usefulness of these questions by examining Jonathan Weiner's paragraph from *The Beak of the Finch*.

THE READINGS

Daniel Goleman attempts to establish a relationship between a physical phenomenon (breaking records, behavior) and a psychological reaction (practiced short-term memory, judgment). Goleman shows how practice affects the mental and physical performance of chess champions, star athletes, and virtuoso musicians.

Anna Quindlen applies causal analysis to human behavior. Quindlen shows how her tendency to run away from home translated itself into more acceptable and rewarding behavior once she was old enough to read. Recounting the many friends and adventures she found between the covers of books, Quindlen recommends the "frigate" of a book to other readers and explains that, in spite of what the media has always said, other diversions have not deterred the bookworms of the world.

Malcolm Gladwell and Eric Schlosser use causal analysis to explain the behavior of corporate giants. Gladwell examines how the success of Stanley H. Kaplan's tutoring for SAT exams has undermined the credibility of the Educational Testing Service and lessened the authority of the exams. Schlosser exposes the proliferation of the flavor industry that results from the increased market for processed foods and reveals that for years McDonald's French fries tasted so good because they were fried in beef tallow.

Ann Beattie's story is about a realtor who attaches mystical significance to a bowl that seems to cause buyers to choose the house where it is placed. At the end of the story, Beattie reveals the cause of the bowl's magic powers—at least in the mind of the realtor.

THE VISUAL TEXT

Frank Hurley was an Australian photographer who accompanied Sir Ernest Shackleton on his journey across the Antarctic from 1914–1916. The ship, the *Endurance*, was trapped in an ice floe. The crew hoped to wait for a thaw aboard their vessel, but the unimaginable cold caused water beneath the ship to freeze, splintering the boat's windows, twisting the deck beams, and breaking the masts. As the ship went down and the men prepared to camp while awaiting rescue, Hurley was forced to destroy about 80 percent of the still pictures he had taken to document the trip. He left the sinking ship with about 120 glass negatives, some motion-picture film, a single camera, and three rolls of film. Such a paucity of supplies caused him to use those last exposures most judiciously, and critics today believe that those three rolls of film represent the best work of Hurley's career. Eventually, the survivors of the *Endurance* were rescued, and Hurley carried the work he managed to salvage through the cold and wet conditions back to the public.

THE WRITING

All the writing assignments have been designed to encourage students to think and write about specific causes and effects. Assignments 1 and 3 ask students to model their work on Quindlen's analysis of the effect of reading on her life by explaining how something, such as lasik surgery or the use of a GPS in their cars, has changed them.

    The second assignment asks students to extend Eric Schlosser's causal analysis about the taste of McDonald's French fries and other processed foods by describing the high calorie menus at restaurants they visit and theorizing about the role of such fast-food fare in the national problem of obesity.

    Assignment 4 asks students to analyze the effect of choosing a particular profession and to anticipate some conflicts the choice will create. Assignment 5 invites students to consider the social ramifications of the movie industry in America upon the aspirations and perceptions of young people. Finally, Assignment 6 asks students to investigate the effects of one community environmental problem and to speculate how it could be remedied or prevented.

ANDREW C. REVKIN "Some Big Ideas Wash Up One Bulb at a Time"

Purpose

Discovering a wreckage of beached light bulbs in the Red Sea more than twenty years ago taught Revkin the lesson that his essay conveys: little bits of litter do add up to significant pollution. Revkin says that the "heaped and piled" litter of light bulbs that he found "was not the fault of any individual." He concludes that many individuals acting independently over time carelessly tossed burned-out bulbs overboard from ships "without a thought." He says that although most people are cognizant of the large-scale "human assault[s] on the planet," such as forest fires and nuclear-reactor accidents, they are inured of tiny, individual instances of carelessness, such as a single burned-out light bulb tossed into the vast sea, a slowly seeping gasoline leak, or a few drops of poisonous contaminate flushed down a toilet. Because ours isn't "an ideal world," people have lost sight of the mounting damage caused by minute amounts of environmental pollution. By raising awareness of the massive effects of minor infractions against nature, Revkin hopes to change the attitudes and behaviors of his readers.

    Finding the light bulbs in such a remote place as Zuqar Island, which Revkin notes was called "terra nullis" on at least one map, demonstrates the far-reaching impact of human pollution on supposedly unspoiled wilderness. Reading this essay, one naturally worries about the "bed-sized manta rays gliding in the shallows" its author observed from the same island where "yardlong fluorescent tubes . . . that had shattered clinked musically away." The juxtaposition of these details reminds readers that many endangered species earn that adjective through human carelessness. Although Revkin wasn't a reporter when he visited Zuqar Island, the "piles of light bulbs on a faraway beach made [him] want to write about the effect of humans on the environment." Ultimately, in this *New York Times* article, he warns about the almost imperceptible changes in world climate caused by the release of greenhouse gases.

Audience

Who hasn't tossed a candy wrapper on the ground or flung a cigarette butt out a car window once in his or her life? Revkin is banking upon the certainty that his readers will be appalled by the accumulations of trash he describes, and then realize that they themselves have likely contributed to the endangered state of the universe. His story of the gasoline leak in the San Fernando Valley demonstrates that passivity about environmental hazards can be as dangerous as throwing garbage into the ocean or intentionally flushing mercury down a toilet. Even the well intentioned, such as the Brazilians who saved nut trees while deforesting parts of the Amazon, committed an atrocity against nature by driving out the bees that pollinated the trees, thus damaging Brazil's nut crops. Revkin is issuing a wake up call to readers lulled into complacency by the slow accumulation of pollution in our sea, land, and air.

Revkin alludes to Sputnik and Pearl Harbor, taking for granted his readers' familiarity with the subsequent surges in scientific education in the United States after Russia and Japan demonstrated their technological savvy and might. He doesn't, however, expect them to know about Zuqar Island; he identifies its location in the "south end of the Red Sea" and describes its "Mars-like" volcanic rock terrain, which "cracked underfoot like pottery shards." Most significantly, though, is his understanding that many of his readers haven't yet realized the cumulative effects of small amounts of pollution. Just as it "dawned on" him on Zuqar Island that "the incessant parade of container and cargo ships plying the Red Sea" shared responsibility for the light bulbs, he hopes that his readers will understand the far-reaching effects of individual actions from exposure to the examples he presents.

Strategy

Examples form the bulk of Revkin's essay as they are offered as proof of his thesis that small incidents result in serious pollution. The light bulb story is his most puzzling and memorable example, so he builds that scene carefully. The tales of the rusted gasoline storage tank, improperly discarded mercury, and endangered bees follow quickly as Revkin's evidence mounts with these more commonplace examples. His last example is really the thesis of his essay: people must wake up to the slowly evolving crisis caused by the release of greenhouse gases into the atmosphere. Like the light bulbs dropped singly into the ocean, the damage caused by burning fossil fuels is "spread over decades and scattered across the globe," so the public does not take it seriously enough.

Toward the end of his essay, Revkin takes on an accusatory, sarcastic tone. Once he knows his readers are outraged, he states their position with vigor and venom. He suggests that people won't respond appropriately to the dangers of burning fossil fuels because it is gradual, and they'll "never read a front-page headline that says, 'Earth's Temperature Soars Overnight—Coasts Flooded, Crops Ruined.'" His conclusion evokes his introductory point that we respond to "sudden calamity," by reacting, rather than by acting responsibly to curtail environmental threats. His final suggestion that global warming may raise the ocean levels and make the light bulbs "float away" mirrors the attitude of individuals who foolishly pretend that polluting the Earth doesn't affect the place where they live.

DANIEL GOLEMAN "Peak Performance: Why Records Fall"

Purpose

Goleman's essay validates the old adage that "practice makes perfect." A distinguished psychologist, he argues that those who wish to excel at a given task, whether athletic or mental, should not neglect extensive preparation. Voluminous evidence substantiates Goleman's thesis that practice at playing everything from chess to baseball to the violin increases virtuosity much more than actual, head-to-head competition. According to Goleman and numerous experts cited in this essay, effective practice involves breaking through "barriers in mental capacities," such as improving short-term memory, concentrating on particular memory "domains," and, as in the case of baseball greats Hank Aaron and Rod Carew, associating opponents' facial expressions with "cues." A lifetime's accumulation of practice is generally a prerequisite to greatness, and Goleman reports that nationally prominent swimmers "started their training at an average age of 10, while those who were good enough to make the United States Olympic teams started on average at 7." He notes that "This is the same age difference found for national and international chess champions."

Not content to simply proclaim that practice is the key to star performances, Goleman also examines the causes of practice in the first place. He suggests that those children with innate talent and a natural proclivity to excel in a skill will self-select (or be selected) for intense practice. Goleman quotes Harvard psychologist Dr. Howard Gardner, who says "You can't assume that random people who practice a lot will rise to the top." Gardner argues that, "Mozart was not like you and me." Pursuing the question of why records continue to be broken, Goleman first credits practice, which has enabled people to "break through ordinary limits in memory and physiology." He also credits "more sophisticated" coaching methods, "improved" equipment, and the greater "pool of people competing." There appears to be no immediately discernable limit to what science and human will can achieve.

Audience

Although everyone from the armchair enthusiast to the dedicated participant has probably wondered why records continue to be broken and how human beings improve their mental alacrity and physical prowess, Goleman's article would be of primary interest to coaches, teachers, athletes, chess champions, parents, and people convinced of their own "star potential." Because he is concerned with general causes and effects behind record breaking, he does not elaborate on any training exercises. Instead he provides encouragement to dedicated practitioners of every skill that "practice, practice, practice" is indeed the way to Carnegie Hall, an Olympic medal platform, the International Chess Championship, and a variety of other venues for performance and recognition.

Goleman recognizes, naturally, that every reader does not have the perseverance, desire, or attitude necessary to commit the years of practice required to achieve excellence. Dr. Neil Charness from Florida State University advises parents and teachers that "It's unlikely you can get just any child to apply themselves this rigorously for so long." And Nobel Laureate and professor at Carnegie-Mellon Dr. Herbert Simon cautions that "It can take 10 years of extensive practice to excel in anything." Dr. Anders Ericsson, who studied "top-level violinists in music academies" and discovered that they "had practiced a lifetime total of about 10,000 hours," perhaps best sums up the enormous cost of record-breaking performances. Admittedly, for most of Goleman's readers, it is too late to embark on such a life-consuming commitment.

Strategy

Goleman dramatically demonstrates that not only are "records made to be broken," but society also keeps superseding itself in doing so. He reports that the time in which the 1896 Olympic marathon gold-medalist completed his race would barely qualify him to start in the Boston Marathon nearly a hundred years later. Neither sports, nor chess, nor music, nor human bodies and brains have changed radically in the last century, so Goleman sets out to determine what has caused the ever-upward trend of record setting in all fields of human endeavor. Time and again, his inquiries lead to one, fundamental cause: practice.

Proof that practice is behind record-setting performances in a variety of sports and mental challenges is amassed overwhelmingly in this essay. Goleman reports the opinions and conclusions of more than half a dozen eminent psychologists in the United States; he cites research studies examining the nature and importance of practice related to performance; and he uses historical evidence, such as Dutch chess grandmaster Adrian DeGroot's demonstration in the 1940s that many chess masters can exactly replicate a chess game in progress that they have glimpsed for as little as five seconds. Where the experts disagree, however, and where Goleman can provide no definitive answer, is in determining whether innate desire and talent or practice is of primary importance in achieving a "star performance." Science cannot measure the depth or importance of human goals and aspirations in breaking records.

ANNA QUINDLEN "How Reading Changed My Life"

Purpose

Using a striking comparison between reading and wild adventure on the road, Anna Quindlen makes a strong case for the exciting life of the "bookworm." She builds upon Emily Dickinson's metaphor, likening a book to a "frigate," or boat, in describing her childhood adventures of literally running away from home or figuratively sailing the big club chair in her parent's living room through England, Canada, and the American South while reading books. Her essay examines the cultural contradiction whereby children are simultaneously encouraged to "read more" and to play outdoors and have a "normal childhood." She cites the differences between what other people regard as reality and her "real, true world," the one she inhabits vicariously through reading. Quindlen explains that voracious readers like herself do not necessarily conform to the stereotypes that are thrust upon them; she says she does not read to achieve a sense of superiority, or because she is "lazy," "aimless" or needs to "grow up." "America is a nation," she argues, "that prizes sociability and community," making the solitary activity and life of a reader suspect. Therefore, she attempts to describe the rich and rewarding, yet invisible, life that readers enjoy. Quindlen's essay is a paean to literacy and to reading for its own sake.

While many essays bemoan the distractions that keep children from reading—everything from video games to soccer practice—Quindlen puts her finger on a more specific threat to literacy in this country: "careerism." She cites the frequent question that philosophy or English majors in college often hear: "What are you 'going to do with it'?" It seems that reading is encouraged only when it is to some pragmatic end. Quindlen lists examples of stories that newspapers print about the demise of reading: "children in public schools reading poorly," "Americans reading less," "the printed word giving way to the spoken one," and "television and movies supplant[ing] books." Ironically, the people who consume those newspaper stories are reading! Providing evidence from as early as 1923, Quindlen demonstrates that the media has long proclaimed that other leisure activities are dangerously supplanting reading in the American agenda. She argues that people are reading a lot these days, although not the kind of texts she read as a child, and the realm of literature is increasingly falling into the control of critics and scholars who do not read for the sheer pleasure the activity affords. As a result, Americans are missing the "comfort and joy" of reading "not to judge the reading of others but to take the measure of [them]selves."

Audience

Quindlen doesn't merely claim to be a reader; she proves it with many allusions to the books she has enjoyed in her lifetime. Her early allusions are identified for her audience when she explains that her exposure to Victorian England was via *Middlemarch*, or that she "went to" Saint Petersburg before the fall of the tsar while reading *Anna Karenina*. Likewise, she identifies Tara, Manderley, and Thornfield Hall, the mansions she "went to" while reading *Gone with the Wind*, *Rebecca*, and *Jane Eyre*. The quotation she faced down for a scholarship to a convent school comes near the end of *A Tale of Two Cities*. Quindlen also makes passing allusions to *Anne of Green Gables*, *Heidi*, *The Great Gatsby*, *To Kill a Mockingbird*, and to characters created by Agatha Christie. As those are books popularly read by young people, Quindlen is presumably reaching out to budding bookworms in her essay, in the way that she herself took comfort in discovering that Caribbean author Jamaica Kincaid, South African journalist Hazel Rochman, and television host Oprah Winfrey shared her early passion for reading.

While self-avowed "bookworms," like the young letter writer whose mother gave her a copy of one of Quindlen's books, might enjoy meeting another member of their "clan" through this essay, the author is also extolling the joys of reading to those who wouldn't choose it as a favorite pastime. Her evocative comparison to travel or running away from home promises escape to all who would take up reading for its own sake. She tries to lure careerists into leisure reading by proclaiming that "an executive might learn far more from *Moby Dick* or *The Man in the Grey Flannel Suit*" than from *The Seven Habits of Highly Successful People*. Quindlen promises that a rich literary life is even better than the "fine" realm of her "pretty, privileged but not rich" childhood neighborhood just outside the beckoning spires of Philadelphia.

Strategy

Elaborating upon Dickinson's metaphor, Quindlen opens with the often-recounted tales of her youthful escapes, running away from home as a toddler or even when she was old enough to take the train or ride her bicycle to distant destinations. She uses her innate "wanderlust" to explain her early fascination with reading, claiming that she came to vastly prefer the escape offered by a good book to the dangers of physically running away. Her own experiences, such as being anchored to the big club chair "with curled arms and a square ottoman" in her parents' living room, are common among bookworms. The essay reaches out to other readers by drawing on the experiences most share: books they have read, favorite places to read, and the nagging of mothers and friends who find it unhealthy to keep one's nose in a book all day. The evidence that Kincaid, Rochman, and Winfrey had similar experiences reinforces the commonality and legitimacy of the experience. Quindlen places her happy memories of the friends she made in books and the places they went together alongside an idyllic description of her suburban neighborhood to show that the world of the imagination exceeds even the most pleasant physical surroundings.

Quindlen, widely known as a newspaper columnist and editorialist, is writing more than a simple narrative. Once she has built her ethos with other readers, she levies complaints against the "careerism" that makes leisure reading suspect or judged a waste of time by many in our culture. She also derides the news media that so often proclaims that reading has fallen out of fashion and the critics and scholars who continuously bemoan the quality of contemporary texts.

There are still readers out there; you can find them in bookstores, libraries, schools, and reading groups. If you want to know if reading has fallen out of fashion, Quindlen says, don't ask the "pundits and professionals" for whom it probably has—ask the bookworms.

MALCOLM GLADWELL "Examined Life"

Purpose

The history and future of the Scholastic Aptitude Tests (SATs) is inextricable from the biography of its nemesis, Stanley H. Kaplan. In his profile of Kaplan, Malcolm Gladwell states, "He loved the SAT." Although his tutoring methods are still considered "somewhat subversive" by the Educational Testing Service and the colleges that use the exams, Kaplan's life's work grows out of the desire to make the exams truly fair. In purporting to measure aptitude, the ETS set itself up for challenges. Kaplan, who always had a penchant for helping struggling classmates in school, created a system that helps test takers raise their scores by as many as a hundred points. Gladwell shows that much of what Kaplan's sessions teach is logical reasoning and insight into the ideology of the exam's writers. For example, he says the questions on the SAT reflect a "kind of decent, middlebrow earnestness" that helps savvy takers eliminate multiple-choice options that are too postmodern, dogmatic, negative, or picayune. While the ETS has continued to insist that their test identifies innate ability instead of measuring achievement, the success of Kaplan's students (including Arthur Levine, the president of Teacher's College at Columbia and Charles Schumer, the senior senator from New York) suggests that one can "cram" for the SATs.

Gladwell says the preeminence of the SAT is now called into question as the University of California system abandons "its heavy reliance on standardized-test scores" in favor of a more "'holistic' admissions system." He credits Kaplan with "puncturing the mystique of the SAT." Kaplan was a tutor, working out of his parents' Brooklyn basement, when he was first approached about helping a student improve her SAT scores. As his business grew, he and his employees were able to discern patterns in the makeup of the tests. Although the ETS insists that its tests measure "innate ability" and are therefore not culturally biased, Gladwell traces the history of standardized entrance exams to anti-Semitic motives of the Ivy League in the early twentieth century. Suspicious about the diligent children of Jewish immigrants who were winning college seats from the supposedly more intelligent WASP population, universities like Columbia turned to measuring "aptitude" as a way of screening out "the typical Jewish student [who] was simply a 'grind.'" Instead of decrying the deception fostered by standardized tests, Kaplan, himself the child of Jewish immigrants, saw the potential of the exam to give "middle-class students of Brooklyn the same shot at a bright future that their counterparts in the private schools of Manhattan had."

Kaplan's tutoring, however, created a "'heavily traveled path' from Brooklyn to Cornell, Yale, and the University of Michigan." He demonstrated quite conclusively that "aptitude was a social matter," that students' measurable potential is influenced by what they know, what they are taught, and the examples and role models around them. The Kaplan method proves that since it is possible to improve one's SAT scores, the tests cannot separate ability from achievement.

Audience

Most everyone who reads this as part of a college writing course assignment will have some experience with standardized entrance exams. Gladwell likewise assumed that his original audience in *The New Yorker* magazine was mostly college educated and shared the usual mistrust of entrance exams. Standardized testing has undergone serious criticism since the 1960s for its cultural biases, and most people on the test-taking end of the exchange regard the weight colleges place on the exams with suspicion or a healthy skepticism. Gladwell's readers will most likely applaud the California university system's decision to rely more on applicants' past achievements than on SATs in making admissions decisions. The UC study shows that SAT II and high school GPA have more predictive validity about a college students' success than the SAT I score, and probably confirms what Gladwell's audience suspected all along.

The hints about taking the SAT that Gladwell passes along from his interviews with Kaplan are intriguing. Many readers may want to enroll in a Kaplan course to learn more exam-taking strategies. A few readers would probably want to re-take the SATs after taking a Kaplan course; suspiciously regarded or not, a person's SAT score continues to define him or her in life, especially if it is close to the perfect 1600. Therein lies the rub: although no one believes the SAT is the definitive statement about a person's intellect or worth, most everyone buys into its validity to some degree.

Strategy

Gladwell begins his essay with a sympathetic portrait of the young Stanley Kaplan, a sensitive, bookish boy who voluntarily took struggling peers aside and patiently showed them the academic skills they needed to succeed. The obliging, uncompetitive Kaplan, however, was serious about his grades. When a professor at City College mistakenly awarded him the C earned by another Stanley Kaplan in his biology class, our Stanley Kaplan protested until the error was corrected. The story of Kaplan's rise to wealth and influence in academia makes it sound like the modest and reliable Kaplan accidentally stumbled upon a social injustice and began correcting it as a way of helping his fellow Brooklyn public school graduates get the chance they deserved at the nation's best universities. First Kaplan's business outgrows his basement, then Gladwell says "in the 1970s he went national," as if the proliferation of the SAT-preparation industry was simply a natural progression based upon national need.

This would be a radically different story if it were a profile of Henry Chauncey, the founder of the Educational Testing Service. The SAT exam is described in this essay as a "virtually useless tool for making admissions decisions," and a test that "would put put [Jews] back in [their] place." Likewise, Kaplan's detractors have called him a "'quack' and 'the cram king' and a 'snake oil salesman.'" According to Gladwell, the long-standing "hostility" of the ETS toward Kaplan is softening. He calls the College Board's invitation to speak at its annual convention "one of the highlights of Kaplan's life." According to Gladwell, though, the fight between the ETS and Kaplan is over because a "grind" from Brooklyn has "killed" the aptitude test.

ERIC SCHLOSSER "Why McDonald's Fries Taste So Good"

Purpose

The revelation that processed food has little or no innate flavor in it would surprise most people about what they eat. In an essay from his book *Fast Food Nation*, Eric Schlosser reveals that the taste of most processed food is entirely synthetic. Add to that the news that "various fats, gums, starches, emulsifiers, and stabilizers" comprise the texture of most prepared foods, and one realizes that the foods Americans commonly think they are buying (and eating) are but the bland basis under an host of natural and manmade chemical compounds. The food item itself, be it French fries or chocolate chip cookies, is but a vehicle for chemicals designed to fool human senses. Additionally, the brand names that consumers know and love are not really the companies responsible for the tastes people crave; the names of the factories where the flavor is manufac-tured for everything from granola bars and popsicles to taco sauce and strawberry milk shakes are closely guarded secrets. Schlosser describes his investigations into such flavor manufacturers as International Flavors & Fragrances (IFF), Givaudan, Haarmann & Reimer, Takasago, Flavor Dynamics, Frutarom, and Elan Chemical. In unmasking these behind-the-scenes companies, Schlosser exposes the staggering number of chemicals, each used in minute quantities, that are hidden behind the words "natural flavor," "artificial flavor" or "color" additives. These products override nature's built-in protection, which uses taste, scent, and visual cues to prevent people from ingesting poisons or spoiled food. Schlosser hopes to create a better-informed, and possibly better-fed, consumer. Given that in 2000 Americans consumed an average of thirty pounds of French fries or that 90 percent of the money Americans spend on food goes to buy processed food products, Schlosser wants to tell people what they are really buying and eating.

Although this piece of investigative journalism has obvious ramifications within the processed food industry, it is the flavor and texture manufacturers that Schlosser is really going after. He chronicles his visit to an IFF plant, which he notes is situated (not ironically, as it turns out) between a BASF plastics factory, a Jolly French Toast factory, and a Liz Clairborne cosmetics factory. This is convenient; the same company that flavors "potato chips, corn chips, breads, crackers, breakfast cereals . . . pet food . . . ice cream, cookies, candies, toothpastes, mouthwashes, and antacids" makes the scent for "Estée Lauder's Beautiful, Clinique's Happy, Lancome's Tresor, and Calvin Klein's Eternity," along with the smells of household products ranging from deodorant to floor wax. Most readers would probably find something vaguely manipulative, if not sinister, in that. Schlosser also reveals that the difference between "natural" and "artificial" flavors is not what most shoppers would assume. In specific cases, the "natural" flavors contain more harmful chemicals than their "artificial" counterparts, and they are often the exact same chemical compound, just derived differently. The essay is critical of the federal Food and Drug Administration (FDA) which "does not require companies to disclose the ingredients of their color or flavor additives," and of the flavor manufacturers themselves who seem both modestly and suspiciously opposed to having their names included on the packaging of the products they manipulate.

Although the book from which this essay is excerpted is called *Fast Food Nation* and its title mentions McDonald's French fries, Schlosser is really examining all processed foods. That includes not only the burger and shake or taco and ice cream that one gets at the drive-up window, but the canned soup, frozen dinner, or popcorn that people buy in the store and microwave at home. Many readers of Schlosser's essay may realize they have forgotten what food really tastes like, having relied upon processed food for a long time. Consider how much of the average grocery store's area displays fresh produce and how much of it displays processed foods. It is evident that most of what people eat tastes, not like the potatoes in potato chips or the butter and flour in cookies, but like what machines that crudely approximate the human olfactory sense or the "mouthfeel" of the mastication sensation say those things are. This essay might change the grocery-buying habits as well as the roadside meal consumption of many of its readers.

Audience

This essay originally appeared in *The Atlantic Monthly*, a literary and news magazine with a relatively small, well-educated readership. It was Schlosser's appearance on *60 Minutes*, National Public Radio, and CNN, and his disclosure that McDonald's was cooking its French fries in beef tallow that made him famous. Schlosser's experience brings to mind the legendary revelations about the meat industry in Upton Sinclair's 1906 novel *The Jungle*, or the contemporary cult following of journalist and filmmaker Michael Moore. Writers who try to debunk large corporations, especially those with influence over the health and safety of the population, always seem to find a broad audience. Schlosser's work has prompted Hindus to riot against McDonald's in India and vegetarians to file class-action suits against the corporation—not to mention causing McDonald's to abandon the secret ingredient that made its fries so irresistible in favor of another secret concoction.

Strategy

Schlosser's essay is biased against the food industry, especially the taste manufacturers, but he demonstrates that his information is based upon facts through the use of informal documentation and the presentation of statistics. For example, he doesn't merely name the flavor factories along the New Jersey Turnpike, but describes their location by exit number or the city to which they are nearest. He presents numbers to describe, among other things, the amount of French fries people consumed on average in 1960 and 1990 (four and thirty), the average number of servings of French fries Americans now eat weekly (four), the amount of their food budget Americans typically spend on processed food (90 percent), the annual revenues of the American flavor industry ($1.4 billion), and the number of chemicals that make, for example, strawberry Pop Tarts smell like berries (350). Most impressive (although largely unreadable) is Schlosser's listing of the nearly fifty actual ingredients that comprise the "artificial flavoring" in a Burger King strawberry milk shake. These rational elements give his essay the appearance of objectivity and factual accuracy, enabling him to guess at the kinds of research and ingredients McDonald's used to replace the flavor of beef tallow in their French fries.

Early in his essay, Schlosser establishes the secrecy in which the flavor industry is shrouded so that readers will appreciate his enormous coup in gaining entry to IFF. He reveals that in order to tour the factory he was asked to sign a nondisclosure form, and that he was still prohibited from visiting the manufacturing areas of the plant for fear he "might discover trade secrets." Schlosser's research process included interviewing Terry Acree, a professor of food science at Cornell University, as well as Brian Grainger, a senior flavorist at IFF. He also apparently had access to several trade publications and the ingredients list for products developed by Red Arrow, among other flavor factories. However, it is what he sees with his own eyes, hears with his own ears, and, ironically, smells with his own nose (including the various fragrance-testing filters for fresh cherries, black olives, sautéed onions, and shrimp) that provides his most convincing evidence.

ANN BEATTIE "Janus"

Purpose

Ann Beattie has crafted a brief yet effective study of loss in her story "Janus." Andrea, the protagonist, is a successful real estate agent, married to an equally successful stockbroker. The story is a variation on the age-old theme that money does not bring happiness. Andrea remembers "the lean years" when she and her husband were graduate students and the early period of their mutual success when he "urged her to buy things she liked." Now, however, they are bored with the trappings of success, and the wife cannot bring herself to tell her husband about the bowl's seeming significance in her accomplishments, although she sometimes longs to. Instead, they "lay in bed at night listening to the stereo and murmuring sleepy disconnections." She wonders if people who live together and love one another must always be classified as a "relationship." Her secrecy about the bowl is almost justified when we learn that it was a final gift from a lover who shared her interest in antiques and art but left her because of her inexplicable devotion to her marriage. That token fidelity is explained early in the story when Beattie says that the husband and wife "were a lot alike, really." She says that "both were quiet people—reflective, slow to make value judgments, but also intractable once they had come to a conclusion." Long ago they concluded that they would marry and this has become an intractable pact. After the lover has disappeared the wife develops an obsession with his symbol, fearing that someone else will break or steal the bowl. Most of all she fears that the bowl will mysteriously disappear as well. Although she is wed to her decision to stay with her husband, the loss of her lover torments her. The narrator reveals that "her lover had said she was always too slow to know what she really loved." That is why he bought the bowl for her. She had been drawn to it, even lingered over it, but walked away in indecision. At the story's conclusion it seems that, once again, she has been too slow to recognize her love of the other man, and it is too late to act upon that.

The title, "Janus," is intriguing as it takes on different meanings as the story progresses. At first it seems to symbolize the husband and wife in the story—she looking backward in her love of antiques and fine furnishings and he looking forward toward technology in his fascination with his new Leica camera. Then Beattie reveals that the husband "sometimes told people that he was fortunate to be married to a woman who had such a fine aesthetic sense and yet could also function in the real world," and it seems that the woman herself is Janus, looking in two improbable directions at once. Only in the ending of the story does the full complexity of Beattie's reference to the Roman god with two faces reveal itself. When we learn that the bowl was a gift from Andrea's lover, we begin to understand the weird significance the bowl has taken on for the protagonist. She was a Janus character, looking back to the early commitment she made in her marriage and forward to her life with her lover. But she is left with the empty bowl, half a sphere or a blank gaze where once she looked toward the future with the man who gave her the bowl.

Audience

Most people of a similar age with Beattie's characters have had the experience of working with a real estate agent. The author writes, "everyone who has purchased a house or who has wanted to sell a house must be familiar with some of the tricks used to convince a buyer that the house is quite special." The story is thus filled with intimations of Andrea's subtle salesmanship, besides her studious placement of the magical bowl in the houses she wishes to sell. She sometimes brings her dog, Mondo, and one of his toys to persuade prospective buyers, or she will light a fire, place "jonquils in a pitcher on the kitchen counter, where no one ordinarily has space to put flowers," scent the air in a house, or move healthy houseplants to a dark corner to convince buyers that there really is sufficient light for things to thrive. The subtle deceptions of Andrea's business help set the tone for the revelation that it is not just her fascination and dependence upon the bowl that she is keeping from her husband; she has taken a lover and suffered the loss of him silently as well.

Nearly everyone, even readers who cannot identify with the common experience of buying or selling a house, has some experience of love, obsession, and loss. Beattie devotes much of her story to developing the odd bond between Andrea and her bowl. She describes her character's panic when she accidentally leaves it behind at a house she has shown, how she very nearly rushes past the homeowner to reclaim her bowl. Andrea notices "the lady glanced at her a little strangely" on that occasion. Her obsession with the bowl escalates from admiration, when "she liked to see it," to when she admits to herself "it was something she loved," and finally to adoration when "She would get up at night and look at the bowl." Finally, the bowl becomes a surrogate for her lost lover and the future that has gone astray with him. She becomes obsessed with the object, irrationally fearful that it would run to another, be broken by someone, disappear, or even be struck by lightning. Some will read this as a cautionary tale about the emotional dangers of romantic entanglements outside of marriage. Others may find Freudian symbolism in the feminine symbol of the vessel or bowl left empty by the departing lover.

Strategy

Beattie tells her readers very little about the bowl. The story opens with the sentence: "The bowl was perfect," and beyond that we know that its glaze is creamy with tiny bits of color flecked in silver. Andrea wants it kept empty, both to protect it and for symbolic reasons. Readers of the story are free to imagine the bowl themselves; we don't know, for instance what size it is, or what unusual characteristics cause the story's narrator to compare it with a mutt dog. The bowl can become a specific bowl in the reader's mind, or it might be supplanted by the object of each reader's own love or obsession.

Throughout the story Beattie prepares her audience for the revelation that Andrea has taken a lover. She establishes the cordial but distant relationship between husband and wife, and describes the unnatural relationship between Andrea and the bowl. We are told that she is protective of the object, that it brings her "luck," and then that she regards it as a friend. Andrea begins to dream of the bowl. She feels guilty that she has not told her husband about her affection for her good luck charm. As her obsession with the bowl builds, "anxiety be[comes] the operative force." The bowl becomes another lover she cannot keep, and she is haunted by her fear of losing it. She cannot bear to think "what her life would be without the bowl." When Beattie finally reveals that the bowl is a gift from a lost lover, the reader is scarcely surprised. It is almost a relief to discover that there is a reason for Andrea's unnatural obsession with the simple object. In the end, Andrea is alone with the bowl in the dark, and it tugs her eye toward an imaginary horizon. Beattie writes again that the bowl is "perfect." It seems to Andrea to represent "the world cut in half, deep and smooth and empty." That is the future she faces.

Persuasion and Argument

THE STRATEGIES

Students usually study persuasion and argument toward the end of a rhetorically based composition course because good persuasive writing requires an author to combine a number of writing strategies in one essay. Most of the essays in this section combine two or more of the forms featured in the previous sections, and students should be able to analyze them more effectively because they will already be familiar with these forms. They should be able to see how the authors marshal those strategies to advance their arguments. In turn, when students begin to compose their own arguments, they should be able to combine into one process the skills they have been learning all semester. When they are able to make such choices, they will be moving toward becoming practicing writers who know what they want to do and who have a systematic method for doing it.

In teaching your students to read and write persuasion and argument, you will need to keep reminding them of one key point: *An opinion is not an argument unless it can be supported with evidence.* Anyone can say, "I think this" or "I believe that," but to persuade an audience a writer must explain *why* he or she thinks or believes something. Students might be asked to examine Nicholas Lemann's example paragraph and list the evidence he uses to show how the view of racism as a southern problem changed after 1950.

THE READINGS

The essays in this section are paired so that students can assess the effectiveness of two arguments on a controversial issue. Although these essays generally mix emotional (persuasive) and logical (rational) appeals, the first six might be classified as personal opinion essays. That is, they make emotional appeals based on personal evidence to persuade their readers to support a cause. The last two are primarily researched writing. That is, they make logical appeals based on extensive research to support their claims.

Martin Luther King Jr.'s "I Have a Dream" relies on powerful metaphors to make an emotional appeal on behalf of black Americans. By contrast, Eric Liu's essay is less emotional, less ceremonial than King's, but he uses his own experience to support his argument that racial factions in the United States must perceive themselves as integral parts of the country at large.

Barbara Kingsolver argues that the popular definition of "family" in our culture does not correspond with the real composition of most American families. She also asserts that so-called "nontraditional" families are in many instances enviably strong units. Barbara Dafoe Whitehead claims that there is an American fatherhood crisis traceable to the dissolution of the traditional nuclear family. She argues that good fathering is impossible for men who live outside of their children's homes.

Joan Acocella makes a very scholarly and convincing argument that the Harry Potter series is based upon folk-tale tradition and theory, stands up to serious literary criticism, and is good reading for children and adults. Harold Bloom deplores Pottermania. His curmudgeonly persona lambastes popular literature in general as he compares the "epiphenomenon" surrounding Harry Potter to the attention J. R. R. Tolkien received over his Middle Earth trilogy.

The last pair of essays presents a sophisticated debate about human nature—whether people are basically good or evil. Francine Prose writes about her childhood celebrations of Passover and her subsequent study of the book of Exodus. She discovers that since biblical times genocide has been practiced as "the killing of other people's children." Natalie Angier, writing just one week after the 9/11 disasters, argues that human beings are basically kind and altruistic. Citing evidence that ranges from the insect world through the heroic actions of firefighters, rescue workers, and airplane passengers on that fateful day in 2001, she finds much to admire about the human species.

Kurt Vonnegut Jr.'s story, "Harrison Bergeron" offers a darkly humorous argument against conformist movements in society. He paints a ridiculous picture of a society in which everyone is forced to simulate disabilities in order to make all people equal. Nothing gets accomplished because there is no competition, and everyone's ability is reduced to the status quo.

THE VISUAL TEXT

The Leo Burnett advertising company offers a visual pun about missing limbs in its ad for Physicians Against Land Mines (PALM). The girl portrayed in the ad lost her left leg while playing on the outskirts of Sarajevo. Ironically, the bare limb of a tree whose trunk is not pictured supports her; that limb is an inadequate replacement for her lost one. The text that fills the space where her leg would be forms a sort of ghost limb, outlining the shape of the amputated leg. It tells readers that millions of land mines are left behind in nearly seventy countries, and that a person is killed or maimed by accidentally detonating one every twenty-two minutes. The audience for the ad realizes that there are just words or eulogies left in the place of many of those victims.

THE WRITING

The assignments at the end of this section provide a range of purposes, audiences, and strategies for composing arguments. Many of the assignments suggest topics to be posted on a class web site, where students' arguments could potentially be tested against a very wide audience. The first essay asks students to consider their own outlook on the American Dream, following the tradition modeled by Martin Luther King Jr. and Eric Liu. The second assignment invites Harry Potter fans to take issue with Harold Bloom. The third and fifth ask students to conduct a rhetorical analysis of specific essays in this section of the book.

Assignment 4 asks students to carefully consider service learning and construct an argument about whether work through one's own church should count toward college credit. The final assignment encourages students to write a letter to the editor of the *New York Times*.

MARTIN LUTHER KING JR. "I Have a Dream"

Purpose

This famous speech, written by America's foremost civil rights leader, is unrivaled in recent American history as an example of eloquent ceremonial discourse. The context for this speech was the commemoration of the one-hundredth anniversary of the signing of the Emancipation Proclamation, but King devotes only his first three sentences to actions of "Five score years ago"; the promise of a joyous future, made attainable by Lincoln's signature on the proclamation, is the subject of King's discourse.

King's purposes are to urge his followers to continue their actions and not allow the nation to return to "business as usual"; to promote changes that will eventually abolish segregation, discrimination, and prejudice across the country, especially in the South; and to convince his followers that their actions must be immediate and nonviolent. King cautions that, although blacks are continually confronted with injustices, including economic disparity and police brutality, they must continue to meet "physical force with soul force." His injunctions against violence warn against indulgence in "physical violence" and "bitterness and hatred."

The equality he envisions cannot be achieved through angry or "wrongful deeds," but King's nonviolent "creative protest" is not meek or tentative. In his speech, he criticizes the government's inadequate administration of democracy and confronts the South with its archaic prejudices, citing the governor of Alabama's obstruction of true justice and directing vitriolic criticism at Mississippi, where blacks were not allowed to vote. King's primary purpose, however, is to inspire his audience, a goal he admirably achieves in his "I have a dream" and "let freedom ring" sequences, which conclude the discourse.

Audience

King delivered this speech before a huge, live, predominantly black audience who had come to Washington, D.C., on a march for freedom and civil rights, but he knew, too, that the eyes of the country were on that gathering, and the words he wrote are intended for the nation at large. The marchers who gathered in Washington, and civil rights activists everywhere, expected to hear their beliefs stated vigorously and with conviction. King's speech inspired people in Washington and elsewhere because he wrote with his audience, as well as his cause, clearly in mind. Early in the speech, he addresses his black followers, saying, "There is something I must say to my people," but in the same paragraph, he welcomes "our white brothers" who have, "by their presence here today," acknowledged the single destiny that people of all races share.

Urging his followers to keep working, to "never be satisfied" as long as blacks are denied the full measure of equality, he recognizes that "great trials and tribulations" have tested some of his audience members, and he lauds, as "victims of creative suffering," those who are "fresh from narrow jail cells" or who are "battered . . . persecut[ed] . . . and staggered" by "police brutality." He unites his audience around this core of martyrs, promising that he and his followers will work, pray, and struggle together, "go to jail together . . . stand up for freedom together," and "be free one day."

King addresses the nation in this speech by naming states and regions from which marchers have come and by creating images of freedom ringing from the "hilltops of New Hampshire" to the "curvaceous peaks of California" and various points, North and South, in between. King's concluding vision unites disparate groups around the country as he puts the words of an "old Negro spiritual" into the mouths of "black men and white men, Jews and Gentiles, Protestants and Catholics." His audience is everyone who thinks, feels, or believes in God or the government of this country.

Strategy

King's speech employs predominantly emotional strategies. His first words echo the Gettysburg Address in tribute to the "great American" whose "momentous decree" the marchers have come to celebrate, and these words set the tone, as well as readers' expectations, for what is to come. Like Lincoln's famous speech, King's is crafted from connotative words and phrases, such as "slaves," "brotherhood," "sacred," "exalted," "bright day," and "warm threshold." His style borrows heavily from the great persuasive traditions of political "stump" speeches and religious sermons;

his "campaign promises" are described as his "dream," and it is King the Baptist minister who exhorts his followers to "continue to work with the faith that unearned suffering is redemptive."

Repetition of key words and phrases is characteristic of oral style, and King uses it extensively, repeating "one hundred years later," "now," "go back," "I have a dream," "let freedom ring," and "free at last." The most prevalent emotional strategy in the speech is King's use of figurative language. Rich with metaphor, some passages of this speech (such as the second paragraph's description of contemporary black status) employ metaphors in nearly every sentence. Evocative examples include "beacon light of hope," "flames of withering injustice," "manacles of segregation," "chains of discrimination," "palace of justice," and "valley of despair." King's analogy comparing the U.S. Constitution and the Declaration of Independence to a "bad check" establishes America's guilt in withholding "the riches of freedom" and automatically aligns the civil rights movement with the lofty ideal of "justice."

King's tone, however, avoids creating enemies or establishing dichotomies. He unites the nation in the pursuit of freedom, using the pronoun "we" and phrases such as "this is our hope . . . our freedom." King's speech is best remembered (and therefore probably most effective) for its "I have a dream" paragraphs (10–18). These psalm-like passages, whose repetitions and refrain of "I have a dream today," incited his audience to act in 1963, and continue to inspire readers today.

ERIC LIU "A Chinaman's Chance: Reflections on the American Dream"

Purpose

Liu argues in this essay that young people are losing sight of the American Dream because they have forgotten what it means to be Americans. We are becoming, Liu fears, a "culture of entitlement" because we have reduced the American Dream to "some guarantee of affluence, a birthright of wealth." Liu concedes to readers in their "twenties and early thirties" that "job opportunities are scarce" and the "threat" of "a lower standard of living than [their] parents" achieved is "real." Although the economy is discouraging and our government is entangled in its own financial problems, Liu asks whether the "failure of the nation thus far to fulfill its stated ideals" should "incapacitate its young people, or motivate [them]."

A second-generation Chinese American, Liu is especially critical of America's "near-pathological race consciousness." He takes issue with young minority people's strong racial identities, which seem to take precedence over their national pride. Liu asks his audience, "How have we allowed our thinking about race to become so twisted?" He explains that he is proud to be descended from Chinese ancestors, but that his cultural pride "does not cross into prejudice against others." We must, he argues, achieve a national image which "represents the kind of color-blind equality of opportunity" that the American Dream truly represents. Our country, he cautions, "was never designed to be a mere collection of subcultures."

Liu celebrates his own Chinese American heritage, which incorporated Chinese school and an Ivy League education. His own experience of playing "Thomas Jefferson in the bicentennial school play one week and the next week [playing] poet Li Bai at the Chinese school festival" demonstrates the sort of balance he wants Americans and America to achieve. All young citizens, he argues, should view themselves primarily as Americans ready to contribute their talents and labors to their country because "so long as there are young Americans who do not take what they have—or what they can do—for granted, progress is always possible."

Audience

Anyone who believes he or she has a stake in America's future might want to second or refute Liu's arguments in this essay, although he appears to write primarily for young minority Americans whose attitudes and behaviors he seeks to change. He speaks to those who seem to see "retreat to one's own kind . . . more and more . . . as an advance." Throughout the essay, Liu appeals directly to "people of [his] generation," "second-generation American[s]," and "peers" who are "coming of age just as the American Dream is showing its age." He alludes to contemporary bands, "Arrested Development" and "Chubb Rock," assuming that readers are at least familiar with "rap and hip-hop music." He empathizes with his audience's desires to "draw strength from [their] communities," but argues that we must not focus on our "diverse heritages" at the cost of forgetting our commonalities. In keeping with his thesis that Americans must think and act together, he addresses all fellow citizens, stressing that "principles like freedom and opportunity" are "necessary" and "vital," "and not just to the children of immigrants." Liu's essay reaches out to "homeboys and house painters and bike messengers and investment bankers," to everyone who wants to restore faith in the American Dream.

Liu translates the Chinese American derogatory label "banana," which refers to persons who are "yellow on the outside, but white on the inside." He is sensitive to criticism that he "speak[s] too much from [his] own experience," that, "not everyone can relate to the second-generation American Story," but he argues that we should not be "paralyzed" by our differences. Liu says that "respect for" divergent "experiences" should not "obviate the possibility of shared aspirations." Echoing John F. Kennedy's famous advice to "ask not what your country can do for you . . ." Liu entreats all Americans to ask not only "What do we 'get' for being American?" but "What do we owe?"

Strategy

Liu employs a straightforward deductive strategy for conveying his thesis in this argument. He begins with the assertion that the "American Dream is" not "dead," and that those who think so are "dead wrong." This is essentially a generative technique because the rest of the essay, then, must back up these strong words. Liu defines "American Dream" at the outset of his argument, as "a sense of opportunity that binds generations together in commitment, so that the young inherit . . . perseverance, . . . and a mission to make good on the strivings of their parents and grandparents." He theorizes that "every generation will reach for success, and often miss the mark," and demonstrates the truth of that through examples. His own parents "were able to build a comfortable life and provide" their son with a quality education and "a breadth of" experiences. The parents of Chinese American author Fae Myenne Ng represent the other half of Liu's equation; they "suffered 'a bitter no-luck life' in America." Liu also holds up the example of the Marine Corps as "a cross section of America," or what he believes America could be: a society that celebrates diversity but strives to reach common goals.

Throughout the essay, Liu draws upon his own experiences "as the son of immigrants," a volunteer for "Marine Corps Officer Candidates' School," a graduate of an "Ivy League" college, a speech writer for President Bill Clinton "on Capitol Hill." These lead him to "believe that America is exceptional" and that it is the duty of his generation to "revive" the "spirit" of the American Dream. He anticipates the arguments of readers who will dismiss his optimism as naive, and ends with a classic speech-writing trope: turning a phrase against itself. Liu's final declaration that "a Chinaman's chance is as good as anyone else's" concedes that the "deck" is "stacked" for everyone. That's why we must all come together to achieve a fair chance at "prosperity and the pursuit of . . . happiness."

BARBARA KINGSOLVER "Stone Soup"

Purpose

Reclaiming the title of "family" for those whose domestic lives don't mimic the popular concept of nuclear family is the purpose of Barbara Kingsolver's essay. She denounces the still widely held definition of family as exemplified by her childhood paper "Family of Dolls" ("Dad, Mom, Sis, and Junior") as a "narrow view" that is "pickled and absurd." The truth about families is that the "typical" nuclear family isn't typical at all. Her examination of family structures throughout recent history (paragraphs 19 through 23) demonstrates that only recently has the "traditional" nuclear family existed as a model for domestic arrangements. Kingsolver points out that, "divorce, remarriage, single parenthood, gay parents, and blended families simply are. They're facts of our time." She argues that those who cling to the notion of perfect families contrived to fit stylized notions have failed to notice the constitution and success of half of the families around. The Family of Dolls is incomplete because even nuclear families usually depend on extended family members to complete their unit. Kingsolver wants her readers to "let go of the fairy tale of families functioning perfectly in isolation."

Kingsolver also wants to destigmatize divorce. She argues that the term "irreconcilable differences" is misleading because it masks the serious grounds upon which most responsible adults seek divorces. Recounting her own experiences, she advises that friends should respond to the newly divorced as they would to a widow. She even suggests, tongue in cheek, that "casseroles would help." After her own divorce, Kingsolver recorded some of the ways people responded wrongly toward her. For example, asking "Did you want the divorce?" strikes her as a particularly stupid question, but it is a better response than that of those friends who simply disappeared when her marriage ended. She notes that her daughter feels uncomfortable about her parents' divorce only "when her friends say they feel sorry for her." Contrary to popular belief, Kingsolver thinks divorce can be good for children. The experiences of the young soccer player described in the essay's opening paragraph and her own daughter bear this out. Children of divorce can be the beneficiaries of a "family fortune": a larger than customary complement of homes, caring parents and grandparents, and siblings.

Audience

If Kingsolver's assertions in this essay are true, at least half of her readers have good cause to share her indignation at society's stubborn refusal to grant full family status to the kinds of real families that populate the United States today. She addresses her readers directly, saying, "We aren't the Family of Dolls. Maybe you're not, either." She empathizes with readers from nontraditional family structures, sharing their shame with being judged as "failures" whose "children are at risk, and [whose] whole arrangement is [seen as being] messy and embarrassing." If half of her readers *are* part of a nuclear family, this essay addresses them, too; Kingsolver says, "Most of us are up to our ears in the noisy business of trying to support and love a thing called family." Basically, since everyone is affected in some way by the social construct of families, this essay addresses a broad audience. If any readers are likely to tune this essay out completely, they are members of the "religious right," which Kingsolver deals with sharply for its much-publicized concept of "family values."

Kingsolver's essay seems to be directed primarily at female readers. She appeals mostly to women when she argues that partners in a marriage have the right to "self-respect and independence" as well as "happiness and safety from abuse." Single parenthood and teenage motherhood, which primarily affect women in this country, are explored in this essay, as is the author's own situation. Kingsolver considers the extended families to which her grandmother and others of her generation belonged, and she reveals that "in many cases they spent virtually every waking hour working in the company of other women." She judges that "a companionable scenario." This essay celebrates the many social advances for women that result from the modern forms that families now take. Women presently are "more likely to divorce" and "plan and space [their] children " yet "less likely to suffer abuse without recourse, or to stare at [their] lives through a glaze of prescription tranquilizers." Given all that, she says, "Hip-hip-hooray for 'broken' [homes]."

Strategy

An extensive argument, this essay draws upon rational, ethical, and emotional appeals to persuade its audience that changes in family demographics are not necessarily bad for society. Kingsolver says that nontraditional families are "statistically no oddity." She reports that "in Colonial days the average couple lived to be married less than twelve years." In present-day America, the "rate at which teenage girls [have] babies" is half what it was in 1957. Since 1979, government support of single parents has steadily declined. Kingsolver draws upon her own experience as a divorced parent, and as a close family friend in other nontraditional households to proclaim the children in some nontraditional families "lucky." She appeals to the emotions of her readers as she describes the agony of the "two terrifying options" available to women considering divorce.

Perhaps only a novelist would put such credence in the words of a fictional character as does Kingsolver, when she quotes Reynolds Price's character Kate Vaiden's advice to the beleaguered: "meet what they send you and keep your hair combed." Kingsolver also evinces a creative writer's gift for inventing metaphors and conceits. Comparing herself to a widow following her own divorce, she complains that "people are acting like I had a fit and broke up the family china." (Consider the pun in that, since dividing the china with her ex-husband would have broken up the set.) She describes "a non functioning marriage" as "slow asphyxiation," and says that "disassembling a marriage . . . is as much *fun* as amputating your own gangrenous leg." Midway through the essay, Kingsolver chastises those who criticize divorcees and other members of nontraditional living arrangements, saying they "should stop throwing stones." Her final tale, about the making of stone soup, suggests what the targets of such stones might do with them to reverse their fortunes.

BARBARA DAFOE WHITEHEAD "Women and the Future of Fatherhood"

Purpose

The success of the fatherhood movement is dependent upon the restoration of the nuclear family, according to Barbara Dafoe Whitehead. She argues that, in order for men to be good fathers, they must be supported by the structure of traditional marriage. Therefore, she calls upon women to wait for marriage before having children and to work to preserve the union so that their children will have resident fathers. Women need to see motherhood as a role that is best carried out within a traditional marriage because, whether they know it or not, "marriage and motherhood are coming apart." Whitehead says that "the traditional bargain between men and women has broken down," and both parties need to negotiate their changing roles as members of a couple. Women, for instance, will need to recognize that men are "less fully committed (to their own) sexual fidelity" than women and that men cannot fulfill the role of husband and best friend simultaneously. Men, on the other hand, cannot be expected to "develop the qualities needed to meet the new cultural ideal of the involved and 'nurturing' father without the help of a spouse." Whitehead insists that "men need marriage in order to be good fathers."

Because "the fatherhood problem will not be solved by men alone," Whitehead argues that men will have to make some compromises, too. Men must recognize the "changed social and economic status of women" by contributing more of the unpaid labor to the maintenance of the household. However, Whitehead is quick to offer that "this does not necessarily mean a 50/50 split of the household chores." She suggests instead that men "do more than one-third of household chores." Men need to recognize that contemporary women have "more exacting emotional standards for husbands," and that women "seek intimacy and affection through talking and emotional disclosure"—not the "physical disrobing" that men prefer.

Audience

Because "women have dominated . . . the debate about marriage and parenthood . . . for at least 30 years," Whitehead primarily addresses them in this essay. She appeals to women to help solve the fatherhood crisis in America, arguing that "men can't be fathers unless the mothers of their children allow it." Quoting poet and polemicist Katha Pollit, Whitehead panders to her female audience with the pronouncement that "'children are a joy. Many men are not.'" Although her arguments urge women to preserve traditional marriage and family ties, the author does admit in the conclusion of this essay that "women can be good mothers without being married." However, the overwhelming point of her essay is to convince women that "the best mothers cannot be good fathers."

Many of Whitehead's younger readers will have grown up in single-parent homes, and a substantial number will have been affected by the current perception of absentee fathers as "'deadbeat dad[s].'" They are a skeptical audience who will find the proofs they require for persuasion missing from this essay. Although Whitehead argues that men cannot be good fathers outside of marriage, she doesn't offer any concrete evidence that resident fathers are necessary to the development of their children. The specific benefits Whitehead promises are for resident fathers, not children: they will be spoken of more highly and they will learn from their more sensitive spouses how to be good parents. Whitehead reveals that a 1994 national survey showed that half of the women questioned believed that "one parent can bring up a child as well as two parents together," and that two-thirds of men disagreed. Nowhere in this essay does Whitehead demonstrate that resident fatherhood is better for wives or children; she simply takes it for granted that resident fathers are best.

Strategy

The language in this essay is strong. Whitehead frequently makes pronouncements such as "Marriage and motherhood are coming apart," and "Men have no positive identity as fathers outside marriage." She wins acceptance for her point of view by presenting it as incontrovertible fact. Subtly, through telling women that they hold the reproductive and nurturing power in our society, she makes them responsible for the parenting opportunities and abilities of men. She argues that "the success of any effort to renew fatherhood as a social fact and a cultural norm . . . hinges on the attitudes and behavior of women." Thus, she appeals to her primary audience of mothers to bear much of the burden of social change.

Whitehead's analysis of the current situation attempts to placate her female readers. She acknowledges that the changing face of the family is paralleled by the changes in women's role is society. As wage earners, women are no longer solely dependent upon their husbands for survival. In a divorce, women generally "enjoy certain advantages" in that they often get custody of the couple's offspring and "do not need marriage to maintain a close bond to their children." Contemporary women also have "more exacting emotional standards for husbands." Whitehead must cautiously exhort women to compromise these privileges and values, because she realizes that "many women see single motherhood as a choice and a right be exercised if a suitable husband does not come along in time." In this delicate situation women have the emotional and reproductive advantage.

JOAN ACOCELLA "Under the Spell"

Purpose

Pundits and serious literary critics are innately skeptical of popular culture. In her review of author J. K. Rowling's Harry Potter books, Joan Acocella admits that she "would love" to inform her audience that *Harry Potter and the Goblet of Fire*, "is a big nothing." However, her purpose is to explain why "it's wonderful, just like its predecessors." The Harry Potter series has received widespread acclaim, including, as Acocella notes, four volumes simultaneously on *The New York Times* best-seller list, the largest advance order ever for its latest volume, and, consequently, the largest-ever first printing of a book. Because children don't comprise the lion's share of the reading public, there must be a significant number of adults who are up past bedtime with Harry Potter books as well. Acocella, who admits to standing in line for two hours around midnight at Books of Wonder in New York on the release date of *Goblet of Fire*, is investigating the reasons behind Pottermania. Her scholarly examination of the Potter series reveals why there is much to admire in them for children and adults alike.

Skeptics of Acocella's thesis that the Harry Potter series is worthy of scholarly attention may be swayed by her application of the tenets of literary criticism and theory to the texts. She holds the Potter stories up against Vladimir Propp's 1928 *Morphology of the Folk Tale* and finds that Rowling has "unabashedly picked up. . . . about every convention ever used in fairy tales." Acocella finds other classic inspirations for the tales of the youthful wizard, including Arthurian legend and the Bible, as well as the work of J. R. R. Tolkien, Sir Arthur Conan Doyle, John Milton, Jane Austen, and Charles Dickens. She praises Rowling's prose for its "wealth of imagination" and "sheer, shining fullness." The Potter books also, covertly at least, raise questions about personal and social problems, including depression and racism; pose difficult questions about whether power inherently corrupts its possessor; and questions whether there is an inextricable connection between good and evil. Clearly, there is much at work behind and between the lines of Rowling's own sorcery to keep a keen critic's attention.

Audience

However, the Potter series is marketed chiefly toward children, many of whom show up at book releases such as the one Acocella describes, wearing Harry's trademark spectacles and sporting temporary tattoos of his distinctive lightning bolt scar. Acocella explains children's, and particularly young boys,' fascination with the books. For one thing, they are rife with adolescent humor, including "toilet jokes, booger jokes," and detailed discussion of Quidditch, a game "with four kinds of players (all flying on brooms) and three kinds of balls." The children in the book indulge in treats that are sure to entertain young readers: "Ice Mice, Jelly Slugs, Fizzing Whizbees—and levitating sherbet balls." But, according to this review, children and adolescents are attracted to the books for deeper reasons than its pure entertainment value. Young readers identify with Harry and his friends as they encounter typical childhood problems such as bad dreams, disappointing Christmas presents, sibling rivalry, uncooperative parents, and monsters under the bed. Harry must strike readers of his own age as particularly daring and realistic; he "lies to adults again and again . . . [and] he hates certain people." Acocella surmises that overall, it is the books' "wised-upness, their lack of sentimentality that must appeal to Rowling's audience." Also, as she notes, there are seven total projected books in the series, and those promise to deal with the escalating problems of maturation, including love and sex.

Pottermania is such a widespread phenomenon that parents cannot avoid curiosity about it. Acocella directly addresses "those parents who have objected to the Potter series on the ground that it promotes unchristian values"; countering superficial understandings of the books' attention to the occult she explains that they exhibit "philosophical seriousness" and model "excellent morals." Harry is an orphan, hunted by an evil man, yet mysteriously endowed with magical powers. Rowling scaffolds a series of intriguing investigations into the nature of life on those facts. According to Acocella, Rowling "asks her preteen readers to face the hardest questions of life, and does not shy away from the possibility that the answers may be sad." Wrestling with Miltonic notions, Harry and his friends will inevitably learn that "loss may be permanent, evil ever-present, good exhaustible." Acocella predicts that in the three volumes yet to be written, "new griefs will surely come." Most parents of "Pottermaniacs" will want to guide their children through such adult lessons, and this review informs those who mistake the Harry Potter stories for simple fairy tales that they may want to stay attuned to what their children are reading and thinking about—and they may enjoy reading along with their kids.

Strategy

Acocella's task in this essay is to review the fourth Harry Potter book, in part because this book is the "central pillar of the projected series of seven," but she discusses the three previous stories as well, and tries to engage readers who have yet to pick up the first volume of Harry's adventures. This review sketches Harry's background, his being orphaned and nearly killed by Voldemort, his loathsome existence with the Dursleys, and his eventual acceptance to Hogwarts School of Witchcraft. Acocella tries to capture the tone of the books for her readers, recounting in detail the gory scenes in which Rubeus Hagrid, the gamekeeper at Hogwarts, "feeds a bucket of brandy mixed with chicken blood" to his pet baby dragon or the transformation of Voldemort from a grotesque baby into an adult villian by his immersion in "a potion made from Harry's blood and someone else's hacked-off hand and various other ingredients." She also describes the "heart-stopping scene" in which the orphaned Harry sees his parents mourning their separation from him in the Mirror of Erised, only to learn that he has not glimpsed another world, but has confronted his own desire. Rowling's mixture of classical horror, mystery, and fantasy elements combines with romantic elements to hold the attention of a wide audience.

This review may at first strike some readers as incongruous. Acocella is holding a children's book to literary and social standards that seem unreasonable for adolescent literature. She examines the books for classical literary influences and finds a plethora of them, including "Gothic paraphernalia . . . purloined letters" and many twists on the timeless struggle of good and evil. When she says "Rowling's books are chock-a-block with archetypes," that their "denoue-ments last for pages and pages," that the ending of *Goblet of Fire* is fraught with "counterintuitive revelations," or that "Voldemort is an avatar of Milton's Lucifer" adult readers can see that these books stand up to scholarly scrutiny. The entire seriousness with which Acocella approaches her analysis of the Harry Potter series is enough to demonstrate that it may be worthy of the attention and anticipation it continues to attract. Or maybe Acocella is just trying to gain admission to Hogwarts School herself.

HAROLD BLOOM "Can 35 Million Book Buyers Be Wrong? Yes"

Purpose

Recognizing that attacking the cult of Pottermania, is like "Hamlet taking arms against a sea of troubles" because the wave of popularity surrounding Harry Potter will not be stopped, Harold Bloom lambastes J. K. Rowling's first volume and her entire series of Harry Potter books. Bloom acknowledges that most will think he is taking the "highbrow," "snobbish," and "nostalgic" position in a battle he is sure to lose. Rhetorically, Bloom seeks a pyrrhic victory by claiming that literary good taste belongs to the minority. He hopes that even those 35 million Harry Potter book buyers who adore Rowling's work will agree with him on principle. Bloom goes on record as disdaining the Harry Potter series for its poor prose, lack of original imagination, and authenticity. He says Rowling "makes no demands upon her readers." In his usual curmudgeonly persona, Bloom throws in sideswipes at *The New York Times*, and the writing of John Grisham, Tom Clancy, Michael Crichton, Steven King, and J. R. R. Tolkien. He also predicts the eventual demise of what he terms "the Harry Potter epiphenomenon." Ironically, Bloom belittled both the Harry Potter series and Tolkien's Middle Earth books just before the final installment in the blockbuster *Lord of the Rings* trilogy of movies was released. The popularity of that, however, only reinforces his thesis that the public has poor taste—at least in his way of thinking.

Our esteemed critic begins his frontal attack on *Harry Potter and the Sorcerer's Stone* by boldly stating, "the book is not well written." However, he concedes that neither was the book upon which the movie *The Wizard of Oz* was based. A list of clichés from the randomly chosen page four of *The Sorcerer's Stone* illustrates one of his complaints against Rowling's style. Although Bloom derides Rowling's writing ability, his chief complaint against the Harry Potter series is its sheer popularity. It signals, for him, a public judgment "proclaimed by the ideological cheerleaders who have so destroyed humanistic study." Bloom laments that there have always been "inadequate works" for adults and children in all ages and suggests that better literature is usually disregarded in favor of that which is sensationalized by the media. He does suggest some "superior fare" such as Thomas Hughes' realistic 1857 novel, *Tom Brown's School Days*, Kenneth Graham's *The Wind in the Willows*, or Lewis Carroll's "Alice" stories. Although he attacks the Harry Potter series specifically, he is really arguing for the public to exhibit better taste in literature in general.

Audience

The Wall Street Journal, where Bloom published this essay, is a conservative newspaper. The majority of his original audience would be more interested in the marketing of the Harry Potter stories than in their literary clichés, and would not be offended by Bloom's complaints about various authors and texts. They might appreciate his designating the liberal *New York Times* as "The official newspaper of our dominant counter-culture." Most of the businessmen who read this in its original context would not have read any of the Harry Potter books themselves, so Bloom summarizes the circumstances of Harry's life and the England he inhabits for his readers. Bloom also takes a swipe at English culture, claiming that Rowling must have invented a mystical England because the actual Britain is so entirely "conventional." Essentially, Bloom hopes to hand a learned opinion about the cultural phenomenon of Pottermania to readers who have little or no firsthand knowledge of the subject.

There is always the chance, however, that Bloom's article will backfire, that readers of *The Wall Street Journal* will be encouraged by what they learn about Harry Potter from this article and join the 35 million book buyers who are reading it for themselves. Doubtlessly, some of those businessmen are former Middle Earth trilogy readers who will find Bloom's comparisons between Rowling's and Tolkien's work intriguing. Certainly some readers would believe that whatever the curmudgeonly Bloom finds "tiresome and grotesque" or "bizarre" might actually be refreshingly light and entertaining. By creating controversy over what appears to be an unanimous approbation of Harry Potter, Bloom is probably inviting some readers who would otherwise ignore the craze to investigate it further.

Strategy

Harold Bloom is a respected literary critic, but he must establish his credentials to critique the Harry Potter books by admitting that he "read[s] new children's literature when [he] can find some of any value." His summary of life at the Rugby school in *Tom Brown's School Days* seems to prove the legitimacy of that claim. Bloom further proves his awareness of popular culture by alluding to the rock-opera *Tommy* by the British pop band The Who. A former professor at Yale, Cornell, Harvard, and NYU, Bloom does not want to embrace popular culture. J. K. Rowling's audience, who accord her the "importance akin to rock stars, movie idols, TV anchors, and successful politicians" does not persuade him otherwise. Essentially, the essay sets up a dichotomy between good taste and popular culture.

Bloom does concede that there is some value in the Harry Potter books: "a host . . . who simply will not read superior fare" reads them. Furthermore, he admits that readers of Harry Potter may appreciate Rowling's "wistful sincerity." They may want to "join her world, imaginary or not," and be distracted for a while from the worse evil of television, or they may simply be reminded of how it feels to turn the pages of "a book, any book." He expresses the hope that those readers will "advance from Rowling to more difficult pleasures." In reality, Bloom's "dire" prediction at the end of his essay has already come true: Harry Potter books are being taught in some colleges—it is being discussed in this class right now.

FRANCINE PROSE "Genocide Without Apology"

Purpose

Exodus, the chapter of the Old Testament that is filled with the stories of the plagues, the enslavement of the Hebrews, and the biography of Moses is the basis for Francine Prose's essay. She tells about her first exposure to it, in the basement of her great-aunt's house in Brooklyn, where she celebrated Passover while growing up Jewish in New York. Then she reads Exodus for herself with the sensibilities of an adult writer, and finds that it is not only shocking but realistic. It is with apparent pleasure, she says, that "the writer of Exodus takes in the gruesome details." She retells the miracle performed by Moses when he cured leprosy on his own hand and remarks, "Anyone would listen to a guy who could do that." Describing the plague of blood, she compares it with our modern-day horror when rust issues from a faucet. The themes in Exodus, she says, "could hardly be more stirring or more beautiful: Oppression and liberation, courage, self-determination: nothing less than the human spirit yearning to break free," as well as "people screwing up, suffering, [and] wandering." She is convincing her audience to read Exodus again for themselves, or at least to attend closely to her retelling of the tale. She wants her audience to see that the suffering described therein is human, and therefore it is real.

Prose recounts the story of Exodus from a uniquely contemporary point of view. She starts her summary of it by explaining "the Exodus narrative begins by striking an ominous note of political anxiety that will echo until the last chapters," and she demonstrates that the same kinds of strife, violence, and revenge enacted in Exodus continue in the world today. She compares the discovery of Moses in the bulrushes with the modern practice of choosing the next Dalai Lama, and the "back-and-forth let my people go" between Moses and the pharaoh to contemporary "end-stage diplomacy." The narrative of Moses' youth is the universal "story of how a hero is chosen and trained." Prose finds the genocide that God brings down on Egypt when he slays all of their firstborn in the night ("from the first-born of the Pharaoh that sitteth upon his throne, even unto the first-born of the maid-servant that is behind the mill; and all the first born of beasts") echoed in the present-day ethnic cleansing of the Palestinians, Afghans, Hutu, and Kurds. There are lessons to be learned in Exodus, such as Prose's observation that "there's always trouble when one population begins to worry about the birthrate of another." She confronts her readers with the facts and tells them, "One would have to be totally unconscious not to realize that all this is as true now as it was when Moses was in Egypt." Once she has established that the story in Exodus is really about "the dark side of human nature," she understands that it was going on even before the events recorded in the Bible transpired.

Audience

Among Prose's readers in *The American Scholar*, where this was first printed, will be people of various religious backgrounds with differing degrees of familiarity with the Bible and the Jewish observance of Passover. Prose explains for some of her readers that part of the Seder, or Jewish Passover feast, includes dipping a finger in wine and placing a drop of it on a plate for each of the plagues over Egypt. She describes the woodcuts in the Haggadah, the book or script for the Passover service, for readers who have never seen the most popular edition of it in America. She lists the ten plagues: "frogs, locusts, boils" as well as lice, flies, blood, hail, fire, the disease of animals, and the deaths of the firstborn. The story of Moses' being spared from the scourge against Hebrew babies is deftly summarized: "Baby Moses is found in the bulrushes and . . . is adopted by Pharaoh's daughter, who knows exactly what she's doing and hands him off to his mother to nurse and raise." When Prose tells of the plague upon the Hebrew firstborn, one need not be familiar with the Bible at all to grasp the horror of the quotation she twice repeats, "For there was not a house where there was not one dead." Her point, that the story in Exodus is universal, suggests that it will be of interest to a wide variety of readers.

The audience for this essay, unfortunately, will be well-acquainted with the word "genocide." It is a commonly used term in international news. From the atrocities of the Indian wars to those of Hitler and Saddam Hussein, genocide continues into the twenty-first century. Prose uses the story in Exodus to demonstrate what is at stake in acts of genocide, namely, "other people's children." She says, "It hardly matters who they are, as long as they are not our own." Harrowingly, she realizes that the slaughter of the firstborn, "just as easily could have been me." Knowing readers will realize that is true, not only in biblical Egypt, but in modern Europe, the Middle East, even North America. Prose argues that Exodus teaches useful lessons about the suffering in the world her readers inhabit.

Strategy

Prose contrasts her experiences with the story of Exodus, as celebrated during Seder through the text of the Haggadah, and with her later reading of the Bible herself. She describes the ritual evocation of the sacred meal's details, during which, she says," Never once, during all those years, during all those Seders, did I think—nor was it pointed out to me—that those plagues had human victims." Her reading of the Bible, however, teaches her that "Exodus involves a series of bloodbaths—outbreaks of state sponsored and divinely ordained carnage directed principally at children." Most of the human victims in Exodus, she adds, are civilians. She finds in Exodus the sentence issued by God that forever separates the Israelites from "other nations and tribes," along with the "detailed protocols" that underlie the Haggadah and the Seder ritual. And, finally, she discovers that the story of Exodus contains "genocide without apology"; the most gruesome detail from all of the plagues is the truth about human cruelty toward others.

The narrator traces her experience from the deliciously adult experience of getting "fairly hammered" along with her cousins on Passover wine to her adult response to Exodus. She says, "As a child, I adored the ten plagues," because during the Seder they are "lovingly listed. . . . And what a glorious list it was! . . . mysterious and thrilling!" The woodcuts in the Haggadah seemed "like watching certain horror films: forbidden and disturbing, therefore sexy and alluring." However, at the end of her essay, Prose says, she finds the book of Exodus "disturbing and depressing." The deep nostalgia that the author reveals for her family and the Seders they celebrated together makes it shocking and bittersweet when she proclaims that she will no longer celebrate Passover, will not "dip my fingers in my wine glass and extract sweet drops for the time when my group, my nation, triumphed at terrible cost." She also says that she does not have to "thank God for . . . killing the Egyptian children, just as God first, presumably, had inspired the Egyptians to attempt to kill the Jews." Her actions are even more persuasive than her words.

NATALIE ANGIER "Of Altruism, Heroism, and Evolution's Gifts"

Purpose

Written immediately after the 9/11 tragedies, Natalie Angier's essay begins with the now familiar litany of heroic acts performed by emergency personnel, passengers on the planes that were used as fire bombs, and inhabitants of the buildings impacted. Amid the horror of the day's occurrences, many people around the world clung to the stories of extraordinary heroism exacted from ordinary citizens to reassure themselves that civilization, as they knew it, had not ended. The stories of heroes also implied something about determinism: the firefighters had willingly run up the stairs to death, laden with 70–100 pounds of equipment; the flight attendants used their training to fight attackers armed with box cutters and made contact with ground control, and the men on the plane that crashed into a field in Pennsylvania had chosen action and resistance over fear. Even those around the country who scrambled to give blood for the injured survivors of the attacks felt the need to respond and take control of the situation as best they possibly could. The profound sense of helplessness that swept the world in the wake of the 9/11 attacks could only be mitigated by the oft-repeated heroic acts that countered the unthinkable, premeditated, and calculated actions of the terrorists. Perhaps that is why Angier's essay, which originally appeared in *The New York Times* just a week after the tragedies, was widely circulated on the Internet. It celebrates not just the actions of the day's heroes, but the impulse toward altruism and heroism that people needed to be assured still existed.

Although Angier's essay is written in response to the 9/11 events, it is also about the good and evil in human nature and that nature itself that is enduring and unchanging. She cites studies of anthropologists who have examined the behavior of tribes and civilizations where people have consistently behaved toward one another in a manner that is "better than good." She recounts the work of biologists since Charles Darwin who have recorded evidence of altruism within groups and observed how it can be "turned off toward members of other groups." The insect and animal world also provide solid evidence of altruistic tendencies; from ants and bees to monkeys, chimpanzees, baboons, and impalas, these innate traits can clearly be seen. Computer simulation studies of herbivores, which have a disturbing tendency to "selfishly consume all of the good in a given patch before moving on," predict that "symbiotic arrangements, even among different species" are likely to form in successive generations. Thus, cooperation and conflict are inbred; benevolent traits may be part of the genetic material of all living things. Angier's essay explains not only the altruistic, heroic behavior the world witnessed on September 11, 2001, but also the previously unimagined atrocious behavior of the attackers; they were one group lashing out at another group that they perceived threatened them.

Audience

The 9/11 attacks rocked the world. Anyone reading this essay, particularly the "postcards" that Angier uses to preface it, will recall how he or she felt in the immediate aftermath of the most shocking terrorist act in modern history. This essay was published while the streets of New York were still adorned with posters seeking information about missing loved ones, while candles still burned in Washington Square, while survivors still camped outside the charred wall of the Pentagon, and while the skies above North America were eerily clear blue and devoid of jet trails. There was no comedy that week; the late-night talk shows and most of prime-time television were swept off the air by coverage of the attacks and the ensuing rescue efforts. People everywhere were trying to make sense of what they had experienced personally and vicariously, and some had doubts that life could ever return to "normal." Angier's essay, like the work of many reporters and journalists during that time, was targeted at a confused and hopeless audience. By telling them that goodness, as well as the tendency of groups to direct evil at others, was inborn in humanity, she could begin to explain what had transpired and offer people hope that the altruistic impulse would prevail.

Strategy

Angier notes that politicians were quick to attribute the spirit of cooperation here in the United States to the "indomitable spirit of rock-solid America," while pastors credited "a more celestial source." Although she admits that "nothing and nobody can fully explain the source of emotional genius that has been everywhere on display," Angier seems to find comfort in biology, in the evidence that the altruistic impulse is "the birthright and defining characteristic of the human species." Her essay demonstrates that altruism does not only emerge in a crisis, but that it is necessary for ordinary survival. Evidence of this abounds in nature. Sterile worker bees, for example, labor unstintingly for their queen, their relatives, and their sister worker bees. Even though those selfless bees do not reproduce, the impulse to work and perhaps sacrifice one's life for the survival of the group perseveres. That, and other examples, demonstrate that selflessness naturally triumphs over greed, envy, sloth, and hatred. In fact, evolutionary patterns suggest that integrity is a persistent trait in many species, and, according to Angier, explains the actions of the firefighters, passengers on the fated planes, and rescue workers. She also predicts that humanity will soon right itself and all will see that goodness is germane to human character in general.

Like any scientist, Angier calls upon objective research and the opinions of leading authorities to prove her thesis that "altruism and heroism" are "twin radiant badges of our humanity." She describes the work of anthropologists because they study human beings. Language, researchers note, gives humans the unique ability to empathize with people they have never met and to "emulate . . . heroic deeds" known only through stories. Humans, animals, and insects are fiercely loyal and protective of their family members. The family structure of various cultures in the natural world promotes cooperation and survival. Angier presents examples from many insect and animal colonies to prove this point. In the words of Dr. Barbara Smuts, a professor of anthropology at the University of Michigan, the cooperation of various species to create "'a mutually beneficial environment'" is a "win-win principle."

Although much of her evidence comes from nonhuman populations, the essay speaks most highly of the human capacity for altruism. "'There's a grandness in the human species that is so striking, and so profoundly different from what we see in other animals,'" says Dr. Craig Packer, a professor of ecology and evolution at the University of Minnesota. In the aftermath of the 9/11 attacks, Dr. James J. Moore, a professor of anthropology at the University of California at San Diego, predicted that "For every 50 people making bomb threats . . . to mosques . . . there are 500,000 people around the world behaving just they way we hoped they would." Humans, he says, "are amazingly civilized." In fact, according to Dr. Moore, "We're the nicest species."

KURT VONNEGUT JR. "Harrison Bergeron"

Purpose

As is often the case with science fiction, Kurt Vonnegut Jr.'s story "Harrison Bergeron" is a comment on contemporary society, although it is set 140 years in the future from the time it was published. Vonnegut creates a scenario in which the constitutional dictum, "All men are created equal" is carried to its extreme, and gifted or beautiful people are literally disabled by being forced to carry weighted bags to reduce their strength, wear grotesque masks to conceal their beauty, and suffer implants in their brains to disrupt their thinking. The leveling of society reduces its achievements to clumsy dancing, unintelligible television announcers, and inane conversations, such as that between George and Hazel Bergeron, whose dialogue makes up most of the story's text. The Bergeron's impassive witnessing of their son's murder suggests that social interaction would be meaningless, were it not for the differences between human beings.

Harrison Bergeron, whose strength and attractiveness are said to rival those of "Thor, the god of thunder," is imprisoned when the story begins, but he escapes and takes over the television station. He tears the 300 pounds of disabling implements from his seven-foot frame and challenges a ballerina to do the same and dance with him. When the couple is free of their fetters, they defy more than the equalizing law of the land; they defy gravity, leaping high enough to kiss the thirty-foot ceiling in the television studio, and they manage to hang suspended in air through a prolonged kiss. Their superhuman agility and athleticism seems to signify their moral superiority; they alone are wise and brave enough to defy the inhuman proscriptions of their government. However, they are permanently brought down by shotgun blasts. Birdshot, like that which is hung about the necks of their physically able counterparts to slow them down, proves to be the death of the self-declared Emperor and Empress of the society.

Audience

As the comment in the textbook points out, this story was published after the repressive Stalinist regime that wiped out thousands of leaders and intellectuals in Russia. Similarly, the Nazis exterminated intellectuals and liberals in concentration camps during World War II, of which Vonnegut himself was a veteran. Vonnegut's fictive attempts to warn the world of the destructive consequences of attempts to level society seem to have gone unheeded in the world. Since this story was published the disastrous era of Mao's Red Guards in China, when hundreds of thousands of intellectuals and artists were killed or imprisoned in the name of equality, has passed.

The story has significance regarding wartime atrocities which annihilate targeted groups. It is also a comment on social conformity on a much more innocuous scale. Vonnegut's story warns individual readers that their contribution to society is valuable. Nearly everyone in the story has differing talents and gifts that must be leveled by mechanical means, enforced by Dianna Moon Glampers, the Handicapper General. The enormous waste of such a ridiculous policy and the immeasurable loss to the society described in the story reminds readers to make use of the skills and talents they have.

Strategy

Dialogue, interrupted by frequent discordant blasts generated by the implant in George's brain to scramble the thoughts of his superior intellect, comprises much of the story. Hazel's "average" intelligence is easily assessed by her lack of empathy for George's suffering with the implant, the simplicity of her thoughts, and the nonstandard dialect she uses. Neither of the Bergerons is able to keep a thought in mind long enough to react to it. Even the death of their son is quickly forgotten, and Hazel cannot explain the tears on her cheeks minutes after it has happened. By disrupting communication between people, the government has shut down their functioning. Fittingly, the story ends with Hazel repeating a phrase she has uttered often in the story, "I could tell that one was a doozy."

Vonnegut's singular, satiric style is well known now, even more so than it was in 1961 when this story was first published. He is a master at social criticism conveyed through entertaining fiction, and this story is no exception to that. The specter of ballerinas performing while burdened by sashweights, birdshot, and cumbersome masks is hilarious to imagine. Only a government with too much power and a misguided sense of justice could command such a thing. The romantic imagery used to describe Harrison Bergeron's gravity-defying dance with his ballerina Empress is exaggerated for humor, and as a contrast with the tragic deaths both suffer for their insubordination. With outlandish humor, Vonnegut conveys serious criticism about governmental policies and actions that seek to limit the aspirations and activities of intellectuals under their rule.

Resources for Writing:
The Discoveries—A Casebook

THE STRATEGIES

As the introduction makes clear, this section recapitulates the whole text by providing an essay in each strategy, plus a story, on a common theme: Discoveries. The purpose of representing these strategies is to demonstrate how they may be seen as thinking strategies, or ways of organizing and manipulating information on a particular subject. Indeed, the point of the section is to use readings to illustrate that thinking and writing are organically linked.

The section has been placed at the end of the anthology to give students the opportunity to master these techniques, one at a time, before they are asked to use them as planning strategies or to mix and match them in a more sophisticated writing strategy. But you could just as easily use this section at the beginning of the course to introduce and underscore the relationship between thinking and writing. Or if you prefer to organize your course thematically (see Thematic Contents), you can use this section as a way to blend your approach with rhetorical strategies.

THE READINGS

Although any theme could illustrate how effective writers use different strategies to explore different aspects of the same subject, discovery is a provocative topic. These readings range from personal discoveries about one's own nature and aspirations to exploring uncharted regions of the world, disentangling questions from history or science, and understanding the ordinary things around us.

Andrew Sullivan, a gay man, writes about self-discovery. He looks for causes in order to determine whether homosexuality is a lifestyle or an orientation.

Colin Evans writes about the clues the FBI used to find the kidnappers of Oklahoma oil millionaire Charles Urschel. The 1933 case was solved, in large part, because of the powers of observation and ingenuity of its victim.

Lewis Thomas surveys the categories of medical technology, and discovers that the best technology is the simplest because it is inexpensive and treats diseases completely. His essay makes a strong argument for more basic scientific research, so that medicine can produce technology that is so perfect patients can take it for granted. Similarly, Witold Rybczynski's essay on the importance of the machined screw in the building of civilization suggests that some of the most common technology around us is the most valuable.

John Fleischman writes about the archeological work of Sharon Stocker and her predecessor at the University of Cincinnatti, Carl Blegen. In 1939 Blegen excavated a ruin in an olive grove in Greece that may have been the palace of King Nestor, who is described in the *Odyssey*. The discovery of charred bones from an animal sacrifice on the site may authenticate a passage of Homer's that has long been thought to be an anachronism, thus suggesting that Homer was a better historian than many anthropologists formerly believed. Dava Sobel also writes about an historical discovery when she reveals what caused English "mechanic" John Harrison to invent a dependable, portable clock for use in navigation onboard oceangoing vessels.

Richard Doerflinger and Peggy Prichard Ross argue opposite sides of the stem cell research controversy. Likening the use of fertilized embryos to abortion, Doerflinger tries to bully conservative politicians who have shown fledgling support for this potentially life-saving technique. Ross is suffering from a form of brain cancer that might someday be cured if stem cell research is funded. Her impassioned plea for hope for future victims includes the disturbing information that no one knows what causes the disease she has, but 20,000 American get it each year.

The final reading in this section, a short story by Arthur C. Clarke, raises moral issues as well. A science fiction story set aboard a spaceship sent to explore the remains of a brilliant supernova, the text is mostly the internal monolgue of a Jesuit astrophysicist. The priest discovers more than he wanted to know about God when he realizes that an artistic and advanced civilization was destroyed by the explosion that created the Star in the East, which heralded the begining of Christianity.

THE WRITING

The pattern of writing assignments in this section is both similar to and different from the other writing assignments in this anthology. As in the other sections, the assignments in this section follow a three-part sequence: (1) writing that asks students to *respond* to the subject and strategies of an essay by drafting a similar composition, (2) writing that requires students to *analyze* the rhetorical strategies in an essay, and (3) writing that invites students to use an essay to *argue* similar or related assertions in another rhetorical context.

The pattern also is different because each selection is followed by three richly contextualized assignments rather than the six that conclude the other sections. In addition, it is different because each assignment encourages students to cycle back through the text looking for specific essays and stories that might serve as additional resources for comparison.

ANDREW SULLIVAN "Virtually Normal"

Purpose

Writing about his own experiences growing up homosexual, Andrew Sullivan says his essay "is an attempt to think through the arguments on all sides as carefully and honestly as possible, to take the unalterable experience of all of us, heterosexual and homosexual, and to make some social sense of it." Sullivan emphasizes that he can't speak for other homosexuals, and what he knows about the topic is confined (as it truly is for everyone) to his own experience. One purpose of his essay, however, is to understand himself, to see if any element of his upbringing or adolescent development contributed to his adult emotional and sexual orientation. He says, "Like many homosexuals, I have spent some time looking back and trying to decipher what might have caused my apparent aberration." He narrates memories of "the first time it dawned on [him] that [he] might be a homosexual," when a girl accused him of being a sissy for not choosing to play soccer in the rain. He analyzes his relationship to each of his parents, and recalls his early pre-sexual attraction to a second cousin, a shirtless man on television, and a fellow high-school student who undressed beside him in the locker room. Repeatedly he finds that, although he did not want to be "one of them," he was undeniably gay, perhaps from the very beginning of his life.

Sullivan is careful to acknowledge that he writes from personal experience, not an entirely scientific perspective. He explains, "When people ask the simple question: What is a homosexual? I can only answer with stories like these." Yet, the evolution of his self-awareness as a homosexual suggests that sexual orientation is not usually a matter of choice for individuals. At some point, he was forced to admit to himself that he "could no longer hide from [his] explicit desire . . . an undeniable and powerful attraction to other boys and men." He says that "when people ask me whether homosexuality is a choice or not, I can only refer them to these experiences [his own]." His admission naturally suggests that no one else really knows, either. Sullivan therefore finds it suspicious when "purportedly objective studies" reduce "opaque and troubling emotions . . . to statistics in front of strangers." When a conservative think tank asked him what made him believe that homosexuality is usually an orientation rather than a choice, he answered, "my life." Ultimately, Sullivan is convinced that "for the overwhelming majority of adults, the condition of homosexuality is as involuntary as heterosexuality is for heterosexuals."

Audience

Writing mainly for a supportive audience, Sullivan tries to explain to heterosexual readers (who by his own reckoning make up 95–98 percent of the population) what it is like to grow up gay. He says, "I relate my experience here not to impress or shock or gain sympathy but merely to convey what the homosexual experience is actually like." He wants heterosexuals to understand what he calls "homosexual hurt," resulting from the difficult situation of having to choose one's friends and lovers from the same social group. He says he learned early on "that love was about being accepted on the condition that you suppressed what you really felt." He writes of his relationship with his father and male friends that he had to constantly "be careful, in case they found out." Complicating matters for young Sullivan was the complete lack of role models or any mention of homosexuality among his family members, in his schooling, or in the media to which he had access. This led him to understand that he "would have to be an outlaw in order to be complete," and that his own "survival depend[ed] upon self-concealment." Through candid and frank discussion of his own adolescent experiences and feelings he tries to explain how growing up homosexual is fundamentally different from growing up straight.

Of course, Sullivan is aware that not all of the world is empathetic with the homosexual experience. He reveals that he once won the admiration of other boys in a debate competition by making a joke about homosexuals. Of his friends and himself he says, "we had learned the social levers of hostility to homosexuality before we had even the foggiest clue what they referred to." Certainly, homosexuality has been one of the last forms of diversity to be protected by political correctness or common courtesy; it has remained okay to joke about or disparage homosexuals in situations where nearly any other overt form of discrimination would be considered unthinkable. Sullivan acknowledges that to many "The homosexual experience may be deemed an illness, a disorder, a privilege, or a curse; it may be deemed worthy of a 'cure,' rectified, embraced or endured." Nonetheless, he counters, "it exists." Although he realizes that others may not agree with him he is as powerless to change human nature as they are.

Strategy

Sullivan's essay is essentially narrative, yet it is also argumentative, and he draws upon causal analysis frequently in exploring the roots and evolution of his own homosexuality. In a particularly complicated passage he examines his distant relationship with his father and his corresponding closeness to his mother. This follows "a typical pattern of homosexual development," but it also raises a sort of chicken and egg conundrum. What is causal? Do overbearing mothers shape homosexual sons? Or are homosexual sons more likely to identify with their mothers? Are homosexual boys threatened by their fathers or fearful of not living up to their expectations? So little is known about the cause of homosexuality, and causal analysis of it yields more questions than answers.

There are underlying similarities between hetero- and homosexual people, as there are among all human beings. Sullivan notes that while growing up he felt most acutely like himself, not like "one or the other gender category." He acknowledges that the accusation of being a sissy is common among "all young geeks, whatever their fledgling sexual orientation." His fears that he might never start puberty, and that his voice might never break are probably common to heterosexual boys as well. Likewise, "sexual implosion" of puberty happens to "gay and straight kids alike." Sullivan writes about the confusion of all people in sorting out their feelings for same-sex friends and loved ones, saying, "It is not always—perhaps never—easy, for either the homosexual or the heterosexual." Still, undeniably, there are huge differences between homosexual people and the majority of the population. Rather than attempt to dismiss that, Sullivan tries to confront it. He says, "There's a lamentable tendency to try to find some definitive solution to permanent human predicaments—in a string of DNA, in a conclusive psychological survey, in an analysis of hypo thalami, in a verse of the Bible—in order to cut the argument short." His own experience, and that of everyone around him, gay or straight, proves that each human life is too complicated for simple explanations. He says that homosexual experience is different from heterosexual life, and "Anyone who believes political, social, or even cultural revolution will change this fundamentally is denying reality" because "the isolation will always hold."

PHOTO ESSAY "The Senses of Place"

Purpose

The excerpt from Patricia L. Price's *Dry Places: Landscapes of Belonging and Exclusion* asserts that "Places . . . are narratives." The essays included in this section of the book invite readers to compose narratives of their own or to recount time-honored tales about the places depicted. From the imaginary landscapes out of the minds of artists to the unblinking eye of the camera, we are reminded that perspective and point of view are everything in the capture and presentation of an image. The visual texts reprinted range from the quaint representational world of Grandma Moses to the dark realism of Edward Hopper, and from the grand-scale tragedy of the wreckage of the World Trade Centers to the shattered family attested to by the grave of "Baby Sonne." The living signified by the names of homeowners on makeshift signs pointing to summer cottages, the dead in the baby's grave, and many centralized and marginalized positions in between are signified by the narratives implied in these images. The private places painted by Rowlinson and Mason contrast with the labyrinths of Hogue's feminine landscape and the maze of office cubicles photographed by Tom Wagner. All of these are places where people's lives play out and the myriad individual and overlapping stories people live and tell themselves take place.

An essay implies a journey with a beginning, a middle, and an end. This photo essay is no exception. It starts with signposts leading in opposite directions, and its audience is free to turn left or right, or to plough right into the bramble, making their own way through the tangle of information that follows. Five paintings invite us to consider the role of the individual in dreams, contemplations, and interactions with others and the landscape. For instance, the one-dimensional painting by Grandma Moses shows the impact of the population on the snowy hills, the houses situated and painted against the stark white snow, the streets ploughed, and the train making its benign way through the town. The Hogue painting of Mother Earth hints at the reciprocal relationship between people and the natural world—the Earth like a fertile woman with an abandoned plough at her knees. Look closely at Ruth Fremson's photograph of Ground Zero, and you will see hundreds of people working the site, framed by the bleak and monumental ruins of the Trade Centers. The power to destroy is balanced by the power to build, as evidenced in the Coles Hairston photograph of "Building an Offshore Rig." The even greater power to imagine is represented by Tolkien's Middle Earth and Harry Potter. Everything is framed and made meaningful by mortality. Every photo in the essay is a story unto itself and part of a larger story as well.

Audience

These photos are especially well chosen for a contemporary audience. Most will be familiar with some of the artwork, images from the 9/11 tragedy, scenes from contemporary life, representations of fantasy from two recent blockbuster movies, and the ubiquitous reminders of death that take us without warning in the grassy, unkempt monuments of graves. Considered individually, most anyone could spin a yarn or recount an autobiographical story based upon one of these images. For example, the photograph of Ground Zero might cause some students to think of the William Langewiesche essay in the Definition section of the book. Or, it might cause someone to remember the published story of a person who was injured or lost on September 11, 2001. Given the magnitude of the event, many viewers of the photograph will have had some firsthand experience with the tragedy or the site. Another legitimate response to that photo is simply for its viewer to recall where he or she was when news of the tragedy broke, and the reverie or reflection that such an unthinkable event spawned.

Strategy

Themes unite the photos in this essay, but so do other elements of visual rhetoric. One interesting way to examine these elements is by concentrating on the color "blue" while paging through them in order. The first, the photo of directional signs, shows that most summer homeowners opt for the stark clarity of black and white, while the blue and red paint used on the signs causes others to jump out of the jumble. Consider that the paint used on the signs might be leftover from the painting of the houses themselves, and they become a clue to imagining the blue houses of "HI-ZI," "Walsh," "T. Dixon," and "I. Simpson." Contrast the bright blues in the painting of a dream or in the fantasy landscapes with the deep and somber ones in the background of "The Porch," or the cool blues in the winter exterior scene with the faded blues inside the diner where the "Nighthawks" congregate. Notice the blue smoke still rising from Ground Zero as rescue workers pick among the ruins, or the breathtaking gradient blue of the sky in the offshore rig photograph. Even the tufts of living grass surrounding the grave of "Baby Sonne" show themselves as impressionistic blue smudges behind the iron marker. Think about the many cultural connotations of "blue," and decide which is represented in each image. Then do the same for white, green, and red, for geometric and curved, and pattern and variation. Clearly, a picture is worthy of more than a thousand words, and these dozen images would take more than the sum of twelve pictures to analyze fully.

COLIN EVANS "The Kelly Gang"

Purpose

Careful powers of observation and the planting of what little evidence was available to him helped Charles Urschel to lead authorities to his captors, and makes his case one of the most interesting in the annals of crime. In his brief essay describing the details of the Kelly Gang's kidnapping of Urschel, Colin Evans deftly sketches significant and insignificant details from the case. There are two processes being analyzed here: the first is the kidnappers' ability to pull off their caper and transport and harbor their victim, and the second is Urschel's attempts to leave evidence of his whereabouts at the scene of the crime.

Significantly, the Urschels and Jarretts are playing bridge when the gunmen come to kidnap the millionaire. Bridge is a game of observation; it requires players to keep the full deck of cards in mind and to remember which cards have been played to surmise which suits opponents are holding. It is also a game of strategy, and its best players respond insightfully to the moves their opponents make. On the other hand, the kidnappers reveal themselves quickly as bunglers. When neither man will confess to being millionaire Charles Urschel, they foolishly take both men along until it occurs to them to search their wallets and release Mr. Jarrett. As Evans notes in his conclusion, it was a mismatch of epic proportions for the Kelly Gang to target a brilliant thinker like Urschel. He says that "In such a lopsided contest, Kelly never stood a chance," and that seems to be borne out by even the most rudimentary details in the case.

Audience

Mystery stories are enjoying a renaissance among contemporary readers, and a tale like this is of interest to a wide audience. Evans tells the story chronologically to give his readers an opportunity to figure out how the FBI will use the details that Urschel supplies to crack the case. There are details here that mystery fans will appreciate and a few they might find amusing. For instance, one might calculate how far from home the kidnappers have transported Urschel by remembering that the events take place in 1933, and that it takes four days for their ransom note to arrive in Oklahoma City by mail. Add to that Urschel's own calculations about how far he was taken, and armchair criminologists can get a pretty good idea of the length of his blindfolded travels. More novel is the Kelly Gang's method for receiving a message from the Urschel family in the form of a precisely worded real estate ad to be placed in the *Daily Oklahoman*. Together, these kinds of details create the sort of story that mystery readers thrive upon.

Strategy

The famous O. J. Simpson case in the last decade, and many high-profile trials since then, have called forensic evidence into question. Many jurors seem to believe that lab work is a new and unproven science, yet the Urschel case was solved, in part through the use of fingerprinting, more than seventy-five years ago. Evans' book, from which this essay is excerpted, is dedicated to demonstrating the long and fascinating history of forensic detection. Although other evidence, such as the marked bills, weather reports, and flight schedules were used to solve the crime, Urschel's own faith in forensic evidence caused him to plant the most incriminating evidence against his captors. While he was handcuffed to a kitchen chair, and while he was released to write a letter to his family, Urschel placed fingerprints everywhere he could reach. Even if his captors had killed him and all of his powers of observation had failed, Urschel knew that some fingerprints might remain to accuse his kidnappers.

Although Evans' telling of this story is brief, it is filled with important details. Like every good mystery, the story contains relevant and useless details. Among those facts that help to solve the case are the marked bills that a family friend leaves with a stranger in a hotel, the amount of time Urschel spends in the two cars used to transport him, the comment about drought made by the woman who puts gas in the second car, the distinctive mineral taste of the water Urschel drinks, the rain that falls on Sunday, the times of the morning and evening airplanes passing overhead, and the fingerprints that Urschel intentionally leaves.

Less important details include the exact text of the ad the Urschel family is commanded to place in the newspaper, the two barns the captors visit, that the second car is a Buick or Cadillac in Urschel's estimation, the location of the hotel in Kansas City where the ransom money changes hands, the Panama hat worn by the man who collects the ransom, and the presence of cows and chickens on the farm where Urschel is held. Mystery fans will enjoy picking out the meaningful details from the red herrings as they follow the tale, and other readers will simply marvel at the FBI's ability to track the path of Urschel and his kidnappers using such evidence. No reader and no detective in the story is probably as ingenious a crime solver as Charles Urschel himself, whose attention to detail, along with his wife's decision to defy her husband's captors and notify the

FBI immediately, brought about the quick and conclusive identification of the Kelly Gang that landed "Machine Gun" Kelly in Leavenworth for the rest of his life.

DAVA SOBEL "Imaginary Lines"

Purpose

The imaginary lines of latitude and longitude that are used to measure distance around the globe are often thought of in geographical or political terms. Certain latitudes are warmer and more temperate, creating ideal vacation spots. Certain longitudes help one understand the relationship of countries or continents to one another. Most people, even contemporary world travelers, spend their time in the air or on land and give little thought to the significance of such measurements upon the ocean. In her essay on "Imaginary Lines," science writer Dava Sobel explains the origin of the latitude and longitude as they came into recorded history, and their significance in navigating the sailing ships that explored the New World and waged war in the Old. Of course, those same lines are still used to guide ships and airplanes today, and contemporary navigational devices, such as Loran or the Global Positioning Satellite, still use latitude and longitude as points of reference. Those global measurements form part of the basic mechanics of science; they predate the birth of Christ by at least three centuries. However, as Sobel reveals, it was the cartographer and astronomer Ptolemy who drew them on the earliest maps extant. Although subsequent map makers moved the prime meridian, its placement today is as arbitrary as Ptolemy's. The zero-degree longitude line now runs, predictably, through London.

People in the modern world can buy an accurate timepiece at a convenience store for less money than we might spend on lunch, so it is necessary for Sobel to remind her readers that the invention of the precise wristwatch is really an accomplishment of fairly recent history. Sobel argues that, without the need of ship's navigators to measure the distance between longitudinal marks using the difference between time in their homeports and time aboard ship, the accurate, portable clock might have been much slower in coming. She tells the story of John Harrison, the English clock maker who, in spite of prejudices that favored astronomers over simple "mechanics," prevailed in winning the prize of a "king's ransom" posted by maritime nations in the eighteenth century. Harrison invented a clock that needed no lubrication or pendulum, that was rust free, and that adjusted itself to atmospheric changes so it could maintain its accuracy aboard ship. Although it took Harrison forty years of struggle to claim his reward, the efficacy of his invention is attested to in the pockets and on the wrists of seafaring and land-loving people alike.

Audience

Nearly everyone can recall the childhood fascination with illustrations and models of the globe that Sobel recounts in the opening of her essay. She reveals the trick she learned for remembering the difference between latitude and longitude. The lines of latitude remain parallel, becoming shorter as they move in either direction from the equator. Longitudinal lines, however, cross one another as they reach the poles; thus, they are all "long." Sobel explains that the significance of this is that the equator is really the only naturally existing line that measures the globe because it marks the widest part of the sphere. The rest are evenly spaced from that. Ptolemy then had the honor of deciding for the world where the lines of longitude would be placed. He arbitrarily drew the first line, or the prime meridian, so that it ran through the Canary Islands, and spaced the others accordingly. This nonscientific anchoring of longitude explains why that measurement is the most difficult to attain without sophisticated instrumentation. All of the principles of navigation come to rest upon Ptolemy's decision; students must understand this in order to grasp the problems that everyone from Vasco de Gama to Sir Isaac Newton to the scientists at NASA must solve in locating themselves or objects upon the Earth.

One of the arguments for continued space exploration is that scientific breakthroughs are spurred by the need to defy gravity, feed astronauts, and bring them safely back to earth. The vitamin drink Tang and Teflon coatings are often cited as spin-offs of the space program. Sobel offers her readers a far more practical and sensible example by explaining that the accurate, portable clock is an offshoot of ocean navigation research. When we think of the widespread influence the watch has had on culture, it makes us wonder what new technology scientists might evolve that could have such far-reaching implications on ordinary life. Certainly it is nice to hope that there are some contemporary "mechanics" whose workshops might give rise in the next two centuries to something as practical and amazing as the dependable portable clock.

Strategy

A science writer who is accustomed to entertaining a wide variety of audiences through her work at The Discovery Channel and *Vogue* magazine, Sobel does a masterful job of captivating her audience. She opens the essay with a personal narrative, describing a toy that many of her readers may have owned: a beaded sphere that collapses and springs back to shape in the hand. She draws upon public imagery when she describes sitting on the shoulders of her father to admire the bronze globe that Atlas shoulders in front of Rockefeller Center, and she alludes to a common educational experience when she describes studying longitude and latitude in school. She demonstrates for her readers how much their lives depend, both romantically and practically, upon the accurate measurement of the globe and the ability to know precisely where a traveler is at any given moment. By describing in detail the problems faced by early ocean navigators, Sobel inspires admiration for those early explorers, astronomers, and "mechanics" who made our modern navigational tools possible.

Sobel's clear explanation of the problems of early ocean navigation further engages her audience. She sets up the need for accurate time measurement to know how many degrees of longitude one has crossed, and then explains why the clocks of Columbus' time were unsuitable for the task. The rolling decks of ships caused pendulum clocks to slow and speed up with their ambient motion. Changes in temperature thickened or thinned their lubricating oils, causing them to run faster or slower as well. Changes in barometric pressure and variations in the Earth's gravitational pull resulted in the same problems. Rust, a perennial peril of the world's oceans, destroyed timepieces altogether. Yet an accurate clock was absolutely necessary to prevent ships from running aground, causing such horrific naval disasters as the one in 1707 when four British warships ran aground, killing two thousand soldiers. By framing the problem carefully, Sobel pits her audience against the prejudiced and corrupt commissioners of the longitude prize, creating a denouement in her story when "mechanic" John Harrison is at long last given his reward in 1773. It makes a reader proud to glance at his or her wristwatch from time to time.

LEWIS THOMAS "The Technology of Medicine"

Purpose

Thomas applies the sort of "technology assessment" that is routine in endeavors such as space, defense, energy, and transportation to medicine, a technology so humane and in such urgent demand that its value is usually considered above the coldly objective measurements of cost analysis. Examining the value of what Americans get for the "$80-odd billion" they spend on health care, Thomas demonstrates that the public takes for granted the most cost-effective technology available. The best medical technology is easily delivered and relatively inexpensive because it is "the result of a genuine understanding of disease mechanisms." Immunizations and the use of antibiotics and chemotherapy are identified as "the real high technology of medicine."

Thomas proves that technology is most costly when its power to heal is incomplete. Those diseases "for which medicine possesses the outright capacity to prevent or cure" are the simplest, least expensive to treat. Effective technology is preventative rather than adaptive, but prevention can only be formulated when a complete understanding of the disease has been achieved. Thomas' classification system demonstrates the need for more "basic research in biologic science." Himself a physician and president of a large cancer research institute, Thomas' purpose in this essay is to persuade government officials and voters who are "interested in saving money for health care over the long haul" to support increased funding of basic research efforts.

Audience

Health care consumers are Thomas' audience for this explanation of the three types of medical technology. He recognizes that such a large audience encompasses persons who remember when diseases such as "diphtheria, meningitis, poliomyelitis, lobar pneumonia, and all the rest of the infectious diseases" were technologically untreatable. Recalling the scourge of polio and the adaptive treatments that evolved in the 1950s, the author asks, "Do you remember Sister Kenny?" Thomas also demonstrates sensitivity toward readers too young to recall diseases and treatments that do not plague modern patients. He describes Sister Kenny's battery of "halfway" technological treatments, and his cost estimates for present-day administration of 1935's "best methods" against typhoid fever include descriptions of the obsolete treatments.

Modern treatments of cancer and heart disease, however, need not be described for this essay's audience. Thomas chooses examples a wide readership is likely to be familiar with. For example, although he "can think of at least twenty major diseases that require" the supportive care of nontechnology, he names such well-known problems as cancer, rheumatoid arthritis, multiple sclerosis, stroke, and cirrhosis of the liver as examples. Similarly, he chooses illustrations of halfway technology that frequently appear in the popular media: heart, kidney, and liver transplants, and "the equally spectacular inventions of artificial organs." Relatively obscure examples are defined in the text; for instance, discussion of chronic glomerulonephritis identifies the problem as kidney disease.

Throughout the essay Thomas acknowledges his audience's vested interest in all technology surrounding modern medicine. Naturally, his readers expect practitioners "to deliver today's kind of health care, with equity, to all people." As consumers, they also want the best available care at the most reasonable cost. But Thomas offers readers an even more compelling reason to push for the development of real technology; anyone would prefer to be cured by a simple vaccination rather than endure complex surgeries and mechanical interventions designed to postpone death.

Strategy

Thomas' categories of medical treatments are distinguished according to the level of technology they represent. The names he assigns to the categories—"nontechnology," "halfway technology," and "real high technology"—demonstrate that the same principle of selection has been applied to each and suggest how each category differs from the others. Thomas describes each level of medical technology by offering a general definition. For example, he summarizes effective technology as "the result of a genuine understanding of disease mechanisms," adding that "it is relatively inexpensive and relatively easy to deliver." He demonstrates the uses, methods, and costs of each level of technology by including several examples representing each category.

Thomas' extensive analysis of treatments for various diseases proves his division of the subject is definitive and complete. Cancer, however, appears in two categories. When the disease is untreatable, it is subject to nontechnological interventions, but when hope of remission exists, it is treated with such halfway technology as "surgery, irradiation, and chemotherapy." The three categories established in the essay are arranged in an emphatic order from the least effective to the most effective. Ironically, the third category, "real high technology," is the most frequently overlooked of the three types of treatments. In calling for basic research that would expand medicine's most effective technology, Thomas acknowledges that such a plea is "like asking for the moon"—a request, he implies, that has already been granted the space program.

WITOLD RYBCZYNSKI "One Good Turn"

Purpose

Witold Rybczynski draws attention to an ubiquitous example of low technology in his essay about the origin and impact of screwdrivers and modern screws. Many of the things we use in a day would not exist in their current form without the common screw. Furniture, automobiles, small appliances, door frames, and wristwatches are just some of the things we encounter daily without giving a thought to the many screws that they contain.

How many times has each of us found a screw on the ground or the floor of our cars and simply thrown it away without considering what an engineering marvel it is? Rybczynski says that "the machined screw represented a technological breakthrough of epic proportions," and that "threaded screws changed the world." His quick recap of the history of screws and screwdrivers demonstrates that technological strides, including the Industrial Revolution, would have been impossible without the invention of this lowly fastener. Most of his readers will be surprised to learn how influential screws have been in civilization. This essay gives readers pause to appreciate a common building material that is often regarded as a nuisance, rather than a modern marvel.

Audience

The naming of various hand tools without describing their functions suggests that Rybczynski is writing for an older generation of craftsmen, who would be insulted if a writer described the function of each. Younger readers who have never used a handsaw, chisel, or brace and bit, however, are almost certainly familiar with screws and screwdrivers and the hammering of nails that Rybczynski describes as "satisfying work." He notes that "if you rummage around in most people's kitchen drawers you will most likely find at least one screwdriver." It may be possible that there are readers who have never used a screwdriver. However, these readers have definitely used one of the household objects that Rybczynski mentions which employ screws: "door hinges, drawer pulls, shelf hangers, towel bars."

Readers who aren't particularly fascinated by tools and building materials might be interested in the history of civilization revealed in Rybczynski's suggestion that a medieval carpenter would be surprised by very few of the hand tools in use today. Or they would be surprised to learn that early screws were expensive and therefore reserved for precision applications, such as clockworks. They might even be fascinated by the "chicken and egg story" of the lathe that makes screws, but needs screws itself to operate.

Strategy

This history of various tools is highly informative, yet it is written in a very friendly tone, as if the reader and writer were working side by side on a building project. It includes building advice, such as the insight that "wood screws are stronger and more durable than nails, pegs or staples." Rybczynski explains how gimlet-pointed wood screws work, drawing planes tightly together, much like a bolt holds pieces of steel together with friction. The essay moves chronologically through history from the Neolithic period, through Archimedes' invention of the screw in the third century B.C., the Middle Ages, the sixteenth century, to the invention of the screwdriver around 1800, and the period when screws became plentiful about fifty years later.

Rybczynski builds his essay from old-fashioned research, piecing together bits of history to reveal the story of the invention and evolution of the common screw. The essay begins with a reminiscence of building a house "from the ground up" using only hand tools. This essay was painstakingly crafted in much the same way.

JOHN FLEISCHMAN "Homer's Bones"

Purpose

Five hundred years and the Dark Ages passed between the battles recounted in the *Iliad* and the *Odyssey* and Homer's writing of those epic poems. The bard worked from oral poetry and stories handed down though generations, writing four hundred years before "the invention of history as a record of facts." The degree to which Homer's stories can be taken literally is a matter of scholarly contention. In his essay about archeological excavations on the western edge of the Greek Peloponnesus, John Fleischman raises historical questions and assumptions about Homer's veracity and anachronisms and attempts to verify a passage in Book 3 of the *Odyssey*. That passage concerns Telamachus, who, early in the quest to find Odysseus, runs his boat aground at Pylos. There King Nestor is sacrificing bulls to Poseidon. Literary and historical experts have tried to locate the cities Homer names, all of which were lost by the time of his writing. There is a modern Greek city named Pylos, but it was named after 1832, when the Greeks won independence from the Ottoman Empire, with only "a rough guess" as to whether it was near the site Homer had described. In his essay, Fleischman objectively examines the claims of several contemporary archeologists who believe they have found the ruins of the real Pylos in an olive grove near the village of Hora. The author of this essay seems guardedly enthusiastic about this potential vindication of Homer's accuracy, but one purpose of this essay is to assert the possibility that the Bard's tale was based upon verifiable facts.

All of the supposition about the veracity of Homer's writing rests upon modern-day archeologists, many of whom mistrust the accuracy of a poet working half a millennium after the events he described. Fleischman's essay celebrates the 1939 work of University of Cincinnati archeologist Carl Blegen. On his first day of digging, Blegen stumbled upon pot shards and tablets inscribed in "Linear B," an undeciphered Bronze Age script that had never before been found on the Greek mainland. During a summer of furious digging he found enough of the tablets to crack the ancient code. However, war intervened, so Blegen labeled the other artifacts his group had unearthed and stored them in a basement at the archeological museum in Hora. Fleischman picks up the story of the dig in 1997 and follows the work of Sharon Stocker, Jack Davis, Paul Halstead, Valasia Isaakidou, and Lisa Bendall as they attempt to authenticate both Homer's description of the sacrifice at Pylos and their claim to have discovered the Bronze Age palace of Nestor to which Homer refers. The essay explains the delicate mix of fact finding and conjecture that archeologists use to discern historical truths.

Audience

It is a common experience among educated people in the Western world to have read the *Odyssey*. Fleischman writes for those who scarcely remember it or scarcely read it. He quotes from the *Odyssey* to remind readers of the description of Nestor's sacrifice and the feast he offers to the throng of "nine divisions, each five hundred strong." In discussing Heinrich Schliemann's search for ancient Troy, Fleischman identifies Priam as "the Trojan King" and alludes to the sequestering of Helen there. He establishes details from Homer's work, such as the "Sacrificing [of] sleek black bulls" which he later echoes in the findings of the archeologists who reassemble the sacrifice-charred bones of "at least 10 animals, primarily bulls, plus one red deer." He calls Homer's verse "a fruitcake" because it mixes Bronze and Iron age details in a dense mixture that is part fiction and part historical writing.

Strategy

Using a similar analogy, Fleischman describes Schliemann's archeological trench digging as the process of slicing through "a wedding cake of lost cities," each built upon the ruins of its predecessor. He quotes Cynthia Shelmerdine, a prehistorian at the University of Texas, who summarizes the 1970s-era prevailing thought about studying history through literature like the *Odyssey*: "if you want to know about the Bronze Age, you don't read Homer. You come and look at the Bronze Age evidence." Archeologists like Sharon Stocker are in the process of changing that, however; new evidence suggests that Homer's accounts of Bronze Age cultural life may be more accurate than once believed. Perhaps Fleischman is trying to kindle the dream of visiting Greece and standing in Nestor's footsteps when he describes the "huge metal shed" that the Greek Archaeological Service erected in 1960 to cover the central ruins at Pylos. There, he says, one can "trace the passages, rooms, and courtyards where the king ruled 3,200 years ago."

Late twentieth-century archeologists unpacking the stored findings of Carl Blegen's work practiced, in the words of Paul Halstead, "an excavation of an excavation." In fact, Fleischman introduces his audience to the archeological process, not with examples of pottery and metalwork from ancient Greece, but American exports from relatively recent history. When Sharon Stocker arrives in Hora to inspect the treasures of her distant colleague's dig, she first sorts through detritus that includes wooden boxes and cardboard barrels of food relief sent by the United States during the Greek civil war and a yellowed newspaper photo of Jackie Kennedy in her trademark 1960s pillbox hat—before she lived in Greece as the wife of Aristotle Onassis. That is archeology of another sort, but it explains to Fleischman's readers how trained scholars date materials by the fashions of the times they represent, how disused things get old and broken or disintegrated, and how age piles upon age so that the walls of one ancient civilization rest upon the foundations of an even earlier one. This modern-day example introduces the problems faced by scholars attempting to recover and identify ancient artifacts.

Fleischman is writing for the inquisitive audience of *Discover* magazine. He is careful to remain objective, if hopeful, about the claims that Stocker and her team are making. Millions of people know of the ancient Greece Homer describes and want to take him literally. Fleischman explains that "Truth be told, Homer is something of an embarrassment to 21st-century archaeology," because "He catches the . . . imagination . . . but complicates science." James Wright of Bryn Mawr College says that "the public love of Homer . . . can be dangerous." Early twentieth-century scientists like Blegen, however, "dug, if not with the *Iliad* in hand, then with a memory of it fresh in mind." Blegen's findings stayed safely stored throughout the post-1960s "backlash" against Homerian archeology, and are now being used by his successors to locate the remains of Pylos "because some legendary bard had the force of imagination, some 500 years after the palace burned, to rebuild it in memory." That is at last, some vindication for Homer and Carl Blegen.

RICHARD DOERFLINGER "First Principles and the 'Frist Principles'"

Purpose

Very few writers have more fun or are more flagrant than those writing for a like-minded audience. Richard Doerflinger illustrates that in his essay criticizing pro-life Republican senator Bill Frist and condemning the "ideologues who want a Brave New World" (namely former President Bill Clinton and Senators Arlen Specter and Tom Harken who have supported legislation permitting exploration of stem cell research). During a congressional hearing on the matter, Senator Frist proposed some guidelines for the funding of stem cell research, a medical procedure that harvests stem cells from unfertilized human eggs, which may be useful in combating certain diseases of the nervous system, including Alzheimer's, A.L.S. (Lou Gehrig's disease), and Parkinson's disease. In Doerflinger's estimation, anyone who supports investigation of stem cell research has "thr[own] away his pro-life convictions." He criticizes Frist for hoping for medical benefits from the research. Openly mocking Frist, whom Doerflinger acknowledges is "the Senate's only physician," he scoffs at the senator's "newfound loophole in respect for life." Doerflinger is clearly disappointed in Frist because, for once, the two do not agree on a moral issue, and he tries to paint Frist's guidelines as a failure because they were not fully supported by some of his colleagues. Finally, he cautions President George W. Bush that if he doesn't stand firm on his opposition to stem cell research, he will suffer a similar loss of respect from conservative constituents.

Audience

Doerflinger says he wants to clarify an issue the news media covered and bring to light one that was covered poorly. However, he is mostly bent on name-calling and haranguing Senator Frist. Doerflinger is one of many conservative opponents of stem cell research who persist in equating the use of unfertilized human eggs with abortion. Throughout the essay he tries to suggest that permitting stem cell research will open the door for easier access to abortions. He brings abortion into the argument through analogy, stating that the used of unwanted human embryos "is like saying that the government will fund abortions only for unborn children not wanted by their parents." He threatens that if the proposed study is approved, "researchers could perform abortions solely to obtain fetal tissue for government research." This ignores the necessary prerequisite that women agree to get pregnant solely to undergo an abortion for government research—an unlikely scenario. Doerflinger draws upon the emotional and divisive abortion issue to fuel the fight against stem cell research. Furthermore, the growth of cells from a single cell is technically cloning, but Doerflinger pretends that permission to explore stem cell cures for diseases would result in people duplicating themselves like human versions of Dolly the sheep; that is a preposterous leap.

Strategy

Notice that Doerflinger does not objectively define stem cell research in his essay. His goal is to align it with abortion in the minds of his readers and ask them to make an uninformed choice in the matter. He refers to the body of beliefs held by "pro-life Americans" in citing Frist's stance against cloning in an attempt to suggest that everyone against abortion shares the same attitude about various reproductive-related issues. Simply put, Doerflinger wants his readers, who already agree with him that abortion is wrong, to trust him on this topic, too. He pokes fun at Senator Frist's comments asking for "respect" for embryos and defines their use subjectively as "suck[ing] out a living being's innards and throw[ing] away the shell." Doerflinger hopes to encourage opposition to stem cell research by attacking the character of anyone who considers it.

Slanting language in his own favor, Doerflinger refers to "destructive embryo research" and "grotesque research" to describe the process of using healthy cells to cure devastating and fatal illnesses in human beings. The victims of the diseases stem cell research purportedly might cure suffer and die degrading and dehumanizing deaths. This raises the question of whether Doerflinger is as compassionate and caring as he seems, or whether he simply wants to demonize some people on Capital Hill to galvanize his followers against them.

PEGGY PRICHARD ROSS "Stem Cell Research: It's About Life and Death, Not Politics"

Purpose

Arguing for "future generations" who will be afflicted by the same disease she has, Peggy Prichard Ross demands that President George W. Bush put his own religious beliefs aside and give the green light to stem cell research. Presumably, her arguments are altruistic, because as she reveals in her dramatic first sentence: "there is a good chance" she'll be dead in six months. She further adds significance to the political debate when she says that her own impending demise "doesn't bother [her] nearly as much as having a president who wants to jail scientists and doctors who are trying to find cures for people with . . . illnesses." Sadly, Ross is without the hope she says that "millions of Americans who fight for their lives every day against life threatening illnesses" deserve and need.

In addition to the inescapably emotional argument based upon her own approaching death, Ross offers a rational reason why representatives, senators, and the president should consider funding stem cell research. She says that, although the president popularly refers to the process as cloning to scare the public, stem cell research asks to utilize egg cells that "have no chance of being fertilized or transplanted into a woman's womb." It is cloning, but not the stuff of science fiction that results in "mutant or butchered babies, "Ross argues.

Audience

Criticizing George Bush's self-avowed stance as a "compassionate conservative," Ross reaches out to truly compassionate readers by telling them that she is about to die, yet in her last months of life she cannot give up the fight to bring stem cell research to the medical community. As a director of communications for a large insurance company, she is well aware of the kinds of arguments that will move readers.

Strategy

Choosing a powerful opening, Ross begins with the information that she is dying. She presents her rational defense of stem cell research succinctly, criticizes the president for mixing his religion with politics, and ends with a call to action. Ross' conclusion names Congress, representatives, senators, and the president in the hope that her readers will write their elected officials immediately to lobby for funding for stem cell research. Given her sharp criticisms of the sitting president, she might also be hoping that her readers will vote as she would have after she is gone.

Ross emphasizes that astrocytoma, the form of brain cancer that is killing her, "is not hereditary" and "has no known environmental cause either." She says there is "no rhyme or reason to who gets it and why." However, "almost 20,000 Americans per year will get the same type of brain cancer." Readers don't have to be good at math to understand that they could be one of the people randomly struck by this disease. It could be the research that leads to their own cure that Ross asks them to champion.

ARTHUR C. CLARKE "The Star"

Purpose

The purpose of Clarke's story is to entertain, but also to perplex its readers by raising questions about religious faith. Like much of science fiction writing, it "solves" a mystery of our universe by using fictional technology that the writer creates as part of his vision of the future. Foreshadowings, such as the spectrophotometer tracings, which measure light intensities in different parts of a spectrum and enable the narrator to calculate the year the supernova appeared to Earth, give readers a chance to predict the Jesuit's devastating discovery before it is revealed in the story's last words.

The story also comments on a current social issue, a frequent characteristic of its genre. The narrator's unspoken entreaties to Saint Loyola suggest that religious faith is the result of ignorance, that the saint believed because a "little world" was all the universe he knew. The Jesuit does not question—as his colleagues do—whether God exists, but whether he is a benevolent God worthy of worship. He wonders how the destruction of a solar system could "be reconciled with the mercy of God" and answers himself with the logic of Catholic dogma: "God has no need to justify His actions to man."

Although it falters, the priest's faith probably remains; he censures himself for the near blasphemy of judging God's actions. Still, in his estimation, the beauty of the sacrificed civilization outshines the supernova above Bethlehem. The story casts aspersions on the fundamental Judeo-Christian belief that God "has a special interest in . . . our miserable little world," and perhaps it even suggests that there is no God by ascribing the Star of Bethlehem to purely physical causes.

Audience

Clarke assumes his readers have some degree of knowledge, if not faith in, Christian religion and that they are at least aware of the Jesuit order and the Star of Bethlehem. The author explains Saint Loyola's importance to the narrator by revealing in the priest's internal monologue that Loyola founded the Jesuit order. The Latin inscribed on the saint's book means "to the greater glory of God." Clarke does not translate it for his audience, probably because the phrase is widely known, and it is not crucial to an understanding of the story.

Clarke also uses his protagonist's thoughts to convey astronomical information. The character reveals that "the Phoenix Nebula is a tiny thing—a tenuous shell of gas surrounding a single star." Comparisons with our own solar system indicate that the nebula was once "a sun like our own" but is now "a White Dwarf, smaller than the Earth, yet weighing a million times as much." The nebula examined in the story is the remnant of a supernova, a rare occurrence "beside which even a nova pales into total insignificance." Clarke avoids intimidating or alienating his audience by communicating within the story the astronomical data necessary to appreciate the unfolding plot.

Strategy

Argument is the strategy Clarke uses to advance the plot in his story. The spaceship's crew wages a good-natured, yet serious, campaign against its Jesuit chief astrophysicist. Dr. Chandler, one of medicine's "notorious atheists," articulates the crew's argument when he agrees that "perhaps *Something*" made the Milky Way but then insinuates it is foolish to believe that *"Something"* is concerned with human life. The crew is amused by the incongruity of a Jesuit astrophysicist, uncertain as to how he can reconcile his religious faith with scientific facts. That problem becomes a moral dilemma for the priest when his greatest scientific discovery tests his faith in God's mercy.

As the spaceship penetrates the realm of the Phoenix Nebula, the astrophysicist collects evidence from the interstellar space debris that proves they are exploring the remains of a brilliant supernova, a "cosmic bomb that had detonated millennia ago." His awe at its "incandescent fragments" is replaced by grief when a planet is discovered and the carefully preserved remnants of a peaceful civilization are found.

Clarke uses emotional appeals to heighten his reader's sensitivity to the ancient civilization. The "civilization that knew it was about to die" and "made its last bid for immortality" had preserved "the fruit of their genius": sculpture, visual records and machines for projecting them, written language, musical speech, and cities built with grace. All the evidence shows they were a warm and beautiful civilization, "so disturbingly human" that pictures of their children playing on "a beach of strange blue sand" remind the narrator of children playing on Earth. In the priest's judgment, "They were not an evil people," and "they could have taught us much." Their destruction seems unspeakably senseless; the protagonist wonders, "Why were they destroyed?"

The third bit of evidence he weighs, his own calculations that verify that the flareup of the supernova coincides with the occurrence of the Star of Bethlehem, shakes his faith and threatens his being. Logical evidence demonstrates that a civilization, by many measures better than Earth's own, was expended to fuel God's pyrotechnics. Clarke establishes in the story's second paragraph that there is no other conclusion; scientists on Earth will certainly confirm the astrophysicist's findings.

Ironically, the priest's unwelcome discovery settles his argument with the crew. God does take special interest in the affairs of men, but the supernova calculated to herald the birth of Jesus on Earth indifferently annihilated another civilization. The Jesuit reasons, "He who built the universe can destroy it when He chooses," but his sympathies lie with the doomed people who raised the monolith over the Vault containing the desperate evidence of their exquisite existence.

Reading Quizzes
and Vocabulary Lists

Name _____   Date _____

NARRATION AND DESCRIPTION

ANDRE DUBUS "Digging"

READING QUIZ

1. How did Dubus lose his leg?

2. How old is the narrator at the time that the story he tells takes place?

3. What was the narrator's job at the time of his father's death?

4. Why did bullies pick on the narrator?

5. What did the narrator's father tell his son about professional wrestling matches?

6. With whom was the narrator assigned to work on his first day at the construction job?

7. To what specific duty was he assigned on that first day?

8. Describe the narrator's lunch-hour activities on his first day on the job.

9. What did the narrator's father purchase for him on that day?

10. Who really "made a man" of the narrator?

Name _____   Date _____

ANDRE DUBUS "Digging"

VOCABULARY LIST

ruddy

ducktails

rebuke

seersucker

Cajun

oscillating

pith helmet

stewardship

exultant

arduous

Name _____   Date _____

JILL MCCORKLE "The Mullet Girls"

READING QUIZ

1. In which U.S. state is Holden Beach, where the story takes place, located?

2. What had eliminated the two rows of beachfront houses that sat in front of the narrator's vacation home in the early 1950s?

3. What phrase did the narrator's cousin like to hear her and her sister say because it revealed their Southern accents?

4. What is one of the other names by which the narrator's family refers to "the Mullet Girls"?

5. For whom did the narrator's father express pity when he released a fish with a hook stuck in its mouth back into the water?

6. In what movie did the narrator's father find Julie Andrews "pretty"?

7. Where did the narrator's father work?

8. What was in the brown paper bag that the narrator used to deliver to her father at his special fishing spot?

9. How does the narrator characterize the Mullet Girls when her mother asks about them?

10. In essence, what does the narrator's father say to the Mullet Girls when they finally find him at home?

Name _____   Date _____

JILL MCCORKLE "The Mullet Girls"

VOCABULARY LIST

meager

convulsive

shrill

Mullet

surrogate

loamy

briney

solace

pavilion

Atlantis

Name _____   Date _____

JUDITH ORTIZ COFER "The Myth of the Latin Woman: I Just Met a Girl Named Maria"

READING QUIZ

1. In which U.S. territory was Cofer born?

2. In which Broadway musical did the song that the man on the bus sings originate?

3. Why was the narrator of this essay in England?

4. What did her Anglo friends and their mothers think of her clothes?

5. Which special day at school caused the narrator to agonize about what to wear?

6. How does Cofer say advertisers generally portray women from her culture?

7. Does Cofer say it is custom or chromosomes that cause Latin women to choose to wear scarlet over pale pink?

8. Which religious tradition has customarily protected Latin women?

9. What are *piropos*?

10. What does the woman in the audience request from the narrator just prior to her public poetry reading?

Name _____ Date _____

JUDITH ORTIZ COFER "The Myth of the Latin Woman: I Just Met a Girl Named Maria"

VOCABULARY LIST

Latina

microcosm

bodega

barrio

coalesced

innuendo

pueblo

proficiency

retrospect

faux pas

Name _____   Date _____

HELEN PREJEAN "Memories of a Dead Man Walking"

READING QUIZ

1. What subject did Helen Prejean teach in various Catholic schools?

2. Roughly, how much time passed between the release of Prejean's book and that of the movie upon which it was based?

3. In the essay's opening scene from the movie, what is actress Susan Sarandon doing in the women's room of a prison?

4. In which U.S. state was Patrick Sonnier executed?

5. What are the St. Thomas Projects?

6. When did Prejean attend a racially segregated high school?

7. What previous experience in prisons did Prejean have when she became spiritual advisor to Sonnier?

8. What "mistake" does Prejean acknowledge in her handling of Sonnier's case?

9. What was the subject of Patrick Sonnier's last words?

10. Which actor played the part of the inmate in the film *Dead Man Walking*?

Name _____ Date _____

HELEN PREJEAN "Memories of a Dead Man Walking"

VOCABULARY LIST

lepers

vengeance

suffrage

fervently

cusp

naïve

assuage

gurney

protocol

transcendence

Name _____ Date _____

GEORGE ORWELL "Shooting an Elephant"

READING QUIZ

1. What did Orwell choose to do rather than complete his education?

2. What is the narrator's job?

3. What is Orwell's attitude toward imperialism?

4. What object does the narrator obtain after discovering the dead man?

5. Besides adventure, what did the locals hope to get from the killing of the elephant?

6. What is the elephant doing when it is found?

7. How many people does the narrator estimate comprise the crowd behind him?

8. In shooting an elephant, where should one aim?

9. How many cartridges does the narrator fire into the elephant?

10. How long did it take the elephant to die?

Name _____   Date _____

GEORGE ORWELL "Shooting an Elephant"

VOCABULARY LIST

perplexing

prostrate

imperialism

labyrinth

conjurer

dominion

sahib

senility

remnant

pretext

Name _____   Date _____

ALICE ADAMS "Truth or Consequences"

READING QUIZ

1. How old was Adams when she published her first book of fiction?

2. Who does Emily learn that Carstair Jones has married?

3. Where is Hilton, the town where the story takes place?

4. How was the dean of the medical school, Dean Willoughby Jones, related to Carstair?

5. What portentous choice does Emily make during a schoolyard game of "truth or consequences"?

6. Who is the author of the flattering notes Emily receives at school?

7. Why did Car Jones leave the seventh grade?

8. What genre of literature did Car Jones write while he was a college student?

9. What was D.K.E.?

10. To whom is Emily married when she tells this story?

Name _____ Date _____

ALICE ADAMS "Truth or Consequences"

VOCABULARY LIST

wisteria

proximity

pandemonium

ambiguous

discomfit

opulence

languidly

partisan

contempt

decorum

Name _____ Date _____

PROCESS ANALYSIS

BARBARA EHRENREICH "Scrubbing in Maine"

READING QUIZ

1. What is the subtitle (or its essence) of Ehrenreich's 2001 book, *Nickled and Dimed*?

2. From what television series does Ehrenreich say she has learned most of what she knows about domestic service?

3. What is the average age of Ehrenreich's fellow employees?

4. What do her fellow employees say they enjoyed eating and drinking over the past weekend?

5. What, according to this essay, can independent housecleaners make per hour, and what are the hourly wages of employees of The Maids?

6. How much does The Maids company charge for its cleaning services?

7. What three cleaning fluids are sprayed on the rags in the housecleaners' aprons, according to procedure outlined on The Maids' training films?

8. What does the inventor of The Maids' special vacuum cleaner announce proudly in the training film after he has strapped on the device?

9. How do the actual Maids get from the office to their work cars and from their cars to the houses they are to clean?

10. In reality, what replaces the thirty-minute lunch break that Ehrenreich has been promised?

Name _____ Date _____

BARBARA EHRENREICH "Scrubbing in Maine"

VOCABULARY LIST

prophetically

egotistical

oafish

decorum

clientele

austere

petulant

cineast

microbes

antagonists

Name _____   Date _____

P. J. O'ROURKE "Third World Driving Hints and Tips"

READING QUIZ

1. What sort of media is *Harry*, for which O'Rourke got his start as a writer?

2. Name two of the legitimate Third World nations where O'Rourke claims to have driven.

3. By what term is the thing that would be considered a road hazard anywhere else in the world known in a Third World country?

4. On which side of the road does O'Rourke say motorists will always be driving in a Third World country?

5. Where does he claim to have seen Christmas tree lights displayed during his foreign driving exploits?

6. What international road sign does O'Rourke say marks dangerous curves in Christian lands?

7. What is an "Egyptian Brake Pedal"?

8. What are the consequences of stopping at a road block in a Third World country?

9. Of what are Third Worlders who will fight to the death over a chicken also "remarkably fond"?

10. What, according to O'Rourke, is the life expectancy of Third World drivers?

Name _____ Date _____

P. J. O'ROURKE "Third World Driving Hints and Tips"

VOCABULARY LIST

gullies

iguana

festive

veritable

coup

insurrection

bogus

antiquities

leghorn

consul

Name _____   Date _____

NIKKI GIOVANNI "Campus Racism 101"

READING QUIZ

1. What is the subject of Giovanni's book *Racism 101?*

2. Where did Giovanni see the statement "TOO BAD IGNORANCE ISN'T PAINFUL"?

3. In which state does Giovanni work as a university professor?

4. To what other institution that also lets participants read books and develop their writing skills does Giovanni compare college?

5. What is Giovanni's first rule for college students to follow?

6. What is Giovanni's attitude toward "extra-curricular" activities?

7. What answer does Giovanni suggest black students give to the question, "What's it like to grow up in a ghetto"?

8. Why does Giovanni believe white students should take African-American studies courses?

9. Who, according to Giovanni, is responsible for making changes in American racist attitudes?

10. How does Giovanni suggest that college students pretend to act?

Name _____   Date _____

NIKKI GIOVANNI "Campus Racism 101"

VOCABULARY LIST

tenured

predominantly

malice

credentials

consistent

syllabus

cultivate

articulation

inquiries

intimidating

Name _____   Date _____

JULIA ALVAREZ "Grounds for Fiction"

READING QUIZ

1. In which country was Alvarez raised?

2. What social phenomena were sparked by the publication of Goethe's *Sorrows of Young Werther*?

3. Of what did Mallarmé tell Degas poems are made?

4. What did Alvarez label the folder in which she stores ideas for future writing projects?

5. What fear does Alvarez report was confessed by an Indiana housewife in *The 1961 Better Homes and Gardens Sewing Book*?

6. According to a newspaper account, what prompted two eleven-year-old girls to "borrow" a car and take a ten-hour drive?

7. Why was Adolfo Gonzales judged to be mentally ill?

8. What, according to Auden, is the correct response to the question "Why do you want to write poetry?"

9. What did the merchant who warned the Mirabel sisters that they would be killed sell to them?

10. Why has Algonquin's lawyer read all of Alvarez's books?

Name _____ Date _____

JULIA ALVAREZ "Grounds for Fiction"

VOCABULARY LIST

luminosity

curiosidades

ophthalmological

cheviot

Scheherazade

litigious

expository

woolgathering

plenary

aspergill

Name _____ Date _____

SERENA NANDA "Arranging a Marriage in India"

READING QUIZ

1. What subject did Nanda teach at John Jay College of Criminal Justice?

2. By what name are Indian marriages which are not arranged called?

3. How did Nanda describe arranged marriage before her first visit to India?

4. How does Sita respond when the narrator suggests that she is missing out on the fun of dating and meeting lots of different people?

5. In addition to studying arranged marriages, what is another of Nanda's intentions upon her second, extended, visit to India?

6. Name one thing that Nanda perceives as an asset that her son's friend has to offer a potential bride.

7. Why doesn't Nanda's friend from her previous trip want to choose a mate for her son from among Nanda's other friend's five very eligible daughters?

8. Why does the boy's mother reject the girl who is "pretty and well educated"?

9. Who finally "finds the match" for Nanda's friend's son?

10. By what name are suspicious deaths among young Indian brides known?

Name _____   Date _____

SERENA NANDA "Arranging a Marriage in India"

VOCABULARY LIST

oppressive

docile

eminently

caste

dowry

deferential

demure

inducement

ambivalence

stigmatized

Name _____ Date _____

ELIZABETH WINTHROP "The Golden Darters"

READING QUIZ

1. Who is the intended audience for Winthrop's books?

2. How old is the narrator of this story?

3. What medical condition has prompted the father to take up his new hobby?

4. In which room of the house has the father established his work station?

5. Why is Emily allowed to watch her father although her brothers are not?

6. Where does the father take his daily naps?

7. What is the "golden darter" designed to imitate?

8. What skill does the father demand that his daughter learn from him?

9. What does Emily allow her friends to convince her to do, in spite of her parents' objections?

10. What unusual fashion accessory does Emily wear to the dance?

Name _____ Date _____

ELIZABETH WINTHROP "The Golden Darters"

VOCABULARY LIST

bodkins

voracious

hackle

proprietary

robust

tippet

barbules

havoc

illicit

mylar

Name _____   Date _____

COMPARISON AND CONTRAST

MARK TWAIN "Two Views of the River"

READING QUIZ

1. With which American president did editor William Dean Howells compare Twain?

2. Which of Twain's several occupations provided him with the expertise revealed in this essay?

3. Presumably, to which river does this essay refer?

4. What time of day does Twain choose for the settings he compares?

5. What floats upon the river?

6. What caused Twain's change in perspective?

7. What qualities are missing from his second description of the scene?

8. What has replaced those?

9. Why does Twain pity doctors?

10. How would Twain probably answer his own question about the doctor—has one "gained or lost most by learning [a] trade"?

Name _____   Date _____

MARK TWAIN "Two Views of the River"

VOCABULARY LIST

acquisition

conspicuous

somber

obstructed

wrought

rapture

reef

shoaling

snag

flush

Name _____   Date _____

SARAH VOWELL "Cowboys v. Mounties"

READING QUIZ

1. To which Internet magazine is Vowell a frequent contributor?

2. In which western states has Vowell lived?

3. Vowell says she got hooked on CBC radio because of dispatches from which region?

4. What do you call a person who is "keen on all things French"?

5. What did comedian Jon Stewart say when asked what Americans *really* think of Canada?

6. Through what means did Canada achieve its independence from Britain?

7. What political boundary was known as "the medicine line"?

8. Which legendary Native American put Canada's Indian laws to the test?

9. Who was James Walsh?

10. To what does Canadian historian Pierre Berton attribute the difference between Canadian and U.S. citizens?

Name _____   Date _____

SARAH VOWELL "Cowboys v. Mounties"

VOCABULARY LIST

swagger

cordially

sovereignty

nonchalantly

inception

anathema

entourage

fetish

lockstep

serge

Name _____ Date _____

PACO UNDERHILL "Shop Like a Man"

READING QUIZ

1. What is the name of Underhill's business that tracks consumers to determine their shopping habits and preferences?

2. What popular dime store chain went out of business, possibly because they failed to take Underhill's advice?

3. What did Underhill's study, designed to allow women to prove they knew the prices for baby products by heart, prove?

4. Are men or women more likely to purchase the clothing they try on in a store?

5. Are men or women more likely to look at price tags while they shop?

6. In which kind of stores do men throw caution to the wind and spend most freely?

7. In which kind of store did 17 percent of male shoppers say they shop more than once per week?

8. What is the prime objection that Underhill can think of to his passive restraint solution for attracting male shoppers with a barber-shop-like atmosphere?

9. What kind of information does Underhill say will make men interested in shopping for furniture?

10. What advice does Underhill offer to drug stores to increase sales?

Name _____ Date _____

PACO UNDERHILL "Shop Like a Man"

VOCABULARY LIST

mundane

virility

profligate

forays

prototype

predominate

crème brulee

seismic

aggregate

zwieback

Name _____   Date _____

ANNE ROIPHE "A Tale of Two Divorces"

READING QUIZ

1. What shirt company was started by Roiphe's grandfather?

2. Name two things Roiphe says frightened her mother as a young woman.

3. Why did Roiphe's father marry her mother?

4. What advice did Roiphe's aunt offer her sister?

5. What one thing did Roiphe's mother do that her daughter describes as "a brave thing."

6. How old was Roiphe at the time of her own divorce?

7. What devastating fact about her husband did Roiphe learn after their child was born?

8. According to Roiphe, on what do Americans wrongly place too much emphasis in choosing a mate?

9. What effect did her parents' divorce have on Roiphe's stepdaughter?

10. Does Roiphe think divorce should be abolished or preserved in the future?

Name _____   Date _____

ANNE ROIPHE "A Tale of Two Divorces"

VOCABULARY LIST

pushcart

statuesque

edgy

confidante

crescendo

masochistic

rends

panacea

asphyxiated

cataclysm

Name _____   Date _____

LAURA BOHANNAN "Shakespeare in the Bush"

READING QUIZ

1. Where has Bohannan traveled on fellowships to conduct anthropological research?

2. Who tells her that Americans often have difficulty reading Shakespeare?

3. Why were there few ceremonies in the homestead Bohannan visited during the rainy season?

4. What seems to be the chief social activity of the tribesmen during the rainy season?

5. Name one sort of paper document with which the tribesmen were familiar.

6. How do the tribesmen explain the presence of Hamlet's father's ghost in Shakespeare's plot?

7. Why should a chief have many wives?

8. According to the tribe Bohannan visited, what two things can make a person mad?

9. What do the tribesmen think the elders of Bohannan's country should have told her?

10. In spite of their differences in interpretations, what does the old man in the hut say that the story of *Hamlet* demonstrates about people?

Name _____   Date _____

LAURA BOHANNAN "Shakespeare in the Bush"

VOCABULARY LIST

hillock

millet

calabash

motif

soliloquy

fratricide

kola

patronage

ardent

unaneled

Name _____   Date _____

WITI IHIMAERA "His First Ball"

READING QUIZ

1. What is Witi Ihimaera's "day job"?

2. What does Tuta's mother think the invitation is when she first sees its envelope?

3. What does Mrs. Simmons, the boss's secretary, assume when she sees the invitation?

4. What is Tuta's job?

5. Who decided to invite Tuta to the ball?

6. Who taught to Tuta to dance?

7. What is Tuta's transportation to the ball?

8. How does the Major Domo pronounce Tuta's name?

9. How do the other guests treat the only Maori at the ball?

10. What does Tuta learn about himself at the ball?

Name _____ Date _____

WITI IHIMAERA "His First Ball"

VOCABULARY LIST

incredulous

cajole

compendium

kai

duly

palpitated

toff

sundry

Maori

langouste

Name _____   Date _____

DIVISION AND CLASSIFICATION

JAMES H. AUSTIN "Four Kinds of Chance"

READING QUIZ

1. What is the subject of Austin's major book?

2. What is the Kettering Principle?

3. According to Louis Pasteur, what kind of person does chance favor?

4. Who discovered penicillin?

5. What had this person discovered before penicillin?

6. Who coined the word *serendipity?*

7. Who said, "We make our fortunes and call them fate"?

8. Who helped Don Marcelino de Sautuola discover the paintings in the cave?

9. Who discovered the cave?

10. What did the discovery of the paintings tell us about our ancestors?

Name _____ Date _____

JAMES H. AUSTIN "Four Kinds of Chance"

VOCABULARY LIST

discernible

fortuitous

nexus

staphylococcal

enzyme

serendipity

sagacity

mirage

circuitously

sentient

Name _____   Date _____

MARY MEBANE "Shades of Black"

READING QUIZ

1. On what subject has Mebane written two volumes?

2. Which of Mebane's college teachers was amazed at her high verbal score on the freshman entrance examination?

3. Which students were held in the highest esteem on the college campus where Mebane attended?

4. Which students did the faculty assume were more intelligent at the primarily black university?

5. What does Mebane wonder about African men?

6. What did "Hazel," a light brown woman, say to Mebane?

7. What amazed teachers about "Ruby"?

8. Why does Mebane think "Rose" was always chosen "best girl scholar" over her?

9. According to Mebane, which group of black males is least interested in black black women?

10. Name one area in which society has traditionally allowed black black women to find self-worth?

Name _____   Date _____

MARY MEBANE "Shades of Black"

VOCABULARY LIST

pinnacle

affirmative

nonplussed

commiserating

stymied

indoctrinated

zealous

nymphomania

religiosity

paradoxically

Name _____   Date _____

PHILIP LOPATE "Modern Friendships"

READING QUIZ

1. What subject did Lopate teach in the New York public schools?

2. Name one famous essayist that Lopate acknowledges has already "taken a crack" at writing about friendships.

3. Where, according to Lopate, do most people attempt to form their first friendships?

4. What romantic notion does Lopate say he finally gave up when he was thirty years old?

5. Name one of the three types of friendship distinguished in *The Nicomachean Ethics.*

6. According to Lopate, what is the most promising indication that friendship is possible during the uncertain early stages of an acquaintanceship?

7. How does Lopate deal with his friend who is habitually late for their meetings?

8. What embarrassed Lopate's "dear old friend" Richard during a conversation?

9. How much time does Lopate think most modern friends spend together at a time?

10. For what reasons does Lopate suspect that his married friends always want him to come to their houses?

Name _____ Date _____

PHILIP LOPATE "Modern Friendships"

VOCABULARY LIST

afflatus

stoic

debacle

dyadic

quintessence

coterie

petulance

epiphany

ebullient

Platonic

Name _____   Date _____

JAMES Q. WILSON "Democracy for All?"

READING QUIZ

1. Name one White House or presidential committee on which Wilson has served.

2. Which century does Wilson say was an era of mass murder?

3. According to Wilson, what social structure was created when agriculture and industry brought people together?

4. What tenet common to most religions has been most successful in fostering and sustaining democracies?

5. In which religion does Wilson say the lack of separation between religious and secular law has helped create authoritarian rule?

6–9. What are the four characteristics that Wilson has identified that are common to successful democracies of the past and present?

10. In the final analysis, and in spite of his careful classification of the characteristics that foster democracy, what does Wilson concede as the probable cause of workable democracy?

Name _____   Date _____

JAMES Q. WILSON "Democracy for All?"

VOCABULARY LIST

regime

salient

dictatorial

genocide

oligarchy

agnostics

conjugal

sundered

cantons

Magna Carta

Name _____ Date _____

GARY WILLS "The Dramaturgy of Death"

READING QUIZ

1. Name two of the former U.S. presidents that Wills has written books about.

2. According to Wills, which great philosopher denied that capital punishment ever arose from a single or consistent theory of its intent or effect?

3. What is the English word for *atimia*, the exclusion of a social offender from rights and legal protection?

4. Where did Plato say criminals should be buried?

5. What common fate was shared by the leaders of the Gowrie Plot in Scotland and Pope Formosus?

6. Why was the burning at the stake of Joan of Arc briefly interrupted?

7. Name one contemporary politician that Wills said has shifted his or her views on capital punishment to gain votes.

8. Why does Wills believe that allowing families of victims to witness executions conflicts with the deterrence defense of the practice of capital punishment?

9. What buzzword does Wills say has been used by everyone from the unmarried mother of Jesse Jackson's child to politicians who support the death penalty to cover base motives?

10. During campaign debates leading to his presidency, who did George W. Bush say is his favorite philosopher?

Name _____ Date _____

GARY WILLS "The Dramaturgy of Death"

VOCABULARY LIST

dramaturgy

coercive

execration

viscera

attic

miasma

empirical

moratoria

atavistic

anodyne

Name _____   Date _____

FLANNERY O'CONNOR "Revelation"

READING QUIZ

1. What occasioned O'Connor's move back to her mother's farm in Georgia?

2. What setting does O'Connor choose to bring together characters of differing backgrounds in one small room?

3. What part of people's anatomy did Ruby always notice "without seeming to" look?

4. Which group ranks highest in Ruby's classification of society?

5. Why does Ruby think American blacks want to move to New York?

6. What does Mary Grace throw at Ruby?

7. What does Mary Grace say to Ruby after the attack?

8. Why doesn't Ruby tell Claud what Mary Grace said?

9. How do the cotton pickers respond to the story of the attack?

10. What does Ruby learn from her vision of souls marching toward heaven?

Name _____   Date _____

FLANNERY O'CONNOR "Revelation"

VOCABULARY LIST

florid

roiling

svelte

tremulous

repudiation

protuberance

solicitous

glowered

paling

hieratic

Name _____   Date _____

DEFINITION

CHRISTOPHER M. PIZZI "Doorways: A Visual Essay"

READING QUIZ

1. In which state has Pizzi spent most of his career as a practicing architect?

2. In which cities are most of the doorways illustrated in this essay located?

3. Name the dictionaries Pizzi cites in the introduction of this essay.

4. Aside from an imposing doorway, what other interior architectural element does Pizzi say often marks and important room?

5. List three of the elements Pizzi lists as being common to most doorways.

6. What part of a doorway does Pizzi call "the site of our bodily engagement with architecture"?

7. Why does Pizzi say organic motifs are often integrated into doorway design?

8. Where, according to Pizzi, do people feel safest?

9. What sort of door does Pizzi find "awkward and disorienting to move through"?

10. Where does Pizzi say the "character, history, and meaning of a place" can be found?

Name _____   Date _____

CHRISTOPHER M. PIZZI "Doorways: A Visual Essay"

VOCABULARY LIST

adjuncts

portal

mediating

facade

motifs

expenditure

promenade

atrium

ingenuity

Carmelite

Name _____   Date _____

JOHN BERENDT "The Hoax"

READING QUIZ

1. In which popular magazine was this essay originally published?

2. At which university was humorist Robert Benchley an undergraduate when he perpetrated a hoax against residents of Beacon Hill?

3. What piece of furniture did Benchley and his friends, posing as repairmen, take from a Beacon Hill home?

4. According to Benchley, from what word is *hoax* derived?

5. Who did David Hampton claim he was in the hoax that inspired John Guare's film *Six Degrees of Separation?*

6. What sort of artistic ability was demonstrated by accused Nazi Hans van Meegeren while under guard in jail?

7. With what famous recluse did "biographer" Clifford Irving claim to have conducted secret interviews for an "authorized" biography?

8. Who made his own replica of the Cardiff giant after the owner of the original refused to sell?

9. Who did millions of Americans believe had landed in New Jersey as a result of Orson Welles's 1938 broadcast of H. G. Wells's *War of the Worlds?*

10. What did the owners of the Beacon Hill sofa send to its recipients a week after the sofa was taken in Benchley's hoax?

Name _____ Date _____

JOHN BERENDT "The Hoax"

VOCABULARY LIST

hoax

ruse

insinuate

czar

ersatz

fraudulent

reclusive

gypsum

comeuppance

forensic

Name _____ Date _____

DIANE ACKERMAN "Pain"

READING QUIZ

1. What is the subject of the book from which this essay was drawn?

2. By what name was the famed "Lawrence of Arabia" commonly known?

3. For what reason have religions encouraged martyrs to experience pain?

4. What pain-defying feat do fakirs perform?

5. Name one of the soccer stars that Ackerman followed during her research on that sport.

6. For what "festive event" were the boys in Istanbul that Ackerman saw dressed in fezzes and silk suits decorated with glitter preparing?

7. What "torture" does Ackerman describe undergoing in a Manhattan beauty salon?

8. What causes expectant fathers in some cultures to take to bed in pain?

9. What medical condition often produces the symptom of pain in the stomach, left arm, or shoulder?

10. What is the title of the essay by Virginia Woolf in which she observes that the English language lacks adequate terminology for describing pain?

Name _____ Date _____

DIANE ACKERMAN "Pain"

VOCABULARY LIST

morphine

martyrs

delirium

fakir

anthropological

hazing

stanchion

fezzes

aberration

histamine

Name _____ Date _____

WILLIAM LANGEWIESCHE "American Ingenuity"

READING QUIZ

1. For which magazine does Langewiesche write?

2. In addition to his hard hat, what clothing does David Griffin generally wear to his job as a demolition contractor?

3. To which tabletop game does Langewiesche compare the dismantling of the World Trade Center ruins?

4. In what sort of business did Griffin's father manage to make a quarter of a billion dollars?

5. How did David Griffin initially gain access to the World Trade Center site?

6. When Griffin went to New York City to volunteer at the disaster site, who did he initially take with him?

7. According to legend, where did Griffin often sleep when he was two years old?

8. Describe the process of "shooting" or "juicing them up" as Langewiesche defines Griffin's terms.

9. In a notorious standoff with a DDC engineer, what is Griffin reputed to have told the official who kept blocking his work because of concerns about safety?

10. When a psychologist tells demolition worker Pablo Lopez to "imagine a safe place," what specific spot does he think she should have suggested?

Name _____ Date _____

WILLIAM LANGEWIESCHE "American Ingenuity"

VOCABULARY LIST

rube

bullion

magnate

respirator

flamboyant

incremental

grapplers

penchant

slurry

anthrax

Name _____   Date _____

STEPHEN HARRIGAN "The Tiger Is God"

READING QUIZ

1. About which football great did Harrigan write a screenplay?

2. What is the most common fatal injury suffered by human tiger-attack victims?

3. To what does Harrigan compare the size of the window through which Tovar was dragged?

4. What subspecies of tiger killed Ricardo Tovar?

5. Where was Miguel, the tiger that killed Tovar, born?

6. What formal training did Tovar have in zoology?

7. Upon which days of the week did the tigers in Tovar's care "fast"?

8. Did the zoo's shooting team fire at the tiger?

9. In about how many seconds does a tiger in the wild usually kill its prey?

10. What slogan was emblazoned upon the imperial banner of Tipu Sultan?

Name _____   Date _____

STEPHEN HARRIGAN "The Tiger Is God"

VOCABULARY LIST

placid

aberrant

ersatz

specter

vestigial

primeval

basso

welter

florid

torpid

Name _____   Date _____

ALICE WALKER "Everyday Use"

READING QUIZ

1. What two social themes are addressed in *The Color Purple* and Walker's other novels?

2. On what celebrity's television show does Mrs. Johnson dream she and her daughters are reunited?

3. What happened to Mrs. Johnson's last house?

4. Who paid for Dee (Wangero's) education in Augusta?

5. What is to be Maggie's future?

6. What is Dee's (Wangero's) reason for changing her name?

7. Who was Dee (Wangero) named for?

8. Who made the dasher for Mrs. Johnson's churn?

9. Why doesn't Dee (Wangero) think Maggie should be given Grandma Dee's quilts?

10. What do Mrs. Johnson and Maggie do after Dee (Wangero) and Hakim-a-barber are gone?

Name _____   Date _____

ALICE WALKER "Everyday Use"

VOCABULARY LIST

inanimate

cunning

turnpike

evolve

plausible

virtually

inherent

conciliatory

barometers

aspire

Name _____   Date _____

CAUSE AND EFFECT

ANDREW C. REVKIN "Some Big Ideas Wash Up One Bulb at a Time"

READING QUIZ

1. Name one subject Revkin is known for covering during his career as a journalist.

2. For which newspaper has he worked since 1995?

3. What kinds of assaults on the planet does Revkin say usually make headlines?

4. Where is Zuqar Island located?

5. Who had discarded the light bulbs that Revkin discovered on Zuqar Island?

6. Why does Revkin say he wanted to become a journalist?

7. What was the source of the gasoline that welled up on a construction site in the San Fernando Valley?

8. What did a Haisla contractor discover while removing a toilet on the Alcan Aluminum property in British Columbia?

9. The loss of what species has endangered Brazil nuts?

10. What final example of slowly accumulating pollution does Revkin give?

Name _____   Date _____

ANDREW C. REVKIN "Some Big Ideas Wash Up One Bulb at a Time"

VOCABULARY LIST

calamity

circumnavigating

lee

terra nullis

windward

incandescent

aquifer

innocuous

denuded

scenario

Name _____   Date _____

DANIEL GOLEMAN "Peak Performance: Why Records Fall"

READING QUIZ

1. For which popular periodical does Goleman serve as an editor?

2. What is the punch line to the old joke, "How do you get to Carnegie Hall"?

3. How does the record of the 1896 Olympic marathon gold medalist compare with qualifying times for the Boston Marathon today?

4. Besides practice, name one other factor Goleman attributes to today's record-breaking performances.

5. What part of memory is best served by practice?

6. How many chunks of information has the average expert in any field learned to recognize?

7. What are many chess masters able to do after staring at a chess game in progress for as little as five seconds?

8. At what average age do most Olympic swimmers and chess champions begin their training?

9. How many years of extensive training does Dr. Herbert Simon estimate it takes to excel at anything?

10. Besides practice, what else do many leading psychologists concede probably plays a role in achieving excellence at any skill?

Name _____   Date _____

DANIEL GOLEMAN "Peak Performance: Why Records Fall"

VOCABULARY LIST

potency

virtuoso

physiology

inexorably

prodigious

cognitive

maxim

capillaries

longitudinal

contentious

Name _____   Date _____

ANNA QUINDLEN "How Reading Changed My Life"

READING QUIZ

1. In addition to journalism, what kind of writing does Quindlen do?

2. What was the subject of stories Quindlen's father liked to tell her dates and then her own children?

3. Where did Quindlen grow up?

4. Name the book in which one of the following mansions is featured: Tara, Manderley, or Thornfield Hall.

5. Name the source of this quotation: "It is a far, far better thing that I do, than I have ever done; it is a far, far better rest that I go to than I have ever known."

6. Where did Quindlen like to sit and read as a child?

7. Name one of the famous women whom Quindlen was delighted to discover was also a childhood bookworm.

8. What question does Quindlen say philosophy and English majors were constantly asked when she was in college?

9. Quindlen quotes *Publisher's Weekly* lamenting that movies have replaced other leisure time activities. In which decade was the sentence she quotes written?

10. In what popular adolescent novel does the heroine proclaim, "Until I feared I would lose it, I never loved to read. One does not love breathing"?

Name _____   Date _____

ANNA QUINDLEN "How Reading Changed My Life"

VOCABULARY LIST

rhododendron

corollary

raucous

eponymous

undersung

hubris

solace

exclusivity

literati

hoi polloi

Name _____   Date _____

MALCOLM GLADWELL "Examined Life"

READING QUIZ

1. What is the subject of Gladwell's international best-seller, *Tipping Point*?

2. How did the young Stanley Kaplan respond to classmates who were having trouble with schoolwork?

3. Why was Kaplan initially given a "C" in his biology class at City College?

4. Where did Kaplan open the first Stanley H. Kaplan Educational Center?

5. How old was the SAT exam at the time Gladwell wrote this essay?

6. According to a University of California study, what is the most reliable predictor of a student's freshman grades in college?

7. What, according to the Educational Testing Service, does the SAT measure?

8. By how many points does Kaplan say his tutoring can boost a student's SAT scores?

9. Describe the "parlor game" invented by critics of the SAT reading comprehension section.

10. What does Gladwell describe as "one of the highlights of Kaplan's life"?

Name _____   Date _____

MALCOLM GLADWELL "Examined Life"

VOCABULARY LIST

studious

holistic

variance

pariah

psychometrics

nefarious

ideology

Pythagorean

isosceles

meritocracy

Name _____   Date _____

ERIC SCHLOSSER "Why McDonald's Fries Taste So Good"

READING QUIZ

1. What is the subject of the book Schlosser is currently working on?

2. What percentage of the oil McDonald's cooked French fries in until 1990 was composed of beef tallow?

3. How much of the money Americans currently spend on food goes toward purchasing processed foods?

4. Name one of the flavor manufacturers situated along the New Jersey Turnpike whose name Schlosser exposes in this essay.

5. To what fanciful location does Schlosser liken the flavor factory he visits while researching this essay?

6. In addition to flavors, for what kinds of products do most flavor factories also manufacture scents?

7. What does the olfactory epithelium do?

8. Of the approximately ten thousand new processed-food products introduced in the United States every year, about how many of those fail?

9. What warning does Schlosser give his readers about the ingredient "natural flavoring"?

10. In what aspect of eating is the science of rheology brought to bear?

Name _____   Date _____

ERIC SCHLOSSER "Why McDonald's Fries Taste So Good"

VOCABULARY LIST

sacrosanct

innocuous

palatable

confectionary

volatile

astringent

olfactory

rancid

emulsifiers

tallow

brasserie

Name _____   Date _____

ANN BEATTIE "Janus"

READING QUIZ

1. In which fiction genres does Beattie write?

2. Who is Mondo?

3. What color is the bowl?

4. What does the realtor ask her husband to refrain from putting in the bowl?

5. What powers does the realtor believe the bowl possesses?

6. What is the profession of the realtor's husband?

7. Where did she once forget the bowl?

8. What did she dream of that startled her?

9. Who gave the bowl to the realtor?

10. Why did the lover leave in the end of the story?

Name _____   Date _____

ANN BEATTIE "Janus"

VOCABULARY LIST

vaporizing

paradox

Biedermeier

ostentatious

aesthetic

intractable

unrequited

scenario

dovetailed

intransigent

Name _____ Date _____

PERSUASION AND ARGUMENT

MARTIN LUTHER KING JR. "I Have a Dream"

READING QUIZ

1. What was King's profession?

2. At which famous site did King deliver this speech?

3. What occasion was commemorated by the 1963 "March on Washington"?

4. To which famous address does King allude with his opening reference to history and time?

5. What "unalienable rights" are guaranteed to every American by the Constitution and the Declaration of Independence?

6. What does King say to those who think the march will mark the end of a movement that needed to "blow off steam"?

7. What particular sort of protest does King caution his followers against using?

8. What have "the veterans of creative suffering" endured?

9. Name one state that King specifically sees "transformed" in his dream.

10. With what phrase from an "old Negro spiritual" does King leave his audience?

Name _____   Date _____

MARTIN LUTHER KING JR. "I Have a Dream"

VOCABULARY LIST

languishing

manacles

inextricably

ghetto

tribulations

hallowed

redemptive

momentous

prodigious

desolate

Name _____   Date _____

ERIC LIU "A Chinaman's Chance: Reflections on the American Dream"

READING QUIZ

1. For which U.S. president did Liu work as a speech writer?

2. According to the poet Robert Browning, what must "exceed a man's grasp"?

3. Which of Liu's ancestors emigrated to the United States?

4. What kind of person is a "banana" according to Liu's sister?

5. What race does Liu's sister believe she is "at heart"?

6. What is Liu's response to T-shirts that say "It's a black/Asian/Latino/white thing. You wouldn't understand"?

7. To what other great American myth does Liu compare the "American Dream" in this essay?

8. Under which branch of the military did Liu volunteer for Officer Candidates' School?

9. How did the fate of author Fae Myenne Ng's parents differ significantly from Liu's parents?

10. What did the young Liu think his father meant when he said that a doomed party didn't have a "'Chinaman's Chance'"?

Name _____   Date _____

ERIC LIU "A Chinaman's Chance: Reflections on the American Dream"

VOCABULARY LIST

demographic

barrios

intractable

petulantly

palpable

fealty

idiomatically

moniker

obviate

inchoate

Name _____ Date _____

BARBARA KINGSOLVER "Stone Soup"

READING QUIZ

1. For what genre of writing is Kingsolver best known?

2. What is the "family fortune" of Andy, the soccer player described in this essay's opening paragraph?

3. Name the members of Kingsolver's childhood "Family of Dolls."

4. Name one of the family types that Kingsolver says are judged by society to be failures.

5. Why does Kingsolver object to the phrase "irreconcilable differences"?

6. What, according to Kingsolver, is the least helpful question to ask someone following a divorce?

7. When is the only time that Kingsolver's daughter is uncomfortable about her parents' divorce?

8. For how long was the average Colonial couple married?

9. How does the current rate at which teenage girls have babies compare with that of 1957?

10. What is "stone soup"?

Name _____   Date _____

BARBARA KINGSOLVER "Stone Soup"

VOCABULARY LIST

harbinger

imperious

caprice

specious

raucous

gangrenous

rogue

venerates

servility

amorphous

Name _____   Date _____

BARBARA DAFOE WHITEHEAD "Women and the Future of Fatherhood"

READING QUIZ

1. What is the title of one of Whitehead's more provocative and controversial articles?

2. According to Whitehead, what was missing from the Million Man March or Promise Keepers meetings?

3. According to Whitehead, who has dominated the debate about marriage and parenthood for the past thirty years?

4. What does Whitehead say men need in order to be good fathers?

5. As divorce rates remain at a historic high, the rate of what related phenomena are declining disproportionately, according to this essay?

6. In 1994, how did men and women respond to the national survey question "Do you agree or disagree: one parent can bring up a child as well as two parents together"?

7. What is the emblem by which absentee fathers are known in popular culture today?

8. What did poet and polemicist Katha Pollitt say represents the prevailing sentiment of contemporary women about marriage and motherhood?

9. What percentage of domestic chores does Whitehead recommend that men perform in a household?

10. What does Whitehead say a good mother cannot do?

Name _____   Date _____

BARBARA DAFOE WHITEHEAD "Women and the Future of Fatherhood"

VOCABULARY LIST

unfettered

emblematic

stigmatize

unassailable

mordantly

proviso

androgynous

suffuses

sovereign

altruism

Name _____   Date _____

JOAN ACOCELLA "Under the Spell"

READING QUIZ

1. As a critic of which visual art form did Acocella begin her writing career?

2. Specifically, what book is Acocella reviewing in this essay?

3. At what time of day was the book released to reviewers and the public alike?

4. What distinctive mark does Harry Potter bear on his forehead?

5. What fairy-tale ending does Acocella think J. K. Rowling will avoid in the last volume of her Harry Potter series?

6. Who does Sirius Black, who has been stalking Harry, turn out to be?

7. To which English boarding school did reviewer Pico Iyer compare Hogwarts school?

8. What does the Mirror of Erised show?

9. When, according to J. K. Rowling, did she first conceive of Harry and his adventures?

10. Name one of Rowling's favorite authors according to Acocella.

Name _____   Date _____

JOAN ACOCELLA "Under the Spell"

VOCABULARY LIST

bildungsroman

purloined

archetypes

denouements

ostracism

basilisks

avatar

rapacious

mendacity

pantheon

Name _____   Date _____

HAROLD BLOOM "Can 35 Million Book Buyers Be Wrong? Yes."

READING QUIZ

1. What subject did Bloom teach at Yale, Cornell, Harvard, and NYU?

2. In which American newspaper did this essay originally appear?

3. Which American newspaper does Bloom call "The official newspaper of our dominant counter-culture"?

4. Which of the Harry Potter books does Bloom say is "purportedly the best of the lot"?

5. In which century was Thomas Hughes realistic novel about the Rugby School published?

6. Name one book that Bloom says is superior children's fare, compared with the Harry Potter stories.

7. To what other well-known series does Bloom compare the Harry Potter books?

8. What, according to Bloom, are the social classes in England as defined in the Harry Potter books?

9. Who does Bloom say is given the same importance in popular culture as rock stars, movie idols, TV anchors, and successful politicians as a result of the Harry Potter craze?

10. Where does Bloom predict the Harry Potter books will be read next?

Name _____   Date _____

HAROLD BLOOM "Can 35 Million Book Buyers Be Wrong? Yes."

VOCABULARY LIST

emulate

epiphenomenon

wane

mundane

consign

sadistic

grotesque

aesthetic

emancipated

beguile

Name _____   Date _____

FRANCINE PROSE "Genocide Without Apology"

READING QUIZ

1. What is the subject of Prose's novel *Judah the Pious*?

2. What is the name of the ritual meal at which Jews celebrate the Passover?

3. What artwork does Prose recall from the Haggadah?

4. How do Moses and his brother Aaron get the attention of their audience in the book of Exodus?

5. Name three of the ten plagues.

6. Which famous film director does Prose say shared her enthusiasm for the drama inherent in the Exodus story?

7. What, according to Prose, results when one population begins to worry excessively about the birthrate of another?

8. According to rabbinical commentary on the book of Exodus, what does the Pharaoh believe might cure his leprosy?

9. Name two cultural groups that Prose says have been the historical target of genocide.

10. What act, according to Prose, is "older than the Bible"?

Name _____   Date _____

FRANCINE PROSE "Genocide Without Apology"

VOCABULARY LIST

seder

vermin

mayhem

ominous

rabbinical

Dalai Lama

diplomacy

genocide

meticulous

exigencies

Name _____   Date _____

NATALIE ANGIER "Of Altruism, Heroism, and Evolution's Gifts"

READING QUIZ

1. What topic did Angier cover for *The New York Times* when she won a Pulitzer Prize?

2. What was the total weight of life-saving gear carried by each firefighter who rushed up the stairs of the World Trade Centers following the 9/11 attacks?

3. To what did politicians ascribe the altruism and heroism exhibited by victims and bystanders of the 9/11 tragedy?

4. According to Dr. Barbara Smuts, a professor of anthropology at the University of Michigan, what do many species recognize as the best way to compete?

5. What enables humans uniquely to empathize with and emulate people they've never met?

6. What, according to Dr. Craig Packer, a professor of ecology and evolution at the University of Minnesota, is the fundamental element of civilization?

7. To what group are worker bees more closely related to genetically than their parents?

8. How do chimpanzee hunters kill red colobus monkeys?

9. Why do baboons and impalas associate together?

10. What group does Dr. James J. Moore of the University of California at San Diego call "the nicest species I know"?

Name _____   Date _____

NATALIE ANGIER "Of Altruism, Heroism, and Evolution's Gifts"

VOCABULARY LIST

harrowed

altruism

indomitable

malign

ostracize

amalgamation

nepotistic

herbivores

symbiotic

amity

Name _____   Date _____

KURT VONNEGUT JR. "Harrison Bergeron"

READING QUIZ

1. Of which wartime atrocity is Vonnegut a survivor?

2. In what year was this story originally published?

3. In what year is the story set?

4. How old is Harrison Bergeron?

5. Which handicaps have been assigned to George Bergeron by the Handicapper General?

6. What are the Bergerons watching on television before the show is interrupted?

7. What disability do all television announcers have in the society described in the story?

8. How much scrap metal is attached to Harrison Bergeron?

9. Besides governmental law, what natural law do Harrison and his Empress defy?

10. How are Harrison and his Empress killed?

Name _____   Date _____

KURT VONNEGUT JR. "Harrison Bergeron"

VOCABULARY LIST

vigilance

sash weights

birdshot

impediment

luminous

grackle

calibrated

hindrances

consternation

synchronizing

Name _____   Date _____

RESOURCES FOR WRITING: THE DISCOVERIES—A CASEBOOK

ANDREW SULLIVAN "Virtually Normal"

READING QUIZ

1. In which country was Sullivan born and raised?

2. What question asked by a girl from school first caused Sullivan to wonder if he might be homosexual?

3. How old was Sullivan when he first felt a vague attraction to his male second cousin?

4. What role models or references to the subject did Sullivan find at home, school, in televison, newspapers, or the books to which he had access as a boy?

5. What profession did Sullivan resolve to pursue after seeing a bare-chested man on televison when he was seven or eight years old?

6. What medical condition caused Sullivan's father to try to calm him down in the middle of the night sometimes?

7. To what experience does Sullivan liken taking off on a plane and then realizing he didn't want to go to its destination?

8. What, according to Sullivan, do gay adolescents have that every heterosexual teenager longs for?

9. Why does Sullivan believe that no political, social, or even cultural revolution will make the experience of gay and straight people equal?

10. What simple answer did Sullivan give when asked by a conservative think tank why he believes that homosexuality is an orientation rather than a choice?

Name _____   Date _____

ANDREW SULLIVAN "Virtually Normal"

VOCABULARY LIST

nascent

inchoate

simulacrum

empirical

subterranean

burgeoning

ambiguity

subjugation

hypothalamus

chimera

Name _____   Date _____

COLIN EVANS "The Kelly Gang"

READING QUIZ

1. Name one of the jobs, besides writer, that Colin Evans has held.

2. During which year did the Urschel kidnapping take place?

3. What card game were the Urschels and Jarretts playing when the gunmen arrived?

4. How had Charles Urschel made his millions?

5. How many days passed between the kidnapping and when the ransom note appeared at the Urschel residence?

6. Why was the Urschel family instructed to place a specifically-worded real estate ad in the *Daily Oklahoman*?

7. To test your own powers of observation, describe the man who takes the ransom money from E. E. Kirkpatrick in a Kansas City hotel.

8. What does Urschel notice about the water he is served at the house where he is held captive?

9. What phenomenon does Urschel observe all but one late morning and early evening of the days he is held captive?

10. What does Urschel leave behind in the house where he is held to aid the FBI in identifying his captors?

Name _____   Date _____

COLIN EVANS "The Kelly Gang"

VOCABULARY LIST

grip

unparalleled

idly

windlass

lair

meteorological

hoodlum

mythomania

hapless

astute

Name _____   Date _____

DAVA SOBEL "Imaginary Lines"

READING QUIZ

1. On what subject did Sobel report for The Discovery Channel?

2. What toy does Sobel remember receiving as a gift from her father when she begins reporting her research on latitude and longitude?

3. Where is the famous sculpture of Atlas that Sobel describes admiring with her father located?

4. Which lines remain parallel—latitude or longitude?

5. How early did man begin to conceive of the world as divided by lines of latitude and longitude?

6. Of all of the lines of latitude and longitude, which is not arbitrarily chosen?

7. Through which major world city does the prime meridian now run?

8. In which two places did early navigators need to know the current time in order to calculate their movement between longitudes?

9. What was the profession of John Harrison, winner of the British Parliament's Longitude Act Prize?

10. How much time passed between the announcement of the Longitude Act and its prize and its eventually being awarded to Harrison?

Name _____   Date _____

DAVA SOBEL "Imaginary Lines"

VOCABULARY LIST

orb

girdle

concentric

cartographer

dilemma

barometric

palatial

impervious

parried

intrigue

Name _____　　Date _____

LEWIS THOMAS "The Technology of Medicine"

READING QUIZ

1. With what sort of medical research does the agency Thomas heads concern itself?

2. Why does nontechnology require the skill of the very best doctors?

3. What characterizes the diseases that doctors currently treat with nontechnology?

4. What example of halfway technology is used to respond to glomerulonephritis?

5. Which kind of technology is most expensive?

6. Which kind of technology attracts the least public attention?

7. Which kind of technology costs the least?

8. What might it cost today to manage a case of typhoid fever by the best methods of 1935?

9. What is the only thing that can advance medical technology?

10. Why does Thomas say it no longer means anything to "ask for the moon"?

Name _____   Date _____

LEWIS THOMAS "The Technology of Medicine"

VOCABULARY LIST

lethal

intractable

coronary

rheumatoid

chronic

catastrophe

therapeutic

fomentations

prudence

priority

Name _____ Date _____

WITOLD RYBCZYNSKI "One Good Turn"

READING QUIZ

1. In which country was Rybczynski born?

2. In which academic field was he educated?

3. What did Rybczynski and his wife build, using only hand tools?

4. What is the English name of the tool the ancient Romans called a *plana*?

5. Which of Rybczynski's tools would have confused a medieval carpenter?

6. Name one task for which the first screws were used.

7. Who invented the handheld screwdriver?

8. What sort of products contained small screws before 1800?

9. Name one thing Rybczynski lists that is attached with screws in the modern home.

10. What is ironic about the lathes that made the first precision screws?

Name _____ Date _____

WITOLD RYBCZYNSKI "One Good Turn"

VOCABULARY LIST

conscripted

neophytes

brace and bit

painstakingly

quintessentially

gimlet

aristocrat

lathes

sextants

theodolites

Name _____   Date _____

JOHN FLEISCHMAN "Homer's Bones"

READING QUIZ

1. Who is the audience for Fleischman's award-winning books?

2. Whose photograph did archaeologist Sharon Stocker find atop some ancient Greek remnants in the basement of the archaeological museum in Hora?

3. In what year did Carl Blegen begin his fortuitous dig in a Grecian olive grove?

4. What did scholars learn from the number of Linear B tablets that Blegen discovered?

5. According to Homeric legend, what was King Nestor doing when Telemachus first saw him?

6. Which ancient Greek city did German scholar Heinrich Schliemann search for in western Turkey?

7. How much time passed between the events narrated in the *Iliad* and the *Odyssey* and when Homer wrote about them?

8. In which Greek city did King Nestor live?

9. When the bones Blegen found were assembled, to which animals did scientists believe they belonged?

10. What is a *kylix*?

Name _____   Date _____

JOHN FLEISCHMAN "Homer's Bones"

VOCABULARY LIST

detritus

incised

bard

Phoenician

vassal

femurs

nonplussed

citadel

assuaged

chaparral

Name _____   Date _____

RICHARD DOERFLINGER "First Principles and the 'Frist Principles'"

READING QUIZ

1. With which Christian religion is Doerflinger professionally associated?

2. Where did the hearing that Doerflinger is reporting on take place?

3. Besides senator, what is Bill Frist's other job?

4. What potential scientific research did Frist say has "huge potential"?

5. What signifies for Doerflinger that Frist has lost his respect for human life?

6. Name one of Frist's principles that Doerflinger says pro-life Americans can and do support.

7. Which embryos did Frist approve for use in stem cell research?

8. Besides Frist, which two other U.S. senators are targets for Doerflinger's criticism?

9. Which U.S. president does Doerflinger deride?

10. According to Doerflinger, what is the only reasonable approach to embryonic stem cell research?

Name _____   Date _____

RICHARD DOERFLINGER "First Principles and the 'Frist Principles'"

VOCABULARY LIST

implications

embryos

hypocrisy

bioethics

contingent

denounced

valid

NIH

grotesque

ideologues

Name _____   Date _____

PEGGY PRICHARD ROSS "Stem Cell Research: It's About Life and Death, Not Politics"

READING QUIZ

1. For what sort of business did Ross work as a director of communications?

2. At the time of her writing about how long did doctors believe Ross would live?

3. What is astrocytoma?

4. Which of George W. Bush's presidential speeches does Ross say she watched from a hospital bed?

5. What did President Bush ask Congress to ban during that speech?

6. What is "somatic cell nuclear transfer" popularly called?

7. Upon what does Ross say the arguments against stem cell research are based?

8. How does George W. Bush describe himself politically?

9. How many Americans per year get the same type of disease that Ross has?

10. What causes people to get that disease?

Name _____   Date _____

PEGGY PRICHARD ROSS "Stem Cell Research: It's About Life and Death, Not Politics"

VOCABULARY LIST

astrocytoma

cloning

therapeutic

mutant

somatic

sectarian

compassionate

Muslim

bipartisan

Name _____   Date _____

ARTHUR C. CLARKE "The Star"

READING QUIZ

1. What did Clarke build when he was thirteen years old?

2. How far is the spaceship from Earth at the story's beginning?

3. To which religious order does the narrator belong?

4. Who is the founder of that order?

5. What did Chinese astronomers witness in A.D. 1045 which reoccurred five centuries later in Cassiopeia?

6. What is a White Dwarf?

7. What did the spaceship's crew find on the small planet it discovered?

8. What had the inhabitants of that planet known?

9. What had the inhabitants of that planet looked like?

10. What "ancient mystery is solved at last" by the narrator's calculations?

Name _____ Date _____

ARTHUR C. CLARKE "The Star"

VOCABULARY LIST

incongruity

tenuous

novae

concentric

eddies

prodigal

monolithic

obliterate

blasphemy

conflagration

Answer Key for Reading Quizzes

Narration and Description Quiz Answers

Andre Dubus, "Digging"

1. He lost his leg as the result of an automobile accident.
2. sixteen years old
3. Marine captain
4. He would not fight back or inform on them, and he would pretend he was not hurt.
5. They were fake.
6. black men
7. digging the foundation for a liquor-store building
8. He vomited, then slept under a tree.
9. a sandwich and a pith helmet
10. His father did it.

Jill McCorkle, "The Mullet Girls"

1. North Carolina
2. Hurricane Hazel in 1954
3. "the ace of spades"
4. "the Bathing Beauties" or "the Beach Walkers"
5. the fish's wife
6. *The Sound of Music*
7. at the post office
8. two cans of beer
9. old, coarse, rough, worn-out, wrinkled, and smelled fishy
10. Thank you very much but no thanks.

Judith Ortiz Cofer, "The Myth of the Latin Woman"

1. Puerto Rico
2. *West Side Story*
3. to study at Oxford University
4. They thought they were "too mature."
5. Career Day
6. as "Hot Tamales" or sexual firebrands
7. custom
8. the Spanish/Catholic system of morality
9. erotically charged street poems composed on the spot
10. a cup of coffee because she thought the narrator was a waitress

Helen Prejean, "Memories of a Dean Man Walking"

1. English
2. three years
3. praying for a death row inmate's strength
4. Louisiana
5. a black, inner-city housing project in New Orleans where Prejean lived with four other nuns
6. 1950s
7. singing and playing the guitar with prisoners
8. She did not visit the victim's families.
9. He spoke "words of love" to Sister Helen.
10. Sean Penn

George Orwell, "Shooting an Elephant"

1. serve with Indian imperial police in Burma
2. subdivisional police officer in Moulmein, Burma
3. He was against it; called it an "evil thing."
4. an elephant rifle
5. meat
6. eating grass
7. two thousand
8. ear hole
9. five
10. one half hour

Alice Adams, "Truth or Consequences"

1. forty years old
2. a famous former movie star
3. American Middle-South
4. distant cousin
5. She says she would choose to kiss Car Jones.
6. Car Jones
7. He was tested and promoted to high school at his own request.
8. a play
9. a fraternity
10. a surgeon

Process Analysis Quiz Answers

Barbara Ehrenreich, "Scrubbing in Maine"

1. *On (Not) Getting By in America*
2. *Upstairs, Downstairs*
3. late twenties
4. pizza and Jell-O shots
5. $15 per hour
6. $25 per person-hour

7. Windex, disinfectant, wood polish
8. "See, I am the vacuum cleaner."
9. They run.
10. a five-minute pit stop at a convenience store

P. J. O'Rourke, "Third World Driving Hints and Tips"

1. an underground newspaper
2. Choose two: Mexico, Lebanon, the Philippines, Cyprus, El Salvador, Africa
3. the road
4. your side
5. around the bumper on a car
6. white memorial crosses
7. a car horn
8. having your luggage stolen or being shot
9. their children
10. forty-five minutes

Nikki Giovanni, "Campus Racism 101"

1. It tells black students how to succeed at predominantly white colleges.
2. on a bumper sticker
3. Virginia
4. prison
5. Go to class.
6. She thinks students should participate to let their presence be known.
7. "I don't know."
8. because black students must take white-studies courses, although they aren't called that
9. both whites and blacks
10. grown-up

Julia Alvarez, "Grounds for Fiction"

1. Dominican Republic
2. suicide and dressing in blue frock coats and yellow waistcoats
3. words
4. *curiosidades*
5. She was afraid to cut the fabric.
6. They wanted to see their newborn niece.
7. No one could understand his native Indian dialect.
8. "I like hanging around words listening to what they say."
9. pocketbooks
10. to make sure nothing in them is libelous

Serena Nanda, "Arranging a Marriage in India"

1. anthropology
2. "love match"
3. oppressive

4. She says that it does not sound like fun at all because American girls spend too much time worrying about whether they will meet a man and get married.
5. She wants to help arrange a marriage.
6. One: military career, joined father's business, college graduate, modern, well traveled, handsome
7. Too many daughters makes a big wedding unlikely, and/or their oldest married daughter wants to visit her parents' home too much, meaning that her mother may be prohibiting her from adjusting to her new home.
8. She is "too educated"; she behaves independently.
9. Nanda
10. "dowry death"

Elizabeth Winthrop, "The Golden Darters"

1. children
2. twelve years old
3. He is recovering from upper back surgery.
4. living room
5. She does not "bounce" as her brothers do.
6. in the grass on the front lawn
7. a small fish as it moves underwater
8. fly tying
9. pierce her ears
10. golden darter flies as earrings

Comparison and Contrast Quiz Answers

Mark Twain, "Two Views of the River"

1. Lincoln
2. riverboat pilot
3. Mississippi
4. sunset
5. a solitary log
6. education, experience as a riverboat pilot
7. romance and beauty
8. a sense of danger
9. The doctor no longer sees beauty.
10. yes and no

Sarah Vowell, "Cowboys v. Mounties"

1. Salon.com
2. Oklahoma and Montana
3. Maritimes
4. Francophile
5. "We don't."
6. polite meetings taking place in nice rooms
7. the border between the United States and Canada

   8. Sitting Bull
   9. a friend of Sitting Bull or Vowell's favorite Mountie
  10. the weather

Paco Underhill, "Shop Like a Man"

   1. Envirosell
   2. Woolworth's
   3. They were mostly wrong.
   4. men
   5. women
   6. supermarkets
   7. computer stores
   8. Other customers don't want to see guys slumped in chairs watching TV.
   9. emphasizing the construction of the furniture and showing that it is well made
  10. create a men's health department

Anne Roiphe, "A Tale of Two Divorces"

   1. Van Heusen Shirts
   2. Two: horses, dogs, cats, cars, water, balls that were hit over nets, tunnels, bridges
   3. for money
   4. "Don't give him an argument."
   5. She went to a psychiatrist.
   6. twenty-seven years old
   7. She had married a man more or less like her father.
   8. romance
   9. She was damaged by it.
  10. preserved

Laura Bohannan, "Shakespeare in the Bush"

   1. East Africa
   2. an English poet
   3. Most of the ceremonies demanded the presence of elders from several homesteads who could not visit while the swamps were wet.
   4. drinking beer
   5. One: tax receipts, bride price receipts, court fee receipts, letters
   6. an omen sent by a witch
   7. to hoe and to prepare beer and food for visitors without the chief's having to collect taxes
   8. witchcraft and seeing the beings that lurk in the forest
   9. the "real" meaning of the story of Hamlet
  10. "People are the same everywhere."

Witi Ihimaera, "His First Ball"

   1. diplomatic officer in New Zealand's Ministry of Foreign Affairs
   2. a court summons
   3. It is a mistake. She accuses Tuta of picking it up on the street and putting his name on it.

4. He packs batteries in a factory.
5. The wife of the Governor-General
6. Drag queens: Desirée Dawn, Alexis Dynamite, Chantelle Derrier
7. a Jaguar festooned for a wedding
8. "Tutae," a rude word
9. as if he is the entertainment
10. that he doesn't want to join the upper classes and that he can best represent his people by acting like himself

Division and Classification Quiz Answers

James H. Austin, "Four Kinds of Chance"

1. how "chance and creativity interact in biomedical research"
2. It urges one not to give up, to keep going because something will turn up.
3. the person who has a prepared mind
4. Alexander Fleming
5. lysozyme
6. Horace Walpole
7. Benjamin Disraeli
8. his daughter, Maria
9. a hunting dog
10. The cavemen were highly creative artists with sentient minds and well-developed aesthetic sensibilities.

Mary Mebane, "Shades of Black"

1. herself, autobiography
2. a light-skinned English instructor who was the wife of the department chairperson
3. children of doctors, lawyers, and college teachers
4. those with light skin tones
5. when they stopped showing interest in black black women
6. "You are *dark,* but not *too* dark."
7. She was dark skinned but could outsing, outdance, outdeclaim everyone else.
8. She was light skinned.
9. college-educated males born before 1945
10. choose one: sex, religion, or career

Philip Lopate, "Modern Friendships"

1. creative writing
2. One: Aristotle, Cicero, Seneca, Montaigne, Bacon, Johnson, Hazlitt, Emerson, or Lamb
3. within their families
4. the idea of having one "Best Friend"
5. One: based on utility, based on pleasure, or "perfect friendship" (based on admiration of another's good character)
6. good conversation
7. He brings a book along to read until she arrives.
8. confessional talk about despair and suicide

9. at most, six hours
10. because as a bachelor he might like to partake in the family nurturing, and they can "kill two birds with one stone," visiting with their family and friend at the same time

James Q. Wilson, "Democracy for All?"

1. Choose one: White House Task Force on Crime, President's Foreign Intelligence Board, President's Council on Bioethics
2. twentieth
3. cities
4. The Golden Rule
5. Islam
6–9. geographic isolation, individual property ownership rights, cultural homogeneity, and traditions that enforce democratic behaviors
10. It is a happy accident.

Gary Wills, "The Dramaturgy of Death"

1. Choose two: Richard Nixon, Thomas Jefferson, Ronald Reagan, Abraham Lincoln, James Madison
2. Nietzche
3. "outlawing"
4. He said they should be denied burial, their bodies cast beyond the land's outer limits.
5. They were symbolically executed after they were dead.
6. The flames were raked away to expose her woman's body and show that no demon had spirited her away.
7. Choose one: Dianne Feinstein, Andrew Young, Hillary Clinton
8. They are not particularly likely to commit violent crimes.
9. "Closure"
10. Jesus

Flannery O'Connor, "Revelation"

1. She discovered that she had contracted the systematic disease that killed her father and, eventually, herself.
2. doctor's waiting room
3. their feet
4. those who own their homes and land
5. to marry whites and "improve their color"
6. her *Human Development* text book
7. "Go back to hell where you came from, you old wart hog."
8. She doesn't want to put that image of herself in his mind.
9. They flatter Ruby.
10. that souls are equal

Definition Quiz Answers

Christopher M. Pizzi, "Doorways: A Visual Essay"

1. New York
2. Washington, D.C. and Jerusalem
3. *Webster's Dictionary* and the *Oxford English Dictionary*
4. a major stairway
5. Choose one: handle or knob, letter slot, peephole, lock, knocker, or doorbell
6. the doorhandle
7. to remind us that we are making the transition from nature to shelter
8. indoors
9. revolving doors
10. doorways

John Berendt, "The Hoax"

1. *Esquire*
2. Harvard
3. a sofa
4. *hocus-pocus*
5. Sidney Poitier's son
6. He painted a fake Vermeer.
7. Howard Hughes
8. P. T. Barnum
9. martians
10. the sofa's slipcovers

Diane Ackerman, "Pain"

1. *A Natural History of the Senses*
2. T. E. Lawrence
3. to purify the spirit
4. They run across hot coals.
5. Choose one: Pele or Franz Beckenbauer
6. circumcision
7. having her legs waxed
8. false pregnancy
9. heart attack
10. "On Being Ill"

William Langewiesche, "American Ingenuity"

1. *The Atlantic Monthly*
2. immaculate golfing clothes
3. Jenga
4. demolition and salvage business
5. He sneaked past National Guardsmen.
6. his wife and children

7. in concrete culverts on his father's job sites
8. "shooting": blasting at the base of ruins to bring them down, "juicing them up": pre-cutting the internal structure of ruined buildings
9. "We're not going to *talk* it down. We gotta do *something*."
10. a steak house

Steven Harrigan, "The Tiger Is God"

1. O. J. Simpson
2. broken neck
3. an average television screen
4. Siberian
5. in captivity at the Houston zoo
6. none
7. Thursdays and Sundays
8. no
9. thirty-five to ninety
10. "The tiger is God."

Alice Walker, "Everyday Use"

1. sexism and racism
2. Johnny Carson
3. Fire burned it to the ground.
4. her mother and the church
5. She will marry John Thomas.
6. She didn't want to be named after a white person.
7. her aunt Dicie
8. Aunt Dee's first husband—Uncle Henry or Stash
9. She'd use them.
10. They sit in the yard, dip snuff, just "enjoy."

Cause and Effect Quiz Answers

Andrew C. Revkin, "Some Big Ideas Wash Up One Bulb at a Time"

1. One: murder in the Amazon, the crash of TWA Flight 800, the plight of the working poor in America, the persistent pollution of the Hudson River
2. *The New York Times*
3. sudden calamities
4. in the south end of the Red Sea
5. lots of people from incessantly passing container and cargo ships
6. He wanted to write about the effects of humans on the environment.
7. a leaking rusted storage tank buried a few hundred yards away
8. about half a pint of mercury
9. bees
10. greenhouse gases that result in global warning

Daniel Goleman, "Peak Performance: Why Records Fall"

1. *Psychology Today*
2. "Practice, practice, practice."
3. It would barely qualify.
4. coaching methods, sophisticated equipment, or the larger pool of competitors
5. short-term
6. approximately fifty thousand
7. replicate the board
8. seven
9. ten years
10. innate talent or desire

Anna Quindlen, "How Reading Changed My Life"

1. She writes novels.
2. stories about Quindlen running away from home as a child
3. in a suburb outside of Philadelphia, Pennsylvania
4. Choose one: *Gone with the Wind, Rebecca, Jane Eyre*
5. *A Tale of Two Cities*
6. a club chair in the corner of her parents' living room
7. Choose one: Jamaica Kincaid, Hazel Tochman, Oprah Winfrey
8. They are asked what they "are going to do with it.
9. 1920s (1923)
10. *To Kill a Mockingbird*

Malcolm Gladwell, "Examined Life"

1. how ideas and trends start and spread
2. He voluntarily tutored them.
3. The professor confused him with another "Stanley Kaplan."
4. in his parents' basement on Avenue K in Brooklyn
5. seventy-five years
6. the SAT II exam
7. innate ability or aptitude
8. 100 points
9. They see how many of the questions they can answer correctly without reading the accompanying passage.
10. speaking at the annual convention of the College Board

Eric Schlosser, "Why McDonald's Fries Taste So Good"

1. the American prison system
2. 93 percent
3. 90 percent
4. Choose one: International Flavors & Fragrances (IFF), Givaudan, Haarmann & Reimer, Takasago, Flavor Dynamics, Frutarom, or Elan Chemical
5. Willy Wonka's chocolate factory
6. perfumes and household products
7. It sends the smell of something to the brain to help determine its taste.

8. nine out of ten
9. It is not necessarily purer or more healthful than an artificial one.
10. chewing

Ann Beattie, "Janus"

1. short stories and novels
2. Andrea, the main character's dog
3. cream-colored with other colors and silver flecks
4. his keys
5. She believes it brings her luck and helps her sell the house.
6. He is a stockbroker.
7. in a house she had shown
8. a clear vision of the bowl
9. her lover
10. She was too slow to know what she really loved, or she would not leave her husband for him.

Persuasion and Argument Quiz Answers

Martin Luther King Jr., "I Have a Dream"

1. Baptist minister
2. Lincoln Memorial
3. one-hundredth anniversary of the Emancipation Proclamation
4. Gettysburg Address
5. life, liberty, and the pursuit of happiness
6. They will have a rude awakening.
7. violence
8. jail, persecution, police brutality
9. One: Georgia, Mississippi, Alabama
10. "Free at last!"

Eric Liu, "A Chinaman's Chance"

1. Bill Clinton
2. his reach
3. his parents
4. those who are yellow on the outside, white on the inside
5. black
6. Increasingly, we don't.
7. the "Melting Pot"
8. Marine Corps
9. They were not successful in America.
10. that "the deck was stacked"

Barbara Kingsolver, "Stone Soup"

1. novels
2. the many members of his nontraditional family
3. Dad, Mom, Sis, and Junior
4. One: divorced people, blended families, gay families, single parents, remarried people
5. It implies that the reason for divorce is insignificant—a "stubborn refusal to accept a spouse's little quirks."
6. "Did you want the divorce, or didn't you?"
7. when her friends say they feel sorry for her
8. less than twelve years
9. It is about half what it was then.
10. a concoction made of the contributions of many people

Barbara Dafoe Whitehead, "Women and the Future of Fatherhood"

1. "Dan Quayle Was Right" or "The Failure of Sex Education"
2. women
3. women
4. marriage
5. marriage and remarriage rates
6. Women split 50/50, but men disagreed by more than two to one.
7. "deadbeat dad"
8. Any marriage is not better than none. Why not have a child on one's own? "Children are a joy. Many men are not."
9. more than one-third, but not necessarily half
10. be a good father

Joan Acocella, "Under the Spell"

1. dance
2. the fourth volume or *Harry Potter and the Goblet of Fire*
3. one minute after midnight on the day of its release
4. a lightning-bolt shaped scar
5. a wedding
6. a good guy, Harry's godfather
7. Eton
8. It shows what the viewer desires.
9. on a train trip from Manchester to London in 1990
10. Choose one: Jane Austen or Charles Dickens

Harold Bloom, "Can 35 Million Book Buyers Be Wrong? Yes"

1. literature
2. *The Wall Street Journal*
3. *The New York Times*
4. the first, or, *Harry Potter and the Sorcerer's Stone*
5. nineteenth century
6. *Tom Brown's School Days*, or *The Wind in the Willows*, or any of Lewis Carroll's "Alice" stories

7. J. R. R. Tolkien's series about Middle Earth
8. the sorcerers or the magical, and the normal or the mean and selfish
9. J. K. Rowling
10. in the college curriculum

Francine Prose, "Genocide Without Apology"

1. religious tolerance
2. Seder
3. woodcuts depicting the ten plagues
4. They turn sticks into snakes.
5. Choose three: frogs, locusts, boils, lice, flies, blood, hail, fire, the disease of animals, the deaths of the firstborn
6. Cecil B. DeMille
7. trouble, violence, or genocide
8. bathing in the blood of Jewish male babies
9. Choose one: Hebrew, Egyptian, Palestinian, Afghan, Hutu, Kurd
10. genocide without apology

Natalie Angier, "Of Altruism, Heroism, and Evolution's Gifts"

1. science
2. 70–100 pounds
3. "the indomitable spirit of rock-solid America"
4. to cooperate
5. the capacity for language
6. families
7. other worker bees
8. pull them off by their tales and slam them to death
9. They use each other's warning calls.
10. human beings

Kurt Vonnegut Jr., "Harrison Bergeron"

1. the fire-bombing of Dresden
2. 1961
3. 2081
4. fourteen years old
5. an implant in his brain that makes loud noises to scatter his thoughts and a bag of birdshot padlocked around his neck to slow him down
6. ballerinas
7. speech impediments
8. 300 pounds
9. gravity
10. They are shot by a shotgun fired by the Handicapper General.

Resources for Writing: The Discoveries—A Casebook Quiz Answers

Andrew Sullivan, "Virtually Normal"

1. England
2. "Are sure you're not really a girl under there?"
3. perhaps 5 or 6
4. nothing—there was a complete absence of mention of it
5. a physician
6. asthma
7. realizing he was gay
8. invisible access to objects of desire in the locker room
9. Gay people will always feel isolated.
10. "My life."

Colin Evans, "The Kelly Gang"

1. Choose one: musician, crime researcher
2. 1933
3. bridge
4. He was an oil millionaire.
5. four
6. to signify their acceptance of the ransom note's terms
7. He was a "tall stranger 'in a natty summer suit with a turned down Panama hat.'"
8. It has a mineral taste.
9. a plane passing over the house
10. his own fingerprints

Dava Sobel, "Imaginary Lines"

1. science
2. a beaded, collapsible wire sphere
3. Rockefeller Center, New York City
4. latitude
5. at least three centuries before the birth of Christ
6. the Equator
7. London
8. at home and aboard ship
9. He was a clockmaker or a "mechanic."
10. sixty-nine years

Lewis Thomas, "The Technology of Medicine"

1. cancer research
2. They're good at coping with defeat.
3. Their cures are unknown.
4. kidney transplant
5. halfway
6. real high technology

7. real high technology
8. ten thousand dollars
9. new information or research
10. Man has been there.

Witold Rybczynski, "One Good Turn"

1. Scotland
2. architecture
3. a house
4. plane
5. the screwdriver
6. Choose one: raising water, pressing clothes, making olive oil or wine, printing press work, torturing enemies
7. That is unknown.
8. luxury articles like clocks
9. Choose one: door hinges, drawer pulls, shelf hangers, towel bars
10. The lathe was made possible by the screw.

John Fleischman, "Homer's Bones"

1. children
2. Jackie Kennedy
3. 1939
4. how to read it
5. sacrificing black bulls to Poseidon and giving a feast from them
6. Troy
7. five hundred years
8. Pylos
9. about ten animals: bulls and one red deer
10. a two-handled wineglass used during the Bronze Age

Richard Doerflinger, "First Principle and "Frist Principle"

1. Catholicism
2. the U.S. Senate
3. He is a physician.
4. stem cell research
5. Frist has proposed some guidelines for stem cell research.
6. Choose one: ban human cloning, ban funding of destruction of human embryos, ban the creation of embryos for research
7. only those that would otherwise be discarded
8. Senator Arlen Specter and Senator Tom Harkin
9. President Bill Clinton
10. not to do it at all

Peggy Prichard Ross, "Stem Cell Research: It's About Life and Death, Not Politics"

1. medical insurance or HMO
2. six months
3. a fatal form of brain cancer
4. 2003 State of the Union Address
5. "all human cloning"
6. SCNT
7. religious beliefs
8. "a compassionate conservative"
9. 20,000
10. no one knows

Arthur C. Clarke, "The Star"

1. his first telescope
2. three thousand light years
3. Jesuit
4. Saint Loyola
5. a supernova
6. the remains of a burned-up sun
7. evidence of life, a vault filled with relics of a lost civilization
8. that the planet, and they, were about to die
9. They were "disturbingly human."
10. the origin of the Star of Bethlehem